The Classic Ballet

ALFRED · A · KNOPF: *New York*   2004

Historical Development by Lincoln Kirstein

Descriptive Text by Muriel Stuart

Illustrations by Carlus Dyer

Preface by George Balanchine

The
CLASSIC BALLET

Basic Technique and Terminology

THIS IS A BORZOI BOOK
PUBLISHED BY ALFRED A. KNOPF

Copyright © 1952 and renewed in 1980 by Lincoln Kirstein

All rights reserved under International and Pan-American Copyright
Conventions. Published in the United States by Alfred A. Knopf,
a division of Random House, Inc., New York, and simultaneously in
Canada by Random House of Canada Limited, Toronto. Distributed
by Random House, Inc., New York.

www.aaknopf.com

Knopf, Borzoi Books, and the colophon are registered trademarks of
Random House, Inc.

Library of Congress Cataloging-in-Publication Data
Stuart, Muriel, 1900–1991
The classic ballet: basic technique and terminology / historical
development by Lincoln Kirstein; descriptive text by Muriel Stuart;
illustrations by Carlus Dyer; with a preface by George Balanchine.
p.   cm.
ISBN 0-375-71077-9
1. Ballet Dancing.   I. Kirstein, Lincoln, 1907–96
II. Dyer, Carlus, 1917–   III. Title.

GV1788.s8   2004
793.32   51-011993

Manufactured in the United States of America

Published February 27, 1952

First Knopf Paperback Edition, October 2004

Preface

I know that this book of Muriel Stuart's and Carlus Dyer's is offered modestly, for I have watched it grow over the last five years, passing through many versions of correction and verification. No one with experience of stage and classroom as extensive or exact as Miss Stuart's could hope to bring into the space of even a library all of the information she has accumulated from the time when, as a small English girl, she became the last protégée of Anna Pavlova. But I do think that Miss Stuart has done more than anyone else to make the academic dance clear to students and amateurs. I know that the drawings of Carlus Dyer are superior to any other illustrations that I have seen in a training-book, and more accurate as an approximation of ideal perfection, because they have been corrected and recorrected, which is impossible in photography, however vivid or charming its accidental results may be.

One cannot learn to dance by reading this book at home by oneself; it would be useless to try to do so. This book represents as much as can be set down in black and white of the technique and terminology of the traditional academic classic dance, as far as the limitations of a flat surface, words, paper, and print permit. Correctness and elegance can be read here; it remains to translate them into action. The dynamics of some of the sequences in movement have been ingeniously suggested in Mr. Dyer's designs, but ultimately the plastic and fluid human body must escape him as it escapes every artist and photographer and even the films. Yet the book stands as a more nearly complete criterion of the classic dance than I ever had when I was a student and wondered sometimes if there was indeed such a thing as an absolutely ideal position or method in moving. In parts of the world where well-trained teachers are not available, the plates in this book will be a challenge, a constant corrective, and a vivid reminder of the classic style. In cities where good schools exist, the book is an admirable source of reference for the highest standard of practice.

The technique and terminology employed are the ones I learned in the Imperial Dancing Academy in Saint Petersburg, which is now continued as the State School in Leningrad, the ones taught in the School of American Ballet in New York City, which I founded with Lincoln Kirstein in 1934. Since then, many of our students from all parts of the Americas have graduated from our school to the stage, and from the stage to their own schools throughout the hemisphere. The teaching of the classic dance is a conservative calling; new departures, new methods are rare even when technical capacity has increased as I have myself seen it enormously increase here in the last eighteen years. There are no short cuts to great dancing, but what is necessary to remember and unalterable in its instruction may be found in this book.

The soundest advice one can give a student of the dance is simply to dance, just as the only advice for someone who wishes to "understand" the ballet is to see it. If there were no books there would still be dancing with audiences to watch; perhaps that would be better, for most books are little help. Either they oversimplify the art so that it seems an amusing game, or they overcomplicate it so that it becomes a sacred mystery.

But a few rewarding books about the ballet exist. Descriptions by poets, or poetic critics (Théophile Gautier, Carl Van Vechten, Edwin Denby, Jean Cocteau) of individual performances give us valuable hints of personal style. Memoirs of famous dancers (Taglioni, Karsavina, Nijinsky) show how the problems of life in the theater are always the same yet always different; the care with which great artists must prepare rôles or performances; and the trials that always beset important careers. Many of the most thoughtful books on the ballet were written in Russian during the last century; unfortunately, few have been translated. I am particularly thinking of one by

Konstantin Skalkovsky, a government mining engineer and art collector, called *Dance and Ballet: Their History and Position in the Fine Arts* (1882). Skalkovsky wrote a foreword to his friend Alexander Pleschaeev's even more famous *Our Ballet* (1899) in which he said:

"There is only one way to begin to love ballet—attend the theater as often as possible. . . . First, one learns about dancing through practice, by comparison. Only by watching the execution of the same dance several times does one begin to understand why one dancer dances it better than another, and to notice the finest nuances in the execution. Second, attending the theater often, one does not see only the performance on the stage, for all the minutiae of backstage life become a performance . . . . In a word, you begin to understand *le pourquoi de pourquoi*, and the ballet acquires for you, as an 'initiate,' an entirely new meaning that remains a secret to the crowd of plain mortals."*

GEORGE BALANCHINE

Artistic Director
The New York City Ballet Company
New York City, September 1951

*Revised from the translation by Anatole Chujoy in "Balletomania in Imperial Russia" (*Dance Index*, vol. 7, 1949).

Acknowledgments

This study, the first of its scope to originate in the United States, was partially accomplished through a grant-in-aid from the Rockefeller Foundation (Division of Humanities; John Marshall, associate director). Other needed funds were supplied by the School of American Ballet (Eugene Ouroussow Lehovich, executive director).

While this book cannot claim to represent the complete opinions of every individual member of the faculty of the School of American Ballet, the system of basic positions, movements, and technique detailed here is that practiced by this school, under the supervision of its chairman of faculty, George Balanchine, who, as dancer, choreographer, and pedagogue, represents the chief modern embodiment of the Franco-Russian academic tradition in the Western world, descending as he does from the Imperial and State Schools of Petersburg, from Ivanov and Saint-Léon, Marius Petipa, and Michel Fokine.

Muriel Stuart wishes to thank Marion Schillo and Donn Driver for their encouragement in the early stages of an endeavor that took four years to consummate, and Kate Forbes, of the Metropolitan Opera Ballet School, for her elucidation of Enrico Cecchetti's terminology, widely used in the United Kingdom and throughout the Empire, but less in the Americas. Above all she wishes to thank David Vaughan, the English dancer and choreographer, who emigrated to New York to study in the School of American Ballet and to aid in the final revisions of this text.

Carlus Dyer, whose difficult task it was to prepare the one hundred and fifty-six plate pages, has designed numerous handsome volumes before for public museums and private publishers, but this may well be his masterpiece. With almost superhuman patience, he redrew the innumerable figures until they were as nearly satisfactory as humanly possible; his many thousands of preparatory studies and alternate drawings are gratefully acknowledged if hidden testimony to his accuracy and devotion.

Lincoln Kirstein

Director
The School of American Ballet
New York City, 1947–1951

Contents

List of Illustrations

*An alphabetical listing of plates including a page reference for details of technique and terminology and for the alternate terms given for the technique illustrated in this work.

The Classic Ballet: Historical Development

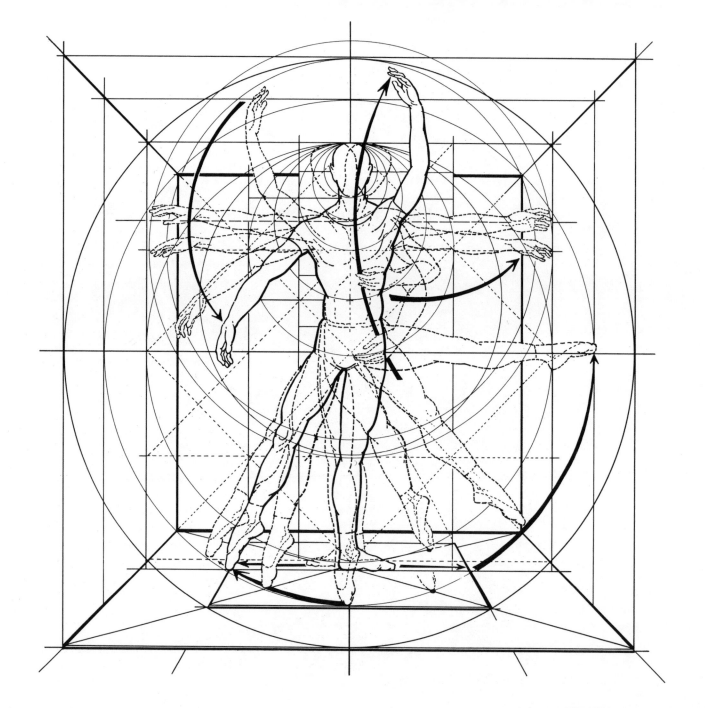

Space Module of the Arms and Legs I   *(front view)*

The Classic Ballet: Historical Development

I. Source and Status

The movement of the human body to rhythmic accompaniment is basic in society. Primitively, it is rooted in the ritual of seasons and sympathetic magic, in which the function of mimicry promises success to hunt or harvest. But the dance must be well danced to ensure victory and food. Dancing around a hero's altar-grave holds the source of our drama, opera, and theatrical dance. At the start, there was no separation between performer and spectator. The focus was central, the ground-plan circular. Tribal ancestors were invoked to sustain their heirs.

Today, in the developed classic ballet, elements of ritual survive. Dancers are ordained by impulse and physical endowment into a rigorous regimen, finally coming of age as members of a professional tribe upon the great platform of an opera-house, in lay ceremonies whose only surprise is in individual performances on given evenings. All else—plot, music, choreography, decoration—is equally familiar. What rests in doubt is the sucessful accomplishment of predesigned movement and gesture, the display of which is not supernatural but superhuman: beyond the physical capacity of those congregated to watch for such signs.

Ballet as an international plastic expression has enjoyed a notable revival in Europe and, more recently, in the United States. This has coincided with an increasing confusion of style and subject, of ends and means, in our drama, prose, painting, and sculpture. Over fifty years ago, Stéphane Mallarmé, critic of the dance through a great poet's eyes, observed "the astonishing but fragmentary extravagance of imagery in the plastic arts, from which the dance, at least, is isolated in its perfection of technique,—alone capable by its concise calligraphy of transforming the ephemeral and abrupt into a concrete absolute."*

The most powerful theatrical essence remains, where it began, in the dance. Its capacity to astonish by brilliance or calm by harmony provides a physical frame in which artist-craftsmen may demonstrate the happier chances of the race, symbolized by the dancer's determined conquest of habitual physical limitation.

Good dancing is never blunted by verisimilitude, nor need it cater to production-codes even in the fiercest or most tender representations of love. Journalistic observation in novels or plays never convinces for long, despite a desperate verbal accuracy. It only debases writers, readers, actors, and audiences into dullness. From it the dance is immune when cleaving to the transparent logic in the classic style. Here what might have degenerated into monotonous acrobatics or banal pantomime has been elevated to humane significance, organized by music and transformed by the visual ambience.

---

* *Divagations: (Richard Wagner, Réverie d'un Poète Français)* 1897. Those critics of ballet whose words last longest are French: Baudelaire, Gautier, Mallarmé, Valéry; as in sculpture, Carpeaux, Degas, Rodin; as in painting, Watteau, Lautrec, Seurat.

II. Toward Spectacle

The classic ballet is a highly artificed craft. Its furthest direct ancestor is Greek choral-drama, precedent for most Western theater. The plays of Aeschylus, Sophocles, Euripides, and Aristophanes utilized semi-professional dance-groups in addition to trained soloists, performing patterned movements within a ninety-foot dancing circle or *orchestra*, often around a central altar, but with the seated spectators finally isolated from the performers. However spectacular, annual dramatic festival seasons maintained an official contact with the state religion. Ritual elements are prominent and persistent through the whole repertory; in the last great surviving complete drama, the *Bacchae* of Euripides, a dancing chorus or *corps de ballet* is itself protagonist in a glorious recapitulation of the sacrificial tragic act.

Roman comedy augmented pantomime—a school of manual gesture, wordlessly legible to an imperial polyglot public, adding virtuoso dumb-show to the acrobat's trade. Down to the last generation, Italy has often revitalized theatrical dancing by an insistence on technical brilliance and clowning. Under the Republic, the profession was dishonorable for freemen. Cicero thought one must be mad or drunk to dance. Even after the Christian interdict, which came from the bad name got by circus and hippodrome, a craft-tradition survived through medieval wandering minstrels who tumbled, juggled, and danced on cords; who sang and mimed ballads—originally, danced songs.

However, what we call "ballet"—a synthesis of human anatomy, solid geometry, and musical composition—commenced in ballrooms during the High Renaissance in North Italy, where social dances acquired intricate floor-plans, swelling out *divertissements* for competitive princely feasts. At first, court guests themselves played principals and chorus, but by the time stages were erected at the far ends of big banquet-halls, and shortly after, when functioning theaters were built, Milanese dancing-masters codified rules for the manner of performing in gallant exhibitions. The twin provinces of professional theatrical dancing were established and analyzed—on the floor and in the air.

Early floor-patterns were quadrilateral, as in the social dances of the West until our grandparents' time, designed equally for four sides of a ballroom that held no single stage-focus. Rapidly, with intrusions from livelier folk and popular dances that lifted heels and skirts off the floor, a vocabulary for the next two centuries emerged. By the time the Medici court was at home in Fontainebleau, indicating the future of a Franco-Italian mannerist art that would dominate Europe and the world, ballet also had been given its idiom, terminology, and aristocratic style.

The development of musical notation—for harmony, counterpoint, polyphony, with dance-suites moving toward broad symphonies—a complex growth from plain song to tone poem, was accompanied, step after step, by the academic dance. There may be other means of tempering the keyboard than those fixed by Bach or geometries other than Euclid's, yet the West settled for single systems of instruction. This was now true of the *danse d'école*, from the foundation of the Royal Academy of Music and Dancing, under Louis XIV.

The development of means of rendering plastic form by painting on a plane surface to simulate light, shade, and color—from Byzantine frontal silhouette and calligraphy through the triumphs of Venetian aerial and atmospheric perspective—enabled the proscenium-framed theatrical tableaux to give stage-dancing its illusion of spatial dignity, accommodated by architecture to a human scale.

The development of European carving, modeling, and bronze-casting was brought to its peak in Baroque ornament. The human body, whose gross anatomy had been supremely delineated in the woodcut illustrations to Vesalius, became familiar as a mechanism of bone, muscle, and nerve, with its own limited if flexible logic of function. Standards of plastic legibility and expressiveness appropriate to this machine were fixed by sculptors in the principle of *contraposto*, a three-quarter view opposition of limbs, the placement of members as an active spiral, denying any flattening symmetrical frontality. Poses of wrist, fingers, head, and neck were adjusted to the ball-bearing sympathy of the fluid torso as a working whole. The climate of the Franco-Italian baroque, from Giovanni da Bologna to Jean Goujon, has remained a criterion for the large profiles of the classic style. Although the antique has been evoked by countless choreographers with the images of poets and the eyes of sculptors, the mean vision (until Nijinsky's archaistic *Faune* of 1912) was usually a late Renaissance recutting of Hellenistic torsion and balance.

The development of manners in European society from tournament-codes, dual-combat, and *Il Cortegiano* through the protocol of the *grande levée* at Versailles to quasi-Byzantine survivals at Tzarsköe-Selo determined the courtesy of performers: how they behaved on stage, bowed before the curtain, took their partner's hands, and gave those airs of conscious elegance to *danseurs nobles*, whose deliberate hierarchy in court- or state-ballet troupes still reflects, as in armies and empires, pyramidal authority.*

The development of European poetry, metrically and philosophically, in lyric and epic, from the Courts of Love to our ultimate synthesis of classicism and contemporaneity in Baudelaire, Rimbaud, Yeats, Eliot, and Auden has provided plots, pretexts and atmosphere. Orpheus's grief and Medea's fury, Don Quixote's confusion and Don Juan's hunger continue to be danced, as they have been for some three hundred years. The poets of each generation have rewoven a net of legend, myth, or fable to which also Aesop and Ovid, Dante and Ariosto, Spenser and Shakespeare, Racine and La Fontaine, Molière and Marivaux, Hoffmann and Heine, Pushkin and Andersen, Cocteau and Claudel have directly contributed.

---

* "The art of dancing has ever been acknowledged to be one of the most suitable and necessary arts for physical development and for affording the primary and most natural preparation for all bodily exercises, and, among others, those concerning the use of weapons, and consequently it is one of the most valuable and useful arts for nobles and others who have the honour to enter our presence not only in time of war in our armies, but even in time of peace in our ballets."

—Letters Patent, from Louis XIV, for the establishment at Paris of a Royal Academy of the Dance, 1661. (From *A Miscellany for Dancers*, edited by Cyril W. Beaumont, London, 1934.)

III. Style and Limitation

Ballet, human action designed toward lyric display, determined by the accompaniment of orchestras, framed in opera-houses, is performed in repertory to the support of loyal audiences. While classic theatrical dancing may have ancient roots, what we recognize as such is comparatively recent. As working idiom and established style, it is about two centuries old; as remembered repertory, barely a century. Only after the French Revolution were court theaters replaced by city opera-houses with subsidized academies of music and the dance serving them. In the big municipal theaters arose the need to amplify movements whose delicacy and finesse had long been attached to their birth in ballrooms. Increased legibility was demanded, and it broadened the language.

This also evoked an arithmetical increase in acrobatic virtuosity, in which succeeding graduating classes of dancers, like athletes, broke all previous records for endurance and capacity. The alliance of opera-house and academy was essential, offering a flexible technical apparatus, official municipal or state subsidy, steady collaboration with musicians, and a more or less consecutive economic stability that freed dancers from the continual need to tour, except on guaranteed invitation. Ballet companies became useful tools of cultural diplomacy and interchange, as dancing, unlike poetry or even painting, was, in most cases, immediately exportable, needing no translation and being independent of local taste.

In the opera-house partnership, first dancers, sharing the scene with virtuoso singing-actors, also glowed into stardom and by force of individual glamour raised the capacity, popularity, and prestige of their craft. And, just as the first viol turned into the *chef d'orchestre*, an experienced controlling performer in his own right of authority, so the *maître de ballet* or journeyman ballet-master developed into a choreographer who commanded collaboration of dancer, musician, and designer, and yet of whom, as of other true masters, there is never more than a handful to a generation.

With an increase of virtuosity, legibility remained the first concern. What was danced had to be not only well danced but also cleanly seen. It was increasingly difficult to read tiny movements without blurring from the upper reaches of the balconies. Dancers have always known that their most faithful friends are nearer the rafters than the floor. Hence, a frank graciousness and compact brilliance determined the apparent ease in the classic style. But this consciously simple breadth, the distinction in disdain of all difficulty, was intensified by pure physical feats, tempered through sustained muscular control. In solos, duets, and trios of joy, love, or rivalry, a bravura stage courtesy was calculated, by alternate stanzas of noble consideration and exuberant display, to capture the public.

The ground of style and technique resides in the five basic school positions of the body, arms, and feet. (Plate 4.) Through them, all other flowering movement is strained; to them it all returns. The five positions are an invisible, or rather transparent, sieve, net, or screen, separating filaments of action into a mosaic of units, consecutive, yet at each step clearly defined. Extension of limbs from the hub of trunk offers elaborate profiles and attenuated silhouettes. (Plates 29-44.) The use of toe-slippers, with their small, sharp fulcrum, provided (from about 1835 on) a means of almost imperceptible floating locomotion across the floor and an increase in elevation for the *danseuse*. Denial of gravity commanded a whole division of schooling, with small foot-beats, air-turns, cross-leaps, and vertical jumps (Plates 70-111), proof positive that a dancer can not only rise through space, but can also perform movements with less friction there than on the floor itself. Pirouettes (Plates 48-62) made clear that front and back of a body have a simultaneous plastic significance in addition to the dialectic brilliance of their blur.

While the increase by innovation, analysis, and instruction developed performers past previous norms of competence, there were and are restrictions of taste, intellectual as well as physical, not always self-evident. Some ideas remain better communicated by other means; others are better left unexpressed or are expressed better in dance terms other than those of ballet. Degas, who was something more than an amateur sonneteer, once complained to Mallarmé that poetry was so difficult to make, yet he was full of ideas. The poet explained that poems are made of words, as pictures of paint. Ballet is made primarily of dancing in the classic style, secondarily of other attractive and ornamental theatrical elements.

With its inherent limitations accepted (one cannot, says Balanchine, explain in dancing that one dancer is another dancer's mother-in-law), there are wide categories of dramatic design in which the developed classic style may be more fully and intensely

communicable than any other visual medium. Animation, the emergence into action of a static body; revelation, the abrupt appearance of an active body; movements reminiscent of the creatures of Prometheus testing their first steps; Pygmalion releasing Galatea; a doll becoming human; or a human becoming animal—these find actions that speak clearer than any ecstatic idiom but song.

Edwin Denby, that American dance-critic whose book deserves a place on the single shelf of useful study (next to Théophile Gautier) gives the best definition:

"Classic dancing is our most expressive development of dance rhythm. It builds long continuities (or phrases) of movement that offer the audience variations of bodily impetus clearly set in relation to a fixed space. And these long phrases of movement convey the specific meaning of the ballet—its drama. As the impetus of successive phrases of music suggests to the hearer a particular quality of emotion and thought, so the successive phrases of a ballet suggest to the observer a particular quality of human action."*

---

* *Looking At The Dance*. Edwin Denby. Pellegrini & Cudahy, New York, 1949.

IV. The Dancer

Dancers are craftsmen. Craft in the classic ballet is not mastered by desire alone, nor even by dedication. It also depends on heredity and temperament, a granted constitutional capacity, always enhanced by pleasant proportions and musical instinct. Inherent limitations may be overcome or put to advantage, as in the case of Taglioni's arms, which were too long, but were disguised by her choreographer father in ingenious *ports de bras*. Exceptional performers have been handed outstanding machines; a great part of their supremacy derives from endowment: firm arms, fine legs, delicate attachments, and a splendid mask, with the added blessing of a clear sense of rhythmic phrasing. Although attempts have been made to establish canons of perfect proportion, an ideal body is a concept more than a fact; schooling compensates for faults and develops gifts.

With an adequate mechanism presupposed or adapted, there remain psychological or moral qualifications too serious and special to discuss briefly. Am I really a dancer? Will I ever become a dancer? Will I ever become a great dancer? What sort of a dancer am I? What rôles do I really want? What rôles do I really deserve? Am I as good a dancer as X, who may be more beautiful, but who is surely weaker than I? Would I be happier in another company, with a different repertory? Am I getting too old to dance? Am I as good, or as bad, as the critics write? Answers to such troubling questions can be found only by individuals at various crises in long careers. When parents have asked about their children's chances, Balanchine has long replied: "*La danse— c'est une question morale.*"

A childhood vision of the dancer's glory must somehow be cradled and preserved, for the daily duty is onerous and the result slow to appear. The balance of encouragement from parents and realistic criticism from teachers is precarious. Fathers often aid their daughters. The profession is no longer dishonorable for girls. For this we have the British to thank, who took to ennobling stage artists late in the last century, and who now recognize (after long years of struggle) their state ballet as an exportable national asset.

The problem of the lack in number and quality of male dancers is distressing. Male actors and singers, painters and poets are enfranchised. The popular dancer of stage and screen, providing he is extravagantly paid and publicized for a personality not necessarily connected with his capacity as a dancer, is also legitimatized. But that American parent is rare who helps his son absorb the craft of the classic dance; Americans barely deserve the few excellent male dancers who manage to get themselves trained. But, indeed, English and American ballerinas are a comparatively recent discovery, and who are the French, German, or Italian male dancers of the last three generations? The honored French weakness for the soubrette all but killed opera-ballet as a serious manifestation, eliminating men except as supports. We have not entirely recovered from the *boulevardier* prejudice.*

Russians maintain their ballet in such esteem that dancers hold the status of civil servants. Their services are recognized as essential and irreplaceable. They are generally exempt from all but emergency military duty. The careers of Western European and American boys who are encouraged to take ballet-classes (a rare occurrence) from the age of nine to nineteen, and who then spend two years in work infrequently useful to the army, may be

---

* The classic Gallic attitude is voiced by Eryximachus, the doctor of Paul Valéry's graceful discourse, *L'Ame et la Danse*. Nine dancing girls are praised at their entrance for grace and beauty—all except Nettarion, "the little boy-dancer, who is so ugly."

wrecked. Bernard Shaw, a man almost alone in his position, appealed (naturally in vain) for the exemption of the British male dancer during the last war. Actually it would take more courage for a dancer to accept exemption on terms of art alone than to escape into the army. It is not the fault of the material that a national ballet lacks impressive men. We have never been poor in Olympic or professional athletes. The Russians, who are neither pacifist nor unrealistic, have raised and maintained the profession of dancer to a deserved prestige, awarding self-respect to working artists which no other success renders entirely secure.

Dancers are committed to hazard. Unless they take all precautions, what they do cannot be well done. Every performance conceals the risk of failure—immediate danger from accident, momentary loss of control, or weakness in obeying the proper law. A dancer's role is sacrificial, like a bull-fighter's or a trapeze-artist's. The physical risk may not be so extreme, but it is serious enough, and few things are sadder than a young girl or boy with a snapped Achilles tendon. Nightly they place themselves in jeopardy for their people, though the aura is more lyric than tragic.

A dancer's manner of projecting the classic style is a helpless reflection of private character, more revealing than handwriting or the quality of a smile. When dancers emerge from the *corps de ballet* to the status of soloist, exposed in naked isolation far from the supports of a classroom, it is only the sum of human nature and digested experience which shapes the muscle-tone to direct a future. They are trained from the start to stare at mirrors. Their preoccupation in correcting themselves need never develop into that flagrant narcissism that often deforms other performers, and sometimes dancers as well.* Most students pray that the monster facing them each morning from their mirror will, by application, grow less monstrous, that its all too visible flabbiness and faults will finally be whipped into at least a decent accuracy.

Theatrical presence, awareness, apprehension, immanence, or magic is not self-love, but an analytical sense that loves to please by releasing the skilled machine. As for virtuosity, there are few living dancers who need fear that their enormous technique may quite overhaul them—their means becoming their only end, a condition that has harassed some of our ablest painters and pianists. The constant crucifixion of dance-training, of submission to new choreography, of risk in performance, which pushes the physique to such sweaty spending, reminds dancers that in great nature there are innumerable elements outside of idiosyncrasy upon which they must depend to ensure the balance of their bodies.

The *danseur noble* and the ballerina are not only idols, but also models. Creations of their instructors, they in turn emerge as professors of style, first on stage, later in classrooms. Dancers as stewards of classicism inspire new ballets. More ballets are designed to frame a resident soloist than for other reasons. Like piano or violin concertos, choreography may be inspired by the personality of one executant, but soon after a début, it enters the general repertory for alternative interpretations. And a performance in varieties of studied roles, as well as differing ideas of the same role, may be as instructive to the student or amateur as the daily routine of academic exercises.

---

* Narcissus, says W. H. Auden, was not a beautiful youth who fell in love with his own image. He was a hydrocephalic idiot who thought: On me, it looks good.

V. Instruction

Progressive training toward a mastery of body mechanics has been developed over the years into a system of practice exercises based on some absolute premises. The daily lesson, in essence the same for beginners as for accomplished professionals, commences with *adagio* (at ease, slowly) supported by artificial correction from the wooden *barre*. Then students are released into the center of the practice-room for a repetition of the identical work, now free from the bar, practicing both to right and to left to gain an easy ambidextrousness contrary to usual conditioning. The lesson terminates with rapid *allegro* combinations, finally launching the body into the air.

At no step in the classic pedagogy is there room for improvisation, experiment, or doubt. The academy is not choreography any more than finger-exercises are music. Without in themselves pretending to art or encouraging premature self-expression, both are stuff from which art derives. But just as there is beauty in a cleanly laid-out palette or a well-played chromatic scale, so the sight of a studio where young aspirants repeat their practice is pleasing.

Training today has advanced, with the dance-theater and choreographic scope as a whole, immeasurably beyond the rudimentary etiquette of Milanese dancing-masters or the simple floor-rules of the French founding fathers. France has always exercised her hegemony; the language of international dancing, diplomacy, and cooking is phrased in French, just as music speaks Italian, science, law, and the Church, Latin. A terminology has been maintained since the early seventeenth century, but while the nomenclature persists, our usage has frequently pushed past original definitions. When we read descriptions of early ballets or attempt to reconstruct antique works from choreographic notation, it is difficult to arrive at any accuracy because the idiom has been so greatly broadened. The vocabulary (and repertory) of even one hundred years ago would seem naïve to us today, that of two hundred uninteresting save for the lost charm of a historic style.

The French inseminated Russia, and while there were very important contributions from the Mediterranean, Scandinavia, and Central Europe (often in regard to *demi-caractère*, or theatricalized folk dancing), the standard for delicacy and dispatch remained French. This was true until the first decade of our own century, when the accumulated results of transplanted French, Swedish, and Italian teaching and practice were returned by the Russians to Paris, then far weaker in dancers than St. Petersburg or Moscow. The Russians established in France and then throughout the world a criterion we continue to recognize. The personal standard for the West is still, long after their disappearance from the scene, Pavlova, Karsavina, and Nijinsky.

As teachers, the most progressive French ballet-masters found more opportunity under the tsars than in Paris, where the dance suffered (along with the opera) from bureaucratic rigidity, the whims of the gentlemen of the Jockey Club, and a severe impoverishment of male material in the second half of the last century. The male principle, dominant in the seventeenth and eighteenth, pursued by Perrot, Saint-Léon, and Marius Petipa before 1850, evaporated into travesty, girls assuming the dress of boys. Petipa, his able assistant, Lev Ivanov, and their disciple, Michel Fokine, are directly responsible for our working style. Their repertory (with Coralli's *Giselle*), as transmitted by White Russian agencies exiled to the West, is our immediate background. The French flowered in Russia, where court and a rising middle-class were avidly francophile, compensating for a comparatively late emergence from demi-Oriental feudalism. Ballet was taken as a symbol of cultural internationalism. Western stars were not slow to attach themselves to so remote, but so rich a province. The splendor of the Russian theatrical and musical apparatus shortly after mid-century was proof that Mother Russia was also a member of the more sophisticated European family.

But those in today's audience who have taken Russian ballet as a fact accomplished for centuries, just like those who accept the present situation in Britain as one of long-standing security, forget the caprice, accident, and agonizing uncertainty that have always dogged the establishment of this art as a separate feature in a new country. More than once, influential managers and critics have called for the suppression of ballet companies in favor of the more ancient opera, and more than once it has happened that the ballet, with its dynamism and ready novelty, has saved an opera house in desuetude. That the ballet has survived is owing to the devotion of dancers and to the innate excitement in the dance.

In the Russian situation traces of byzantinism were preserved. The Russians remained imperial in their formal autocracy and spiritual orthodoxy longer than other states. The tsar was autocrat of all the Russias, including French Russia. Dancers were taught to make their *révérence* first in the direction of the sovereign's loge; the ballet was guaranteed by one million gold rubles a year from his privy purse. Ballerinas were awarded to grand dukes as tutors in love and taste. This court retained its absolutism up to the débacle. It never deigned (or was too blind and spoiled) to save itself by transformation into Western county-family gentility. Dancers were members of a royal household, raised in an atmosphere of such paternalistic security from childhood that they would always assume, even in remote exile and quite unconsciously, an absolute authority as their due, by virtue of their own gifts and training to be sure, but also because of an almost blood kinship with the crown.

Pervasive elements from the patristic philosophy of humility, compassion, and personal nihilism (responsible also for the supremacy of Russian character-acting), certainly touched academic precincts, and must be responsible for some of the constant greatness in anonymous assignments in their stage and film.* In the ballet, the atmosphere of feudal responsibility, aristocratic tenderness without flirtation, ostentation, or affectation—a ritual

---

*In 1915, Diaghilev projected a ceremonial ballet, *Liturgy*, decor by Larionov and Gontcharova, based on gestures in ikon painting. Dancing would have been unaccompanied by music but linked by Stravinsky's orchestral interludes. The project was not realized, but Stravinsky's later *Symphony of Psalms* and *Mass* recall the planning.

elevation of human sympathy, subduing but never extinguishing the Tartar violence beneath—contributed incalculably to the dignity, richness, and power of the Slavic style in its Great Russian epitome. And Russians first developed a specialist audience of passionate amateurs with a clinical if conservative, rather than sentimental, connoisseurship.*

When Diaghilev transported the main elements of the St. Petersburg and Moscow companies to Western Europe in 1909, he was aided by the political climate that made England, France, and Russia establish the Entente Cordiale. But official subsidy was withheld at the last moment, and he was forced to depend at the start (as he was throughout his career until he was kept for a few seasons, and then only in part, by the gaming-tables of Monte Carlo) on the support of individual patrons. Diaghilev settled in Paris to pollinate all our fine and applied arts, and this was, in a sense, a homecoming. For French post-Impressionism was responsible for décor and music, French precedent adapted by Russian, Swedish, and Italian hands for choreography and performance.

And when Diaghilev refused Lunacharsky's invitation to return to head the Soviet State Theaters after the consolidation of the Bolshevik Revolution, modern Russia seems to have shut herself off from progressive dance-design, together with the whole early, middle, and late repertory of Igor Stravinsky, the most evocative body of dance music available today, the single

inspiration to contemporary choreography comparable to Adam, Delibes, or Tchaikovsky. Diaghilev understood that the new bureaucracy, though revolutionary, remained Russian. Even under tsarist tyranny he had been forced to the West to fulfil his earliest collaborations. He felt he could not pursue them even in the comparative openness of the Soviet 'twenties. Over a century ago, Chadaev wrote that "Russia belonged to the number of nations that somehow do not enter into the regular complex of humanity, but exist only to teach the world some important lesson." The lesson she taught in ballet was irreplaceable; it seems to have been learned.

Ballet in Russia may be the strongest in the world today: economically, from generous popular and state support; technically in instruction; in male dancers; and in the prestige of the art and craft as a legitimate and honored expression. But, at least through the evidence of films, the present theater-style, disassociated from French-derived internationalism, has become heavy, over-emphatic, and coarse-grained. It is difficult to maintain universal elegance in cases of hermetic intellectual suspension; certainly Russians are now uninterested in accommodating Western notions of good taste. Nevertheless, when international exchange is not permitted full scope a national manner quickly grows defensively and complacently provincial. Elegance resides in an intensely individual reflection of voluntary behavior; it must still smack of dandyism, and dandyism must always smack of revolt against the ordinary, the level, the average. Elegance is homage to personal rather than national or class distinction. It

*See Anatole Chujoy's excellent article "Russian Balletomania," *Dance Index*, Volume VII.

frames *la côté épique de la vie moderne*, as Baudelaire conceived it, which cannot be imposed by the patriotism of theatrical commisars from artistic supervision by the political police.*

Theatrical dancing persists everywhere as a craft. Academies are reservoirs of information; great teachers are as precious as great dancers. In fact, the authority of instructors may be determined in large part by previous careers as performers. Girls and boys profit by a combination of men and women teachers; a single professor, however able, in one studio, has severe natural limitations. While several excellent male dancers recently prepared in Paris are largely the product of four ex-imperial ballerinas and an ex-first-dancer who all maintained separate classes, this amounted to an informal academy-in-exile, for students shifted from one to the other. Men are better teachers for boys (who nevertheless can always learn a great deal from women) simply because they are themselves stronger in legs and arms for leaps and lifting; male specialties do not instinctively suggest themselves to women, any more than males are expert on *pointes*. A varied and balanced faculty, possibly young in years, but already mature in stage-experience, combined with authoritative and acknowledged personalities, provides the broadest base.

Teachers fall into two categories: instructors by analysis and models by example. It is rare to find a patient analyst and a brilliant stylist combined in one body. While students are temperamentally prone to prefer a single quality that somehow is felt to correspond to their own individual, if as yet undeveloped, character, it is important that they be subjected to as many stylistic and technical facets as are available, so that when they may with sureness determine their special direction they can have some choice from serious standards.

Those schools are most efficient which are attached formally to a ballet company (just as the best medical schools are linked to hospitals), for here is continual association with performance from the very start of training. In Russia, children were not (and are not) corrupted by being presented as prodigies before they know what they are doing. They made anonymous débuts as blackamoors in *Aida* or rats in *Casse-Noisette*. From familiarity with make-up, the wearing of wigs and costumes, theatrical emergency, and an opera-house climate, they gradually assumed the quality of professionals, for which there is no other schooling. The virtue of our French-Russian-derived academy is in its unbroken teacher-to-dancer-to-teacher descent. It is the only practical floor for a great national ballet.

---

*Working conditions in the Russian state theaters have not changed appreciably. In 1824, Charles Louis Didelot, a French founder of the St. Petersburg academy, was threatened with arrest by Prince Gagarin because ballet intermissions were too long; his resignation was accepted. At the dress-rehearsal of *The Sleeping Beauty* in 1890, Alexander II so disparaged the greatest music ever written for the classic dance that Tchaikovsky was convinced of its failure. Diaghilev was in continual difficulty with a bureaucracy largely composed of retired army officers; the engineering of Nijinsky's dismissal as first dancer to Nicolas II was at least in part a protest at the petrifaction of artistic policy which produced great technicians without a progressive repertory. The suppression of the early Shostakovich ballets continues the story.

VI. Choreography

Dances designed for dramatic presentation as ballets are an extension by combination and ornament of the academic vocabulary, with conscious violations and intensifications. The grammar is first learned in classrooms by individual students. These increase their capacity to assimilate chains of movement by the aid of remembered exercise combinations that, at the same time, have extended and strengthened their muscular memory. The unit is the dancer-student, who has only a single body to manage and one set of motions to master. Choreographers must manipulate many bodies, rarely in unison, working contrapuntally all over the stage-surface within the vast cubic space framed by a proscenium. The unit is a large company, broken into groups: soloists, *corps de ballet*, and musicians, fused in a visual orchestra.

The dominant style in classic choreography has shifted over the last twenty-five years towards a purist, or more purely balletic, tone. The traditional academic dance has reasserted itself with startling vigor after certain useful intrusions from extreme idiosyncratic sources, three of the most memorable being Isadora Duncan, Mary Wigman, and Martha Graham. There have always been, and always can be, important contributions from outside the stricter confines of the academy, but personal innovation (extension, inversion, deformation, reformation) usually affects manners in dance-composition and individual styles in movement rather than any basic training in the syntax or vocabulary of ballet practice. It is not difficult for a trained classic dancer to absorb varieties of idiosyncratic idioms; it is impossible for a dancer trained only in a personal method to perform in classic ballet.

In Diaghilev's middle period (1915-25), after his first nationalist or pan-Slav repertory had been exhausted of novelty or shock, the great impresario depended more upon painters and composers of the School of Paris than on new dancers or dancing. He was now separated by nearly a decade from the schools of Great Russia. Western academies had yet to be reanimated by his own dancers' dispersal into teaching a decade thence. His novelties, from the replacement of Nijinsky by Massine to the replacement of Massine by Balanchine, were predominantly in the style of *demi-caractère*, ornamental revivals from historic epochs transformed through contemporary Parisian eyes—such national or period pieces as Massine's *Three-Cornered Hat* or *Good-Humored Ladies*. While the music was often remarkable, the décor delightful, and the individual performance excellent, the dancing itself tended to be decorative and even secondary to the other theatrical elements, with the result that few of the works then invented persist in repertory.

The most recent chapter in the development of classic choreography, that branch of theater-dance composition which deliberately exploits the expanding possibilities and elastic limitations of the clear academic tradition, commenced in 1928, with Diaghilev's collaboration of Stravinsky and Balanchine in *Apollo, Leader of the Muses*. This remains a neo-classic masterpiece with affinities to the plastic philosophy of Nicolas Poussin.

Diaghilev had become bored by character-numbers, atmospheric revivals, and that domesticated and diminutive modernity which Parisian chic breeds with such relaxed and monotonous taste. Before his death in 1929, this animator of all our aural and visual pleasures attempted, as a kind of coda to his career, a return to unaffected nobility. He was no longer in possession of a fine *corps de ballet*, so he determined a veritable novelty employing three ballerinas and a single *danseur noble*, technically the most brilliant executants left to him. For Massine, who had enjoyed little formal academic training, he substituted Balanchine, a product not only of the Imperial and State dancing academy (1914-20), but also of the St. Petersburg Conservatory of Music. George Balanchine, of Georgian origin, the son of a well-known musicologist and composer, combined in one person virtuoso capacities as classic dancer, choreographer, and musician. Not yet twenty-five, he invented, to Stravinsky's exalted homage to Handel, Delibes, Tchaikovsky, and Terpsichore herself, a new synthesis of classicism, the first in the repertory since Fokine's *Les Sylphides* of twenty years before.* It was enriched by details that, on its début, may have seemed astonishing or bizarre, but which long since have become the normal lyric idiom of the subsequent generation of dance-designers. Certain tendencies that guardians of the tradition may consider heterodox at one moment are incorporated, sooner than one might imagine, into the catholicity of the flexible idiom. Traces of seeming novelty became imperceptible within a few seasons, having not only expanded the vision of the audience but also extended the capacity of performers.

---

* The complete revival of Tchaikovsky-Petipa's *La Belle au Bois Dormant*, magnificently undertaken by Diaghilev, Bakst, and Stravinsky with a great cast in 1921 as an act of pious faith in the classic ballet, failed gloriously, but it was the prototype of the triumph of the Sadler's Wells version of the 'forties, which consolidated the present position of that company, and of the power of the pure academic dance over all intervening and untraditional intrusions.

For an excellent reconstruction of this production, and a comparison with others, see *The Complete Book of Ballets* by Cyril W. Beaumont, Putnam.

Those choreographers, like Balanchine, who are most familiar with possibilities inside their tradition are the first to realize when extreme essays at innovation or reversal are no longer needed. One moment in history demands that dullness or over-decoration be shocked by spare elegance; another calls for formal symmetry unshadowed by deformation. It takes a master to lead in either direction against even so-called advance-guard taste. It was Diaghilev's great gift to anticipate such change, offering the next step, which he knew how to make seem at once shocking and inevitable, in the form of a theatrical idea incarnated in a dance.

Today classic choreographers have been given a universal language so specialized, inflected, and unexploited—cleansed and revived by half a century's experiments and research—that they can spend whatever time may remain to them merely filling the repertory with useful works, heedless of any immediate need for greater freedom in expression. To invent a useful work is, in itself, a heroic task. Theatrical use is severe. A ballet's survival for even three seasons is unusual.

Choreography is the supreme contribution of the dancer, its invention even more than its execution, for without design there could be no concerted dance. The dancer is to a choreographer what the dancer's own body is to himself. A ballet-master is not necessarily a choreographer (even though he may have enough skill to arrange numbers), of whom there has been but a handful to an epoch. Ballet-masters remain useful rehearsalists and arrangers. A choreographer is a composing symphonist with personal concepts of movement. He conceives in terms of formal physical activity, as a musician in sound or a painter in line and color.

VII. Contemporary Classicism

The classic style, supported by its academic technique, depends upon rigid criteria and severe discipline for even a modest executant efficiency, like our music, medicine, and architecture, but unlike our prose, poetry, or painting. It has also become true that unless the ordinary run of female dancer is already a budding virtuoso she is inacceptable even for the *corps de ballet*. Virtuosity is almost presupposed, as it is in candidates for a major symphony orchestra. It is beauty and expressiveness that enters the dancer. While good (that is, excellent) performers are not yet quite, as one is sometimes told, a dime a dozen, nevertheless, in America at least, dance-training is on about as high a level as the schooling for the best college or professional athletes.

Their classic training as performing artists, however, has removed from them the need of strain towards feverish personal vindication. They husband for extra energy and projection in performance whatever idiosyncrasy survives their schooling. They practice their craft in the same spirit as those nameless guildsmen who made most of the antique artifacts that continue to please us, without themselves ever claiming to be innovators. Even famous dancers or choreographers hesitate to consider themselves "creative," a word few artists of any sort dared use before Romanticism, for Creation was considered a property of the unique Creator, and the fact was in itself historic and irreversible. Tradition was a living chain that permitted, or rather propelled, inspiration from roots inextricably linked to the past.

In liberal democracy and anxious anarchy, the traditional classic dance, compact of aristocratic authority and absolute freedom in a necessity of order, has never been so promising as an independent expression as it is today. At the moment, when representational art has declined into subjective expressionism, and its chief former subject, the human body in space, has been atomized into rhetorical calligraphy, the academic dance is a fortress of its familiar if forgotten dignity. To it future painters and sculptors may one day return for instruction in its wide plastic use.

Through our 'twenties and 'thirties there was still, under the aegis of Diaghilev, contact with advance-guard easel-painters. At the present, the vanity of dealer- and museum-sponsored decorators tends to overwhelm all classic choreography. Many painters insist that they wish to design for ballet, which usually means they may want to work on cloths larger than those permitted to hang on walls assigned them. There is hardly a handful whom a sensible choreographer could trust to create the illusion of space within which, rather than against which, dancers may be seen to move. As never before, our interest is focussed on classic frankness, elegance without ornament.

The repertory of contemporary classicism depends largely upon what survives from the nineteenth century rather than from the initial shocks and glories of the twentieth. Fokine's huge repertory has diminished after its prime historical service into the faint visibility of provincial disrepair. Massine's work is chiefly recalled in a few character-numbers; his big symphonic extra-illustrations have proved improbable revivals. Our practical background is that of Petipa, Ivanov (from Sergeyev's memories and adaptations of the Tchaikovsky ballets for the English companies); Coralli's *Giselle;* possibly the Fokine of *Les Sylphides.*

The development of classicism through the centuries, as distinct from character-dances that tend to get themselves remembered as solo numbers, has usually depended on one or two choreographers at a time. Today, at least for the West, it is most fully seen in the works of George Balanchine to music from Bach, Mozart, Bizet, Chabrier, and Tchaikovsky, through to Prokoviev, Hindemith, and Stravinsky—scores whose relentless motor suggestion and support propels his insistent metrical drive. This music is Franco-Russian with Italian and Central European fertilization, as is the technique of the traditional dance itself.

The subject of Balanchine's ballets, apart from love (of music, of the human body, of human beings) is the physical act or presence of the dance itself, not "abstractly," for the sake of detached, dessicated, or decorative motion, but concretely, representing and demonstrating the conscious mechanism in its preparation and animation through mastery of time, space, and gesture.

Balanchine has not transformed the style. He does not classify himself as an innovator or original. He has inherited his language, as Valéry and Yeats inherited theirs. Like a hereditary prince, he has extended its domain through an assumption of its duties and prerogatives, by virtue of his historical position and his innate genius. But he has also defined an intensely personal manner so faceted that it often appears related only to the specific piece of music which is the springboard for the occasion. There are as many Balanchine manners as there are aspects of classic or neo-classic formality and sentiment, which bear no resemblance within his manipulation to anything save his own taste and integrity. His unmistakable signature is in his masterful designs for tenderness, regret of loss, mystery, exuberance, and human consideration.

He has encouraged schools of dancers, a generation of choreographers here and abroad who recognize in his gifts and sensibility the direction in which their own latent invention may be best fulfilled. He has found in the bodies of American-bred dancers, with their professional coolness, resourcefulness stemming from a pioneer heritage of competitive risk and sportive improvisation, answers to his own demands. He seldom considers dancers as personalities according to the Western fashion of stardom, but rather thinks of them in the Byzantine tradition, to which he also adheres, as messengers sent, angelic presences who embody certain capacities for the communication of categories of movement.

Some dancers avoid him. They hold that extra-classic elements, naïvely histrionic or earnestly expressionist, suit the troubled times. Others have turned to him in the midst of successful careers, recognizing that their luck to date depended on dangerously accidental factors that they wish to exchange for the more durable support of the lively academy. For Balanchine has transformed what was once an ephemeral amusement into a continuous amazement. Over the last twenty-five years he has endowed us with a library of models as well as of methods of composition which may be used by his distant heirs.

Lincoln Kirstein

New York, September 1951

Since the labour and life of one man cannot attain the perfection

of knowledge, the wisdom of the tradition is that which inspireth

the felicity of continuance and proceeding.

BACON: *The Advancement of Learning.*

The Classic Ballet: Basic Technique and Terminology

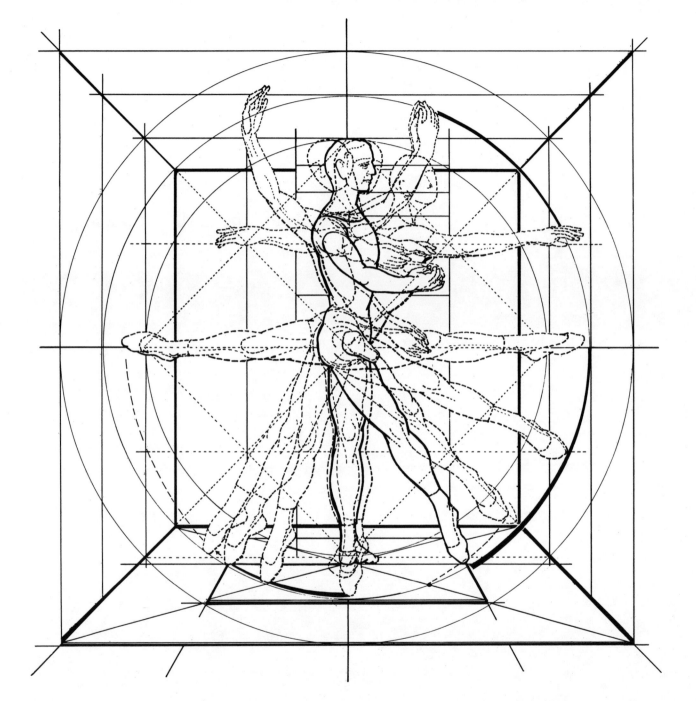

Space Module of the Arms and Legs II   *(side view)*

The Classic Ballet: Basic Technique and Terminology

Introduction to Basic Technique

The traditional technique of the classic dance has developed over centuries and constitutes an academic craft and style that serve both as a basis for the logical physical training of the dancer, and as a medium of expression, or vocabulary, for the choreographer.

The young aspirant who starts to work in the classic idiom submits to a discipline that at once begins to mould his or her personal anatomy for its ultimate function of stage performance. The development of a student's initial endowments of physique and temperament toward a professional career must largely depend upon a correct approach in his or her earliest training. The author-instructor of this work is of the strong opinion, based on the experience of many years, that foremost among the essentials is the conscious and constant application of certain principles of balanced and integrated muscular control (see pp. 26-27).

The terminology employed in the classic dance comprises a body of terms that represent definite positions, steps, and movements generally recognized and agreed upon among responsible instructors, performing artists, ballet masters, and choreographers. It is this "language" that permits the transmission of ideas in dance-terms, from the simplest combination of practice exercises to the complicated variations of these movements in extended sequences that go to make up a ballet.

The author-instructor of this book has chosen to use the terminology most familiar to her in each instance. But where it is known that some other term may be in use among her associates, or by other responsible and recognized schools, an effort has been made to indicate the alternative term in a footnote, to afford as wide reference as possible.

The author-instructor and the artist have tried to achieve a close collaboration, presenting their material in a clearly graphic form that will offer to the beginner an initial chart for the understanding of traditional steps. The form of presentation here attempted has been deliberately designed to give as direct a visual comprehension as possible in a technique that uses static figures in a related sequence to represent both static *positions* and a complete phase of movement. There are inevitable limitations in any attempt to teach a kinetic art through verbal or graphic (yet always stationary) demonstrations on a printed page, but they are less serious than would be imposed by the use of necessarily accidental photographs or cursory film-strips, which so far are not remotely analytic or capable of any instructive breakdown. Author-instructor and artist have directed their labors to recording the sequence of positions that a given movement comprises by means of a simplified "stop-motion" technique that is at the same time not limited to the mere description of which arm or leg should be moved in which primary direction, but also permits, wherever possible, the recording of details of elementary technical finesse, though of necessity the actuality of tempo, accent, and phrasing must be sacrificed.

Innumerable revisions of each plate were made before publication, to attain the highest degree of accurate representation possible on a two-dimensional surface. The typographical design of the pages was considered of prime importance. Thus each term is given its own text and illustration as a separate unit, in order to eliminate the confusion that might arise from an overlap of preceding and succeeding material.

Any temptation to include possible attendant observations of an inspirational or even of a general nature has been resisted in order not to obscure the laconic message of the drawings themselves and to avoid confusing their strictly practical intention. The advice presented has been maintained consistently on the level of the basic facts essential to the execution of a given movement, without invading the vague if fascinating province of personal taste and esthetic theory.

MURIEL STUART

Instructor:
The School of American Ballet

CARLUS DYER: *Designer*

New York City, 1947-1951

[22]

Basic Anatomy: Principles of Posture and Muscular Control

Plate 1. Correct Posture (angle of pelvis)

The pupil must be taught to stand correctly before she starts to move. The placement of the torso over the legs is of great importance: the pelvis must be centered *(fig. 2)*, not tipped forward or backward *(fig. 1 or 3)*. The abdomen is slightly drawn in and the diaphragm raised; the shoulders are dropped naturally, resting downward; and the head is held straight, with the eyes looking forward. The arms are held down and rounded from the shoulder-blades to the finger-tips, slightly forward from the body *(fig. 2)*.

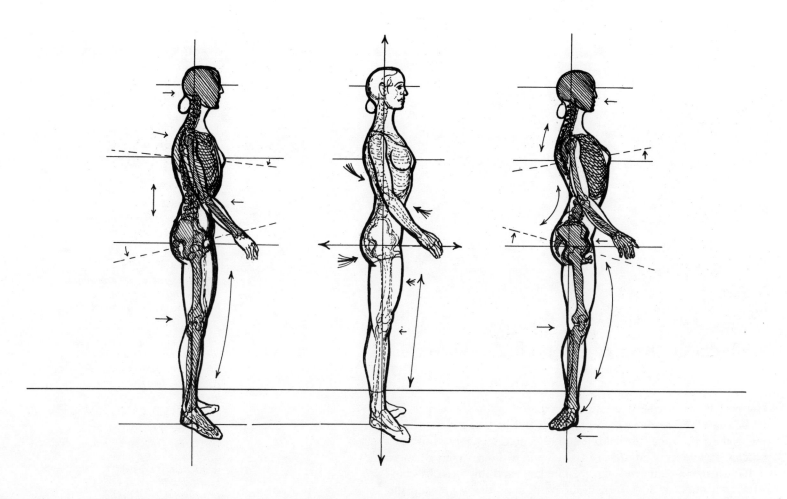

fig. 1   pelvis backward (incorrect)   *fig. 2   pelvis centered (correct)*   *fig. 3   pelvis forward (incorrect)*

CORRECT POSTURE

SKULL
a.   *Nuchal line (base of skull)*

SPINE
b.   *Cervical Vertebrae (7)*
c.   *Thoracic Vertebrae (12)*
d.   *Lumbar Vertebrae (5)*
e.   *Sacrum*
f.   *Coccyx*

RIBS AND SHOULDERS
g.   *Clavicle (breast bone)*
h.   *Thorax (rib structure)*
i.   *Scapula (shoulder blade)*

ARMS
j.   *Humerus (upper arm bone)*
k.   *Radius (lower arm bone)*
l.   *Ulna (lower arm bone)*

PELVIS
m^1. *Iliac anterior superior (pelvic crest, front)*
m^2. *Iliac posterior superior (pelvic crest, back)*
m^3. *Ischium (lower pelvic region)*
n.   *Sacro-iliac joint*
o.   *Pubic bone*

LEGS
p^1. *Head of femur (thigh joint)*
p^2. *Great Trochanter (muscle terminal)*
q.   *Femur (thigh bone)*
r.   *Patella (knee cap)*
s.   *Tibia (lower leg bone)*
t.   *Fibula (lower leg bone)*
u.   *Medial Malleolus (inner ankle)*
v.   *Lateral Malleolus (outer ankle)*

HANDS
w^1. *Carpal bones (wrist)*
w^2. *Metacarpal bones (palm)*
w^3. *Phalanges of the fingers*

FEET
x^1. *Talis (arch)*
x^2. *Navicular and Cuniform bones*
x^3. *Metatarsal (fore arch)*
x^4. *Phalanges of the toes*

Plate 2. Turn-out for Beginners (first position)

The perfectly turned-out position is acquired *gradually*, and should not be forced. Elementary students should not be required to achieve the ideal 1st position (turned-out at 180 degrees) *(fig. 1)* until their muscles have been conditioned to assume it without strain; an angle of 100 degrees is sufficient *(fig. 2)*. The knee and thigh can be comfortably maintained in a turned-out position at this angle, and the danger of the students' forcing their feet to turn out while their knees rotate inwards (resulting in "rolling over" on the front of the foot) can be averted *(see Pl. 1, fig. 3)*.

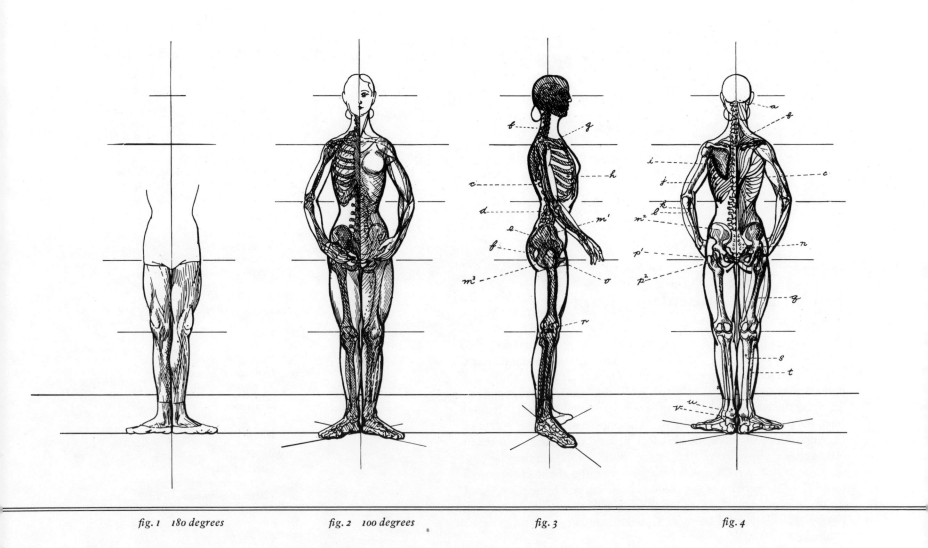

fig. 1   180 degrees   fig. 2   100 degrees   fig. 3   fig. 4

TURNOUT FOR BEGINNERS *(first position)*

a. *Sterno-cleido mastoid (frontal neck)*
b. *Trapezius muscle (upper shoulder)*
c. *Deltoid muscle (crest of the shoulder)*

CHEST AND ABDOMEN

d. *Pectoralis major muscle (breast muscle)*
e. *Rectus abdominis muscle (upper)*
f. *Rectus abdominis muscle (lower)*

THIGHS

g. *Crest of the Ilium*
h. *Tensor fasciae latae*
i. *Sartorius muscle*
j. *Rectus Femuris muscle (front)*
k. *Biceps Femuris muscle (back)*
l^1. *Vastus Lateralis muscle (side)*
l^2. *Vastus Medialis muscle (inside)*

BACK

m. *Trapezius muscle (upper shoulder and back)*
n. *Latimus dorsi muscle*
o. *Infra-spinatus muscle*
p. *Sacrospinalis muscle*

BUTTOCKS

q. *Gluteus Maximus muscle*
r. *Gluteus Medius muscle*

LOWER LEGS

s. *Tatellar ligament*
t. *Gastrocnemius muscle (calf)*
u. *Tibialus anterior muscle (shin)*
v. *Extensor digitorium muscle*
w. *Flexor digitorium muscle*
x. *Achilles tendon*

ARMS AND FEET

y^1. *Biceps muscle*
y^2. *Triceps muscle*
z^1. *Extenso digitorium communis
and related muscles (Extensor, Flexor, Abductor)*
z^2. *Ball of the foot*

Plate 3. Centers of Muscular Control

The muscles of the abdomen, buttocks, and thighs are the dancer's center of muscular energy and control. The muscles in the thighs are pulled upward, causing a slight tension in the buttocks and abdomen; this frees the torso above the waist from strain and eliminates tension from the neck, shoulders, and arms. The pupil must be made aware of the importance of this control before making the first movement in classic dance, the *demi-plié* in the five positions. It will then be possible for her to execute this movement with the slight counter-pull upward in the muscles of the thighs, abdomen, and buttocks which I speak of in my note on Posture and Muscular Control. As training progresses, this control becomes an unconscious part of the dancer's equipment.

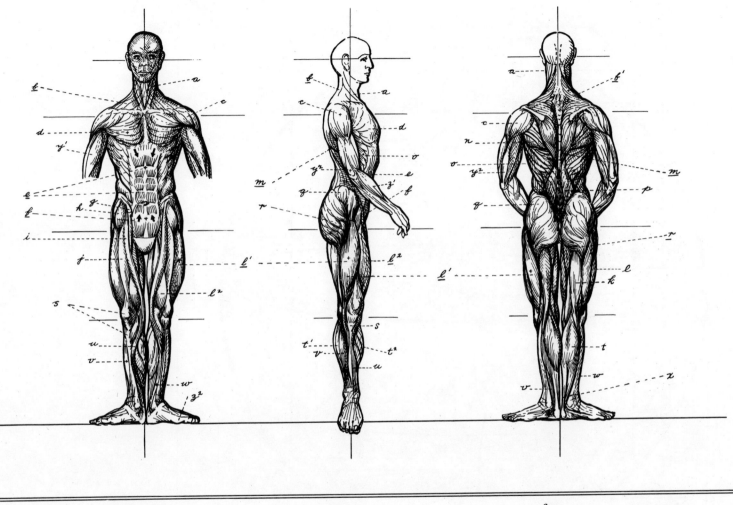

fig. 1   fig. 2   fig. 3

CENTERS OF MUSCULAR CONTROL

[29]

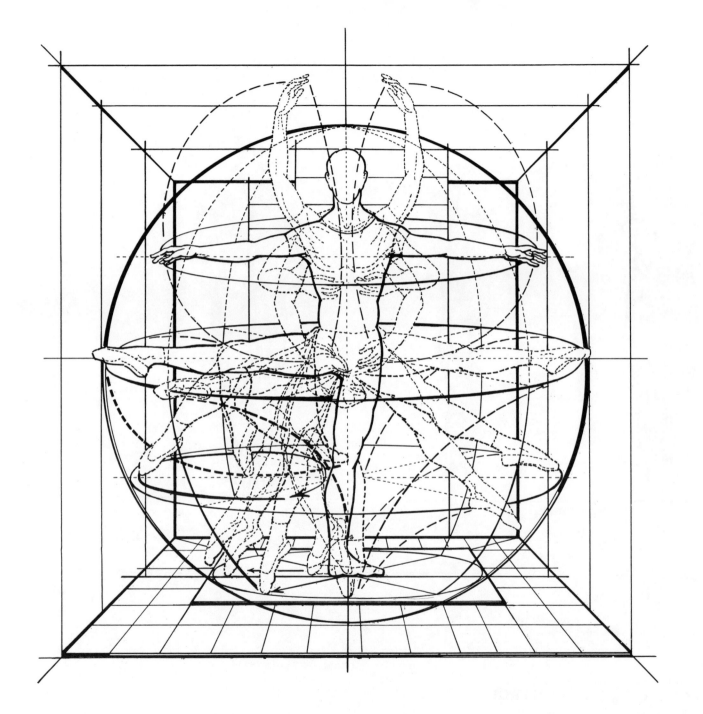

Space Module of the Arms and Legs III (front view)

Part I: Exercises at the Bar

Introduction to Bar Technique

The dance student begins her training at the bar, executing a series of exercises carefully designed to prepare the body for the exacting demands of the classic dance. Each exercise has the function of strengthening specific parts of the torso and legs: *e.g.*, *plié* stretches the Achilles tendon, *battement tendu*, the feet; *grand battement* gives freedom of movement to the entire leg from the hips; and *port de bras* gives flexibility to, and develops co-ordination in, the entire body.

These exercises, correctly approached, develop the student gradually, giving her the ability to achieve a balanced and integrated control of her movements.

The support afforded by the bar relieves the student of the undue strain of maintaining independent control of the entire body before her muscles are sufficiently prepared. Bar practice remains an important part of the dancer's technique throughout professional life. It is invariably employed as preparation for every class or performance.

Exercises at the bar are preceded by the following arm preparation: the free arm is raised to the level of the diaphragm and outward to the side, elbow slightly lifted, palm held inward, where it remains throughout the exercise. The supporting hand rests lightly on the bar and should be held slightly forward of the body, in line of vision, with the elbow relaxed. The bar should not be gripped, or leaned upon, or pulled away from. At the conclusion of each exercise and final return of working leg to 5th position front, release arm from the bar. The free arm is raised slightly, turning palm downward. Both arms are returned to preparatory position. Remain in 5th position momentarily before turning to repeat movement with left leg.

During the first and second years of training, each exercise should be performed slowly and as simply as possible: for example, elementary students should master the *demi-plié* in all five positions thoroughly before attempting *grand plié* with its accompanying arm movement.

In the text, each exercise is given in its simplest form. At a later stage in training, the student begins to perform the exercises in varying tempos and combinations. In some instances, some of the many possible variations have been indicated. I have also suggested how many times each exercise may be performed, but this may be and often is varied by the teacher, according to the student's need. An exercise that is to be executed, for example, eight times in each direction may *either* be executed eight times to the front, eight times to the side, eight times to the back, and eight times to the side, *or* once to the front, once to the side, once to the back, and once to the side, and this combination performed eight times. The note on Posture and Muscular Control will, I hope, be of further assistance in the execution of the exercise described.

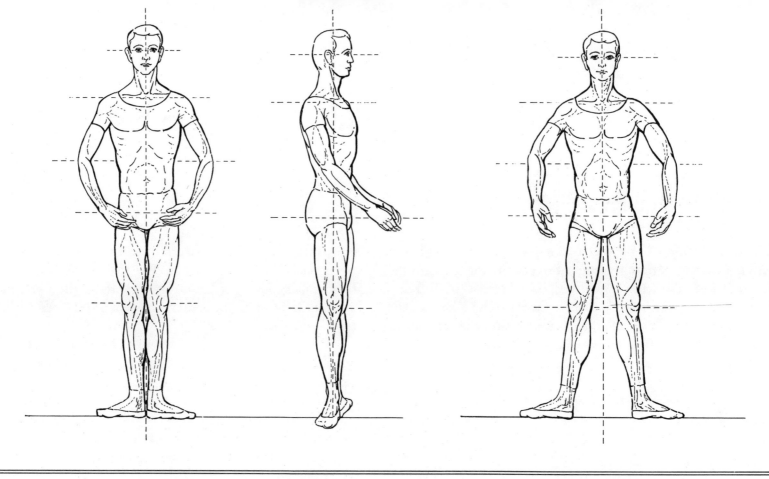

fig. 1   *First Position*   *fig. 2*   *First Position, side view*   *fig. 3*   *Second Position*

Plate 4. Five Basic Positions

All leg movements proceed from these five basic positions and have their logical termination in them.

1st Position: Keep heels together, turn feet outward in straight line.

2nd Position: Turn feet outward in straight line, separated by distance of one foot.

3rd Position: Turn feet outward, place heels together one in front of the other.

4th Position: Turn feet outward, place one foot in front of the other on parallel line, separated by a distance of one foot. Heels and toes are in line forming a square.*

5th Position: Turn feet outward, place one foot directly in front of the other, the first joint of the big toe projecting beyond either heel.

---

*4th Position Ouvert: Advance one foot forward from 1st position, feet separated by a distance of one foot.

[32]

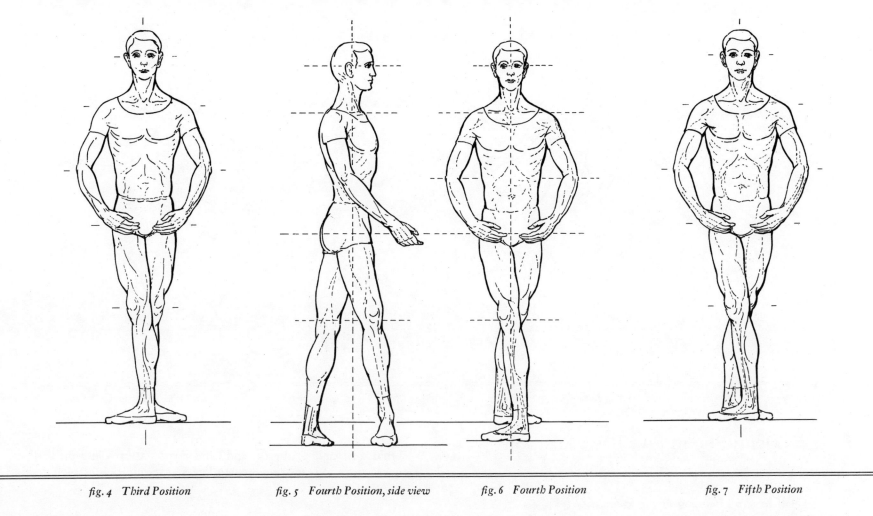

fig. 4 *Third Position* fig. 5 *Fourth Position, side view* fig. 6 *Fourth Position* fig. 7 *Fifth Position*

POSTURE AND MUSCULAR CONTROL

1 Center weight equally between the feet.

2 Tighten muscles in thighs and buttocks. Draw abdomen in and lift diaphragm.

3 Turn thighs outward, keep knees straight and in direct line with center of turned-out feet.

4 Hold shoulders down.

5 Arms are rounded, slightly advanced from body, elbows lifted, palms held inward. Fingers relaxed, thumb held inward, 3rd and 4th fingers held lightly together. Arms are slightly forward of body.

6 Keep head centered, neck free from tension, eyes straight ahead.

[33]

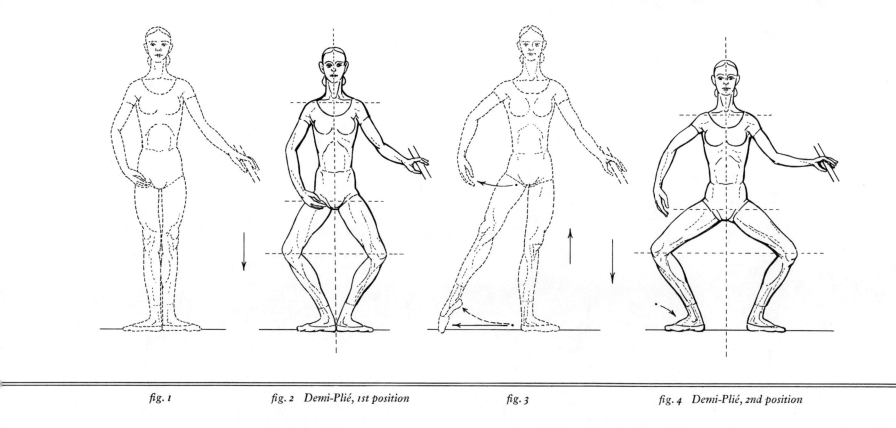

Plate 5. Demi-Plié in Five Basic Positions

(Half or small bending of the knees.)

This basic exercise turns out legs and develops the tendons and muscles of thighs, calves, ankles, and feet, increasing flexibility and strength in the Achilles tendon. The spring-like action of *demi-plié* is essential to all jumping movements as preparation before jumping upward and upon return of feet to the floor.

Exercise

In 1st position: *demi-plié* is a slow, continuous bending and straightening of knees without lifting heels from floor during exercise.

Hold torso and head erect and bend knees outward in a direct line over center of feet, straightening knees at termination of each *demi-plié (figs. 1-2).*

Execute *demi-plié* four times in all five basic positions. Transitional movements from 1st position through the five basic positions are outlined below, demonstrating their logical development from one to the other.

Moving from 1st to 2nd position: Weight on supporting leg, slide toe of working foot on floor, heel thrust forward, in a straight line to point in 2nd position. Lower heel to floor, distributing weight equally between the feet. (Toe of working foot must keep contact with floor in moving from one position to another.) Free arm moves to side as leg slides to point. Feet are now separated by a distance of one foot *(figs. 3-4).*

[34]

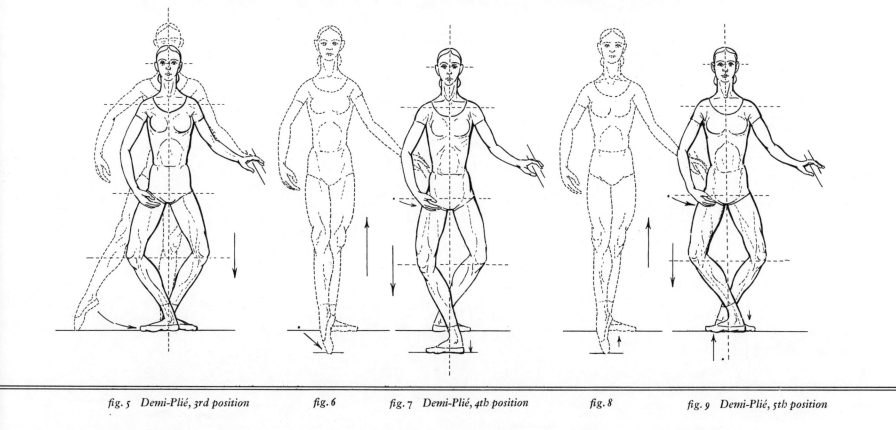

fig. 5 *Demi-Plié, 3rd position*   fig. 6   fig. 7 *Demi-Plié, 4th position*   fig. 8   fig. 9 *Demi-Plié, 5th position*

Moving from 2nd to 3rd position: Point foot of working leg, heel thrust forward. Slide foot back, placing heel of working foot in front of heel of supporting foot. Free arm moves back to preparatory position as leg returns to 3rd position *(fig. 5).*

Moving from 2nd to 4th position: Point extended foot, shifting weight to supporting leg. Move working foot, heel thrust forward, toe on floor, in a quarter circle to point front; heel is lowered and brought forward. In lowering heel, bring torso slightly forward to maintain balance. Move arm to side as working leg describes quarter-circle forward (not illustrated).

Moving from 3rd to 4th position: Keep weight on supporting leg. Slide working foot forward, heel thrust forward, toe on floor, until reaching point. Lower heel. As heel is lowered, torso is brought forward slightly to maintain balance. Move arm to side as working leg moves forward *(figs. 6-7).*

Moving from 4th to 5th position: Point toe of working foot, shifting weight to supporting leg. Bring foot back, toe on floor; heel brought forward directly in front of supporting foot. Move arm back to preparatory position simultaneously with working leg *(figs. 8-9).*

POSTURE AND MUSCULAR CONTROL

1   As body descends and knees bend there must be a slight counter-pull upward in muscles of thighs, abdomen, and buttocks. Executing *demi-plié* in 4th position, hold torso erect, slightly forward, distributing weight equally between the feet.

2   Turn knees out in direct line over feet, preventing them from bending forward. *Keep weight in center of feet,* avoid pressing and rolling forward.

3   Hold free arm down, rounded and slightly advanced from body in 1st, 3rd, and 5th positions, and down to side and slightly forward in line of vision in 2nd and 4th positions.

[35]

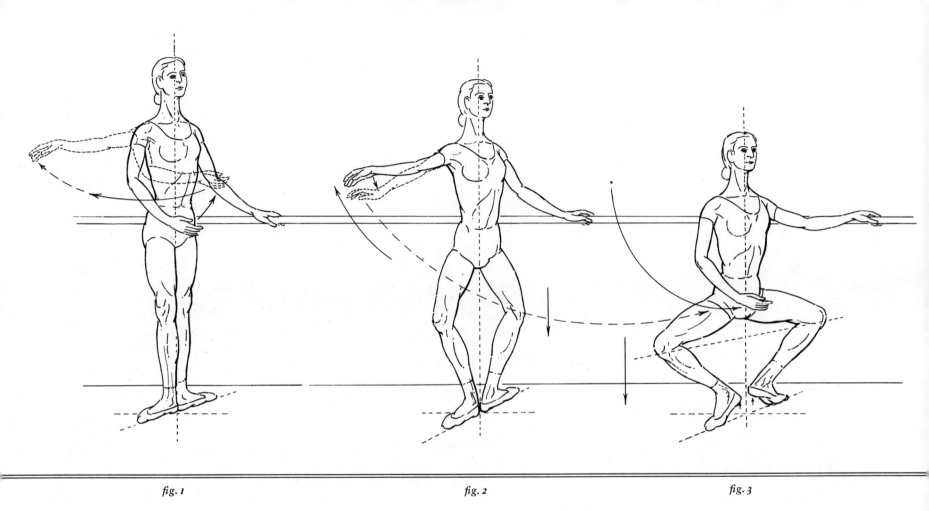

fig. 1   fig. 2   fig. 3

Plate 6. Grand Plié

A slow, continuous movement, bending downward and rising upward without pause, co-ordinating movement of free arm with movement of legs.

EXERCISE

Move knees outward in direct line over center of feet; keep heels on floor when descending until reaching *demi-plié (fig. 2)*, continue *plié* downward, lifting heels a slight distance from floor *(fig. 3)*: upon reaching maximum bend of *grand plié*, press heels to floor and rise *immediately (figs. 4-5)*. Straighten knees at termination of each *plié (fig. 6)*.

Extended arm accompanies leg movement. Raise arm slightly, turning palm downward *(fig. 2)*, as body descends, and carry arm downward in front of body *(fig. 3)*. As you rise and straighten knees, carry

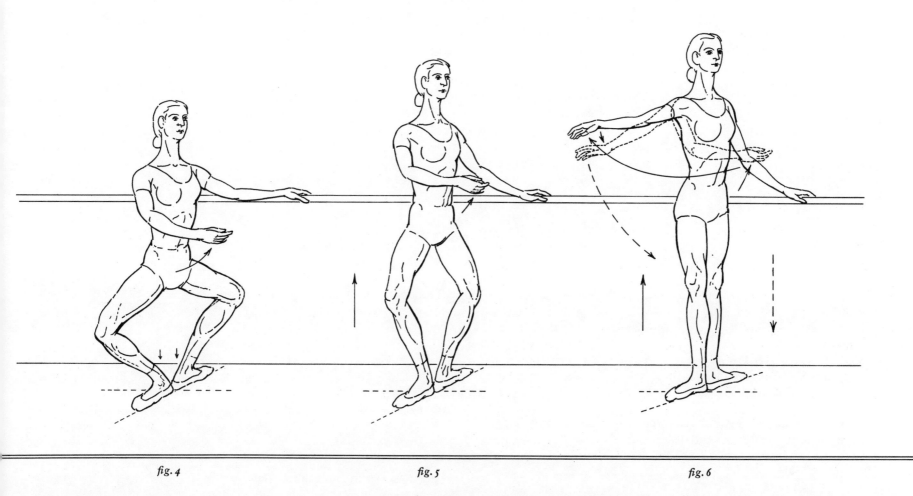

fig. 4   fig. 5   fig. 6

POSTURE AND MUSCULAR CONTROL

arm upward, rounded and extended, fingers in line with center of body, to chest level *(figs. 4-5)*. When body is erect, carry arm outward to side *(fig. 6)*.

Usually performed twice in each position, terminating with *relevé* and balanced on *demi-pointes*. Heels are raised and returned to floor in 1st, 3rd, 4th, and 5th positions; they remain on floor in 2nd position.

1   Center weight equally on the feet, hold torso and head erect, turn knees and thighs outward. Move knees outward in a line over center of feet, preventing them from pressing forward.

2   As body descends and knees bend there must be a slight counter-pull upward in muscles of thighs, abdomen, and buttocks. As body rises and heels press into floor, slightly increase tension in buttocks and abdomen.

3   Executing *plié* in 4th position, hold torso erect, slightly forward, distributing weight equally between the feet.

[37]

Plate 7. Port de Bras (at the bar)

Gives flexibility to and develops co-ordination in entire body. The movements are flowing and continuous.

EXERCISE

In 5th position: (extended arm accompanies movement of body). Raise arm slightly, turning palm downward *(fig. 1)*. Arm accompanies movement of torso bending forward. Head moves with body until parallel with floor *(fig. 2)*. As body rises to upright position, carry arm upward, rounded and extended, fingers in line with center of body, to a position above head in line of vision. Bend torso backward (arm remaining in line of vision), until chest and face are parallel to ceiling *(fig. 3)*. As body returns to upright position, lower arm to side *(fig. 4)*.

This *port de bras* is executed once in 5th position and once on the *demi-pointes*, and from many other positions.

POSTURE AND MUSCULAR CONTROL

1 As body bends forward, draw abdomen in, keeping neck and shoulders relaxed.

2 Returning to upright position, and raising free arm to position above head, lift diaphragm, hold shoulders down.

3 Hold knees straight, turned outward and firmly together.

4 *When body bends backward*, thrust hips slightly forward. When returning to upright position, tighten abdomen and hold shoulders down, controlling movement and direction of arm as it opens, returning to the side.

[38]

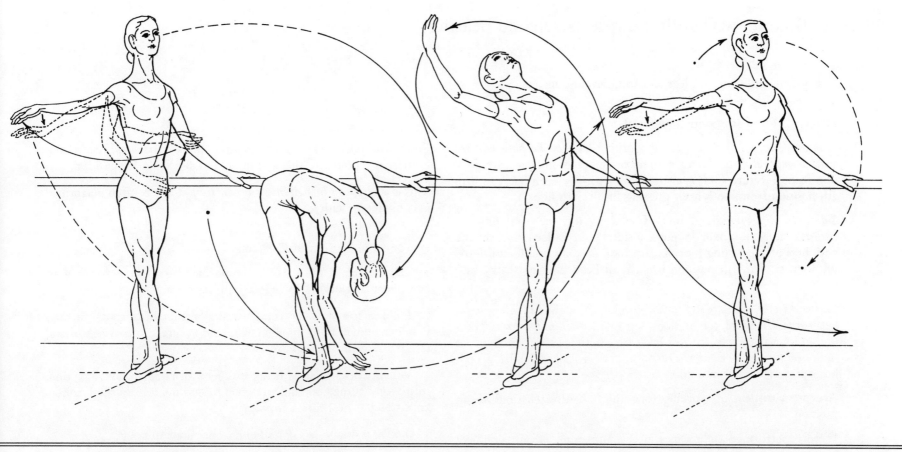

fig. 1   *fifth position*   fig. 2   *bend forward*   fig. 3   *rise—bend backward*   fig. 4   *(continue movement from fig. 1, etc.)*

PORT DE BRAS *(at the bar)*

Plate 8. Battement Tendu Simple (stretched beating)

Strengthens and turns out legs and feet, develops insteps.

EXERCISE [From 5th position *(fig. 1):*]

Forward (fig. 2): Extend foot of working leg, *toe keeping contact with floor, heel thrust forward,* to maximum point in front (4th position front). Return foot, *keeping heel forward,* toe on floor, to firm 5th position front, both heels pressing firmly into floor.

Sideways (fig. 3): Extend foot of working leg, toe on floor, *heel thrust forward,* to maximum point at side (2nd position) in direct line with heel of supporting foot. Return foot, *keeping heel forward,* toe on floor, to firm 5th position back, both heels pressing firmly into floor.

Backward (fig. 4): Extend foot of working leg with *toe leading back,* heel turned forward, toe on floor, *leg well turned out from thigh to toe,* to its maximum point in back (4th position back). Return foot with *heel turned forward,* toe on floor, to firm 5th position back, both heels pressing firmly into floor.

Accent movement of working foot upon return each time to 5th position.

Usually performed eight times in each direction (front, side, and back).

BATTEMENT TENDU DEMI-PLIE

Upon return of working foot to 5th position, keep both knees straight, then execute *demi-plié,* with muscular counter-pull upward, keeping weight equally distributed between the feet, heels remaining on floor.

From *demi-plié* working foot extends to point *(battement tendu)* and exercise is repeated to side and back, and also from 1st position.

This is a variation of *battement tendu simple,* and is often performed in conjunction with it.

POSTURE AND MUSCULAR CONTROL

1   Center weight of body on supporting leg to give freedom of movement to working leg. Hold both legs straight.

2   Hold torso and head erect, draw abdomen in, lift diaphragm, hold shoulders down. Both shoulders are held in direct line over hips and face forward throughout exercise.

3   When working leg is being extended to point in any direction, entire leg is turned out and stretched to maximum from thigh to toe, knee straight, heel thrust forward.

4   Toe of working leg *slides lightly* over floor to point.

5   When working leg is returned to 5th position keep both knees straight, legs turned out, heels pressed firmly into floor.

6   When executing *battement tendu* to back, move torso slightly forward, hold shoulders down. Lead with toe to point in back. Turn working leg out from thigh to toe, heel turned forward. Hold hips down.

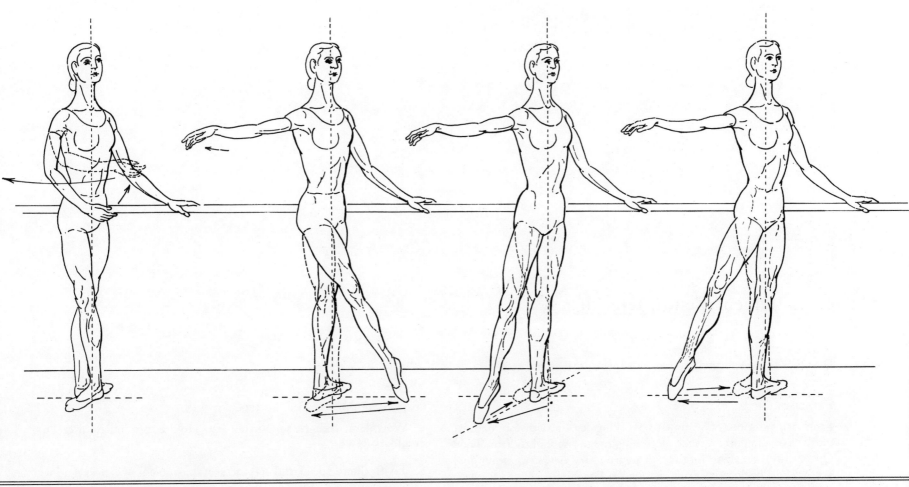

fig. 1 *fifth position*   fig. 2 *front (en avant)*   fig. 3 *side (à la seconde)*   fig. 4 *back (en arrière)*

BATTEMENT TENDU SIMPLE *(stretched beating)*

Plate 9. Battement Tendu Jeté (dégagé)*

Develops speed and precision in movement of legs and feet.

EXERCISE

From 5th position. Slide foot of working leg, heel thrust forward, until maximum point is reached, forcing toe to rise slightly from floor. On return of working foot to 5th position, *toe is first to touch floor* as foot slides back to 5th position *(fig. 1)*. The movement of *battement tendu jeté* is brisk and continuous, accented upon each return of foot to 5th position. Repeat to side and back *(figs. 2-3)*.

Battement tendu jeté is also executed from 1st position.

Usually performed eight times in each direction.

*According to Cecchetti, *battement dégagé*.

POSTURE AND MUSCULAR CONTROL

1 Weight on straight supporting leg. Hold torso and head erect, shoulders down.

2 To facilitate speed and lightness of movement when executing *battement*, tighten buttocks, draw abdomen in, lift diaphragm.

3 When working leg is extended, it is straight and stretched to maximum *from thigh to toe*. Turn out working leg, thrust heel forward.

4 When executing *battement tendu jeté* to back, move torso slightly forward, hold shoulders and hips down, working leg turned out *from thigh to toe*.

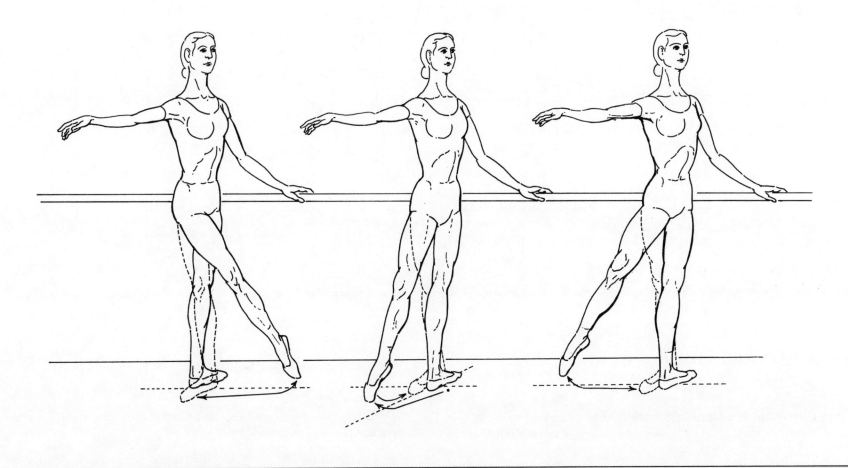

fig. 1 front (en avant)   *fig. 2 side (à la seconde)*   *fig. 3 back (en arrière)*

BATTEMENT TENDU JETÉ *(dégagé)**

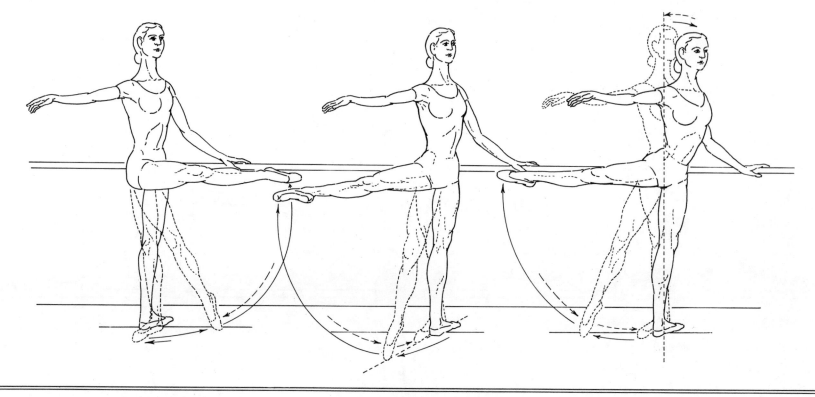

fig. 1   front (en avant)   fig. 2   side (à la seconde)   fig. 3   back (en arrière)

Plate 10. Grand Battement Jeté*

Develops freedom of leg movement from hips.

EXERCISE

Briskly swing working leg with foot sliding on floor to maximum point upward and outward to 90 degrees. Returning working leg, point toe on floor, slide foot back, bring heel forward to 5th position (fig. 1). Repeat to side and back (figs. 2-3).

Usually performed eight times in each direction.

*According to Cecchetti, grand battement.

[44]

POSTURE AND MUSCULAR CONTROL

1   Hold torso erect and both legs straight, weight on supporting leg.

2   When executing grand battement, draw abdomen in and lift diaphragm; hold shoulders down.

3   During battement movement, hold hips down and facing forward. Turn thighs outward. Hold knees straight and firm. Bring heel of working foot forward with toe fully pointed. Control descent of working leg to 5th position.

4   When executing grand battement jeté to back, move torso slightly forward, holding shoulders down as working leg moves upward to back (fig. 3). Slight muscular tension in buttocks and thighs controls descent of working leg to 5th position.

fig. 1 *Battement Jeté Pointé en avant*

Plate 11. Grand Battement Jeté Pointé*

Strengthens torso and legs from thigh to toe.

EXERCISE

From 5th position. Executed in same manner as *grand battement jeté*. Working leg descends to point on floor forward, and continues *battement* movement from this position. Working leg returns to 5th position *only* when making a change of direction.

Usually performed four times in each direction; also combined with *grand battement jeté*.

POSTURE AND MUSCULAR CONTROL

1 Weight on straight, firm supporting leg.

2 When executing *battement jeté pointé*, move working leg, stretched from thigh to toe, as a *single unit*. Touch floor lightly with descending pointed toe, keeping toe pointed and heel forward.

3 When executing exercise to back, move torso slightly forward, holding shoulders down as working leg moves upward to back. Muscular tension in thighs and buttocks as working leg *descends* to point in any direction.

---

*According to Cecchetti, *grand battement* from the *pointe tendue*.

Plate 12. Grand Battement Jeté (sur les demi-pointes)

Develops balance, strengthens legs and insteps.

EXERCISE

From 5th position. Execute *grand battement* from *demi-pointes*. Performed four or eight times in each direction.

POSTURE AND MUSCULAR CONTROL

1   5th position *demi-pointes:* hold torso and head erect, tighten buttocks, thighs, and knees; press legs firmly together and turn them outward; bring heels forward.

2   When executing exercise to back, move body slightly forward, holding shoulders down as working leg moves upward to back *(fig. 3)*.

fig. 1 front (en avant, 90 degrees)   *fig. 2 side (à la seconde, 90 degrees)*   *fig. 3 back (en arrière, 90 degrees)*

GRAND BATTEMENT JETÉ *(sur les demi-pointes)*

Plate 13. Grand Battement Jeté Balancé*

Gives freedom of movement to hips, torso and legs.

EXERCISE

From 4th position pointing back *(fig. 1)*. Energetically swing working leg through 1st position forward and upward to 90 degrees *(fig. 2)*. Swing working leg through 1st position to back and upward to 90 degrees *(fig. 3)*. (The force of the action inclines torso slightly forward.) *Grand Battement Jeté Balancé* is a continuous swinging movement forward and backward, usually performed eight times.

---

*Also known as *grand battement en cloche* and *en balançoire*.

POSTURE AND MUSCULAR CONTROL

1   Weight on supporting leg. When working leg swings forward, hold shoulders down, head facing extended arm. When working leg swings backward, hold shoulders down, head inclining slightly forward and facing extended arm *(fig. 3)*.

2   As working leg descends from front or back, *pointed toe first* touches floor lightly, *heel brought forward and lowered to floor* as foot passes each time through 1st position *(figs. 2-3)*.

3   Turn thighs outward, hold knees straight, bring heels forward.

fig. 1 *fourth position (pointing back)*   fig. 2 *swing forward*   fig. 3 *swing backward*

GRAND BATTEMENT JETÉ BALANCÉ*

[49]

Plate 14. Battements Frappés Pointés

Develops strength in legs, ankles, and insteps.

PREPARATION

From 5th position point working foot to 2nd position and return to position *sur le cou-de-pied* front of supporting ankle *(fig. 1)*.

EXERCISE

Extend working foot to point forward, return to position *sur le cou-de-pied in front* of supporting ankle *(fig. 2)*. Extend working foot to point in 2nd position, return to position *sur le cou-de-pied in back* of supporting ankle *(fig. 3)*. Extend working foot to point back, returning to position *sur le cou-de-pied in back* of supporting ankle *(fig. 4)*. Accent all pointed positions. This exercise may be executed on the *demi-pointe (relevé)* of supporting foot with working leg extended 45 degrees.

Usually performed eight times in each direction.

POSTURE AND MUSCULAR CONTROL

1 Weight on supporting leg. Hold torso erect, draw abdomen in, lift diaphragm, shoulders down.

2 Position *sur le cou-de-pied*. Bring heel forward. Turn knee of working leg outward. When extending to point outward, stretch and turn legs outward to maximum from thigh to toe.

3 *Executing exercise to back*, move torso slightly forward, holding shoulders down. Lead with toe to point in a direct line in back of the body, heel turned forward *(fig. 3)*.

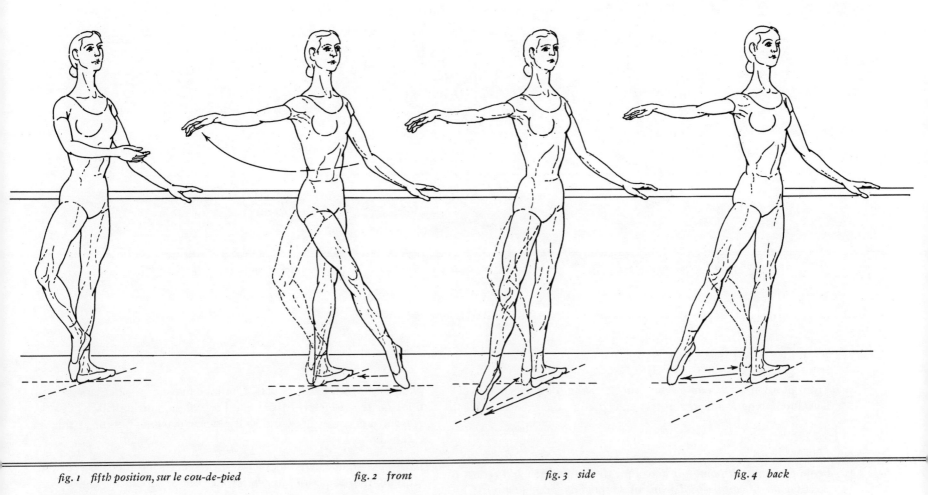

fig. 1   fifth position, sur le cou-de-pied   fig. 2   front   fig. 3   side   fig. 4   back

BATTEMENTS FRAPPÉS POINTÉS

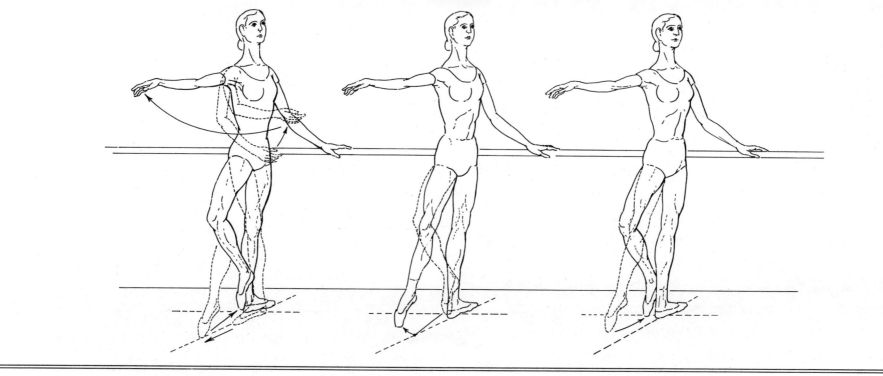

Plate 15. Battements Frappés (single and double)

BATTEMENT FRAPPÉ SINGLE

From position *sur le cou-de-pied* (neck of the foot, or ankle joint)
Develops strength in legs and feet and speed in their movement.

PREPARATION

From 5th position point working foot to 2nd position and return to position *sur le cou-de-pied front* of supporting ankle *(fig. 1)*.

EXERCISE

Move working leg briskly sideways to maximum point. Toe strikes floor on outward movement and "ricochets" a slight distance from the surface *(fig. 2)*. Return working foot to position *sur le cou-de-pied, back of supporting ankle*. Continue movement, alternating positions *sur le cou-de-pied* front and back of supporting ankle *(fig. 3)*. Accent movement of working leg when maximum point at side is reached.

Battement frappé may be executed with accent on the *return* of the working foot to position *sur le cou-de-pied* of supporting leg.

This movement is also executed forward and backward; when the leg is moving backward it is stretched to maximum from thigh to toe, in a direct line in back of the body. Usually performed twice in each direction. *Battement frappé* is also executed on the *demi-pointe* (*relevé*).

[52]

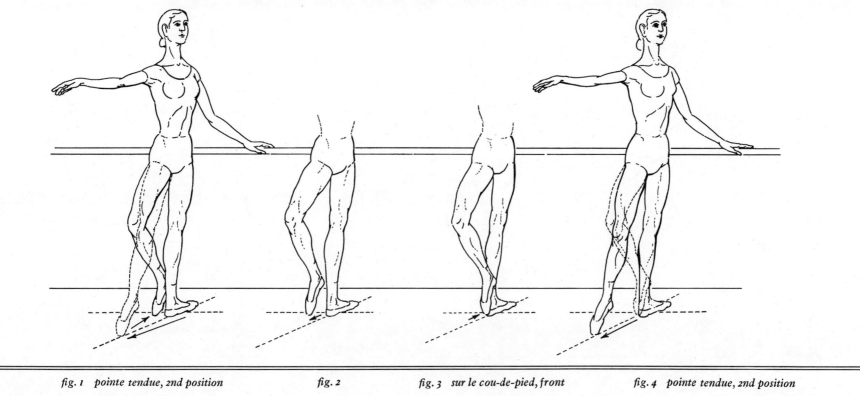

fig. 1 *pointe tendue, 2nd position*   fig. 2   fig. 3 *sur le cou-de-pied, front*   fig. 4 *pointe tendue, 2nd position*

BATTEMENT DOUBLE FRAPPÉ

EXERCISE

From *pointe tendue* 2nd position *(fig. 1)*, make an additional small beating movement from position *sur le cou-de-pied* back to front *(figs. 2-3)*, or front to back of supporting ankle before extending each time to point in second position *(fig. 4)*. (The "beat" is a small, quick movement, foot opening slightly to side in passing from back to front or front to back of ankle.) This movement may also be executed extending working foot to point front and back.

Usually performed once to the 4th front, once to the 4th back, twice to 2nd position; this combination repeated four times and on *demi-pointes*.

POSTURE AND MUSCULAR CONTROL

1 Weight on supporting leg, shoulders down, abdomen drawn in.

2 Position *sur le cou-de-pied front*. Bring heel well forward, foot wrapped around ankle, toe pointing *down and toward back of supporting heel*. Position *sur le cou-de-pied back*, bring heel *forward against ankle* of supporting leg, toe pointing *down and away from heel (fig. 3)*.

3 When accenting movement *outward*, stretch leg to maximum from thigh to toe.

4 Keep thigh of working leg stationary, well turned outward. *Beating movement takes place from knee downwards.* When working leg is extended, straighten knee, toe fully pointed, heel forward. When returning working foot *sur le cou-de-pied*, keep knee stationary and *turned outward*.

[53]

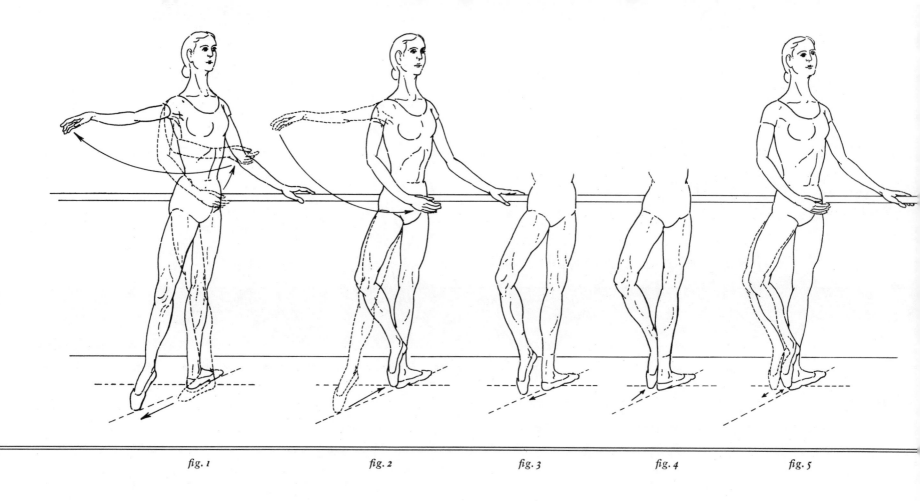

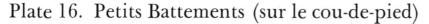

fig. 1   fig. 2   fig. 3   fig. 4   fig. 5

Plate 16. Petits Battements (sur le cou-de-pied)

Develops precision and speed in movement of feet.

PREPARATION

From 5th position. Point working foot to 2nd position *(fig. 1)* and return to position *sur le cou-de-pied* in front of supporting ankle *(fig. 2).*

[54]

EXERCISE

From position *sur le cou-de-pied* front, *slightly open* working foot to side *(fig. 3)* in passing to position *sur le cou-de-pied* back of supporting ankle *(fig. 4)*; return working foot to position *sur le cou-de-pied* front *(fig. 5)*. Execute with working foot a series of small beating movements *sur le cou-de-pied* from back to front, accenting *front position*. First executed slowly and distinctly, then with increasing speed and varied accents. Repeat movement on *demi-pointe (relevé)* of supporting foot *(figs. 6-9).*

Usually performed with two slow and three quick movements.

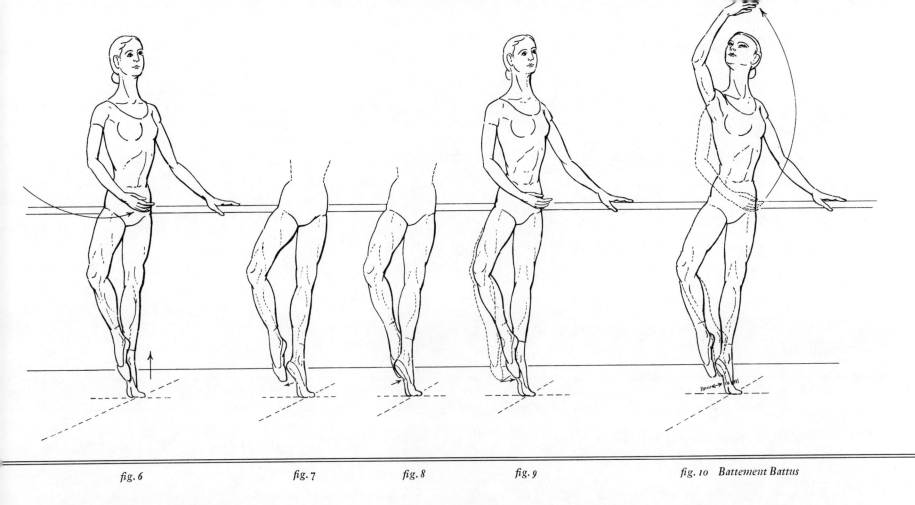

fig. 6   fig. 7   fig. 8   fig. 9   fig. 10   Battement Battus

BATTEMENTS BATTUS (fig. 10)

EXERCISE

From 5th position *demi-pointe*. Carry extended arm upward to a position above head in line of vision, palm held inward, head turned upward towards palm of hand. Execute with pointed toe of working foot a series of small rapid beatings in front on ankle of supporting foot on *demi-pointe*.

Usually executed eight or sixteen times.

POSTURE AND MUSCULAR CONTROL

1 Weight on supporting leg. Hold torso erect and shoulders down; draw abdomen in; lift diaphragm. Hold *thigh and knee of working leg stationary* and turned outward.

2 When rising on to *demi-pointe*, hold shoulders down. Make small beating movements with *fully pointed toe* in front of supporting ankle.

3 When executing *battements battus*, keep working knee turned out, calf and heel forward. The leg, from knee to toe, moves as one unit; from knee to hip, is held stationary. The movement becomes smaller with increasing speed, but remains even, distinct, and precise.

[55]

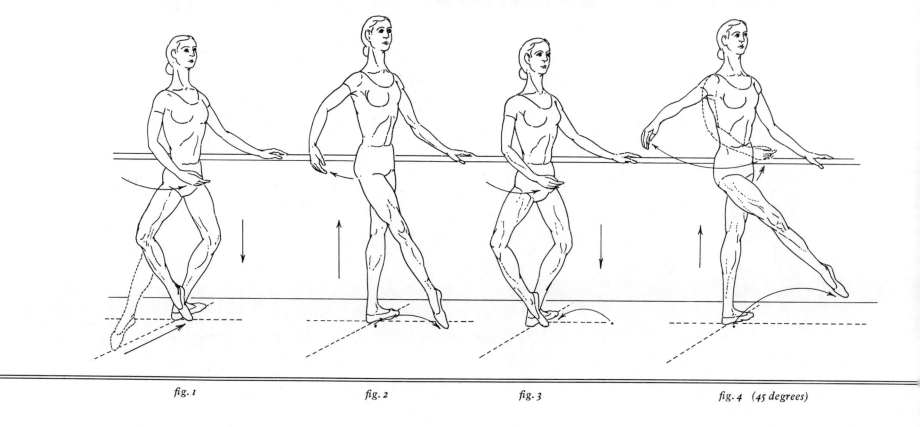

fig. 1   fig. 2   fig. 3   fig. 4 (45 degrees)

Plate 17. Battements Fondus*

A slow bending of supporting leg with working foot pointing in front of supporting ankle, simultaneously unfolding and extending to point on floor or in the air as supporting leg slowly straightens.

Each movement usually performed once in each direction.

BATTEMENT FONDU SIMPLE*

From 5th position point working foot to 2nd position *(fig. 1)*:

EXERCISE

Execute *demi-plié* on supporting leg, *simultaneously pointing* extended foot in front of supporting ankle. Point working foot on floor in front, simultaneously straightening supporting leg *(fig. 2)*.

[56]

BATTEMENT FONDU DÉVELOPPÉ (45 degrees)

EXERCISE: *(figs. 3-4)*

Simultaneously execute *demi-plié* on supporting leg and bring extended foot back, toe pointed in front of supporting ankle. Straighten supporting leg and *simultaneously extend working leg* in air forward to 45 degrees. Execute *demi-plié* on supporting leg, simultaneously pointing extended foot in front of supporting ankle.

BATTEMENT FONDU DÉVELOPPÉ (90 degrees)

EXERCISE: *(figs. 5-6)*

Straighten supporting leg, bringing pointed toe in front of supporting knee, and extend working leg in air forward to 90 degrees. Execute *demi-plié* on supporting leg, simultaneously pointing extended foot in front of supporting ankle.

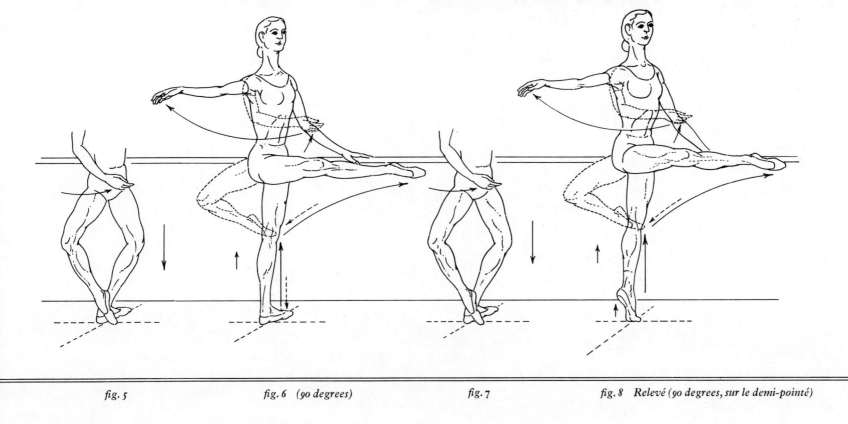

fig. 5   fig. 6   (90 degrees)   fig. 7   fig. 8   Relevé (90 degrees, sur le demi-pointé)

BATTEMENT FONDU DÉVELOPPÉ RELEVÉ
(90 degrees)

EXERCISE: (figs. 7-8)

Straighten supporting leg and rise to *demi-pointe (relevé)*, bringing pointed toe in front of supporting knee, and extend working leg in air forward to 90 degrees. Lower heel to floor and execute *demi-plié* on supporting leg, returning extended leg, toe pointing in front of supporting ankle.

ARM MOVEMENT

Arm is lowered and brought back to preparatory position as working foot returns to position *sur le cou-de-pied* (supporting leg executing *demi-plié*). Arm accompanies leg extending outward, moving first to *chest level* and then outward to side as leg is extended each time.

---

*According to Cecchetti, a series of *développés* from *demi-plié*.

POSTURE AND MUSCULAR CONTROL

1   When executing *demi-plié*, weight on supporting foot, hold torso erect, draw abdomen in, lift diaphragm. Move knee of supporting leg *in direct line over center of supporting foot*, heel remaining on floor throughout *plié*.

2   When working leg is extended, straighten and turn knees outward; bring calf and heel forward. Returning working leg to position *sur le cou-de-pied*, bring heel forward.

3   Rising on to *demi-pointe* of supporting leg. Increase muscular tension in thighs.

4   In *battement fondu développé, working leg moves evenly and continuously* from start of movement until reaching angle of 45 or 90 degrees, and is *momentarily sustained* in this position before slowly returning to position in front or back of ankle of supporting leg executing *demi-plié*.

[57]

Plate 18. Battement Soutenu

From 5th position *(fig. 1)*, simultaneously execute *demi-plié* on supporting leg, lift and extend working foot to point in front *(fig. 2)*. Rise to half toe on supporting leg, simultaneously drawing extended leg back to supporting leg 5th position *demi-pointes (fig. 3)*. Repeat movement to side *(fig. 4)* and in back.

Usually performed once in each direction, and combined with *grand développé*.

Posture and Muscular Control

1 Weight on supporting leg in *demi-plié* and equally distributed when legs are drawn together on *demi-pointes*.

2 When executing *demi-plié* on supporting leg, hold torso erect, draw abdomen in, lift diaphragm. Move bent knee outward in direct line over center of supporting foot, heel remaining on floor.

3 Extending working leg to point in any direction, turn calf and knee outward, bring heel forward.

4 Drawing legs together 5th position *demi-pointes*, tighten and turn thighs outward, hold legs straight and feet firmly together.

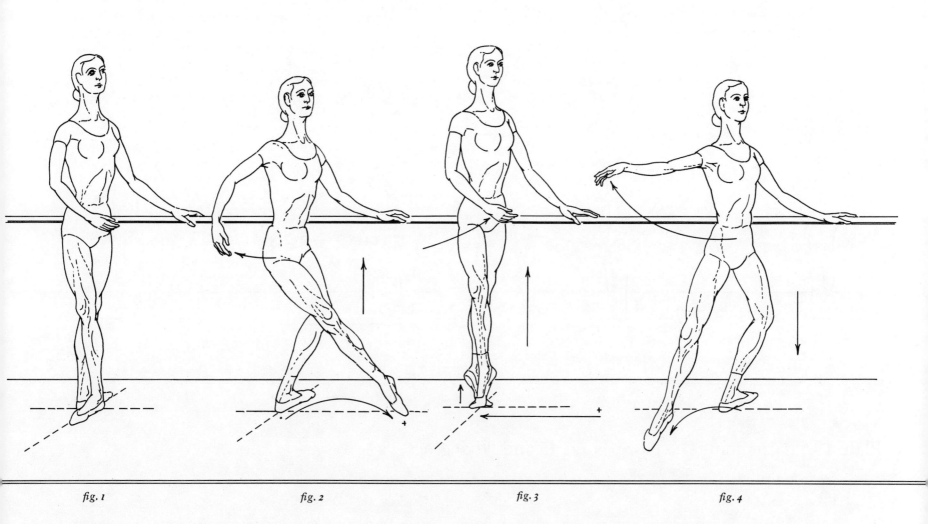

fig. 1   fig. 2   fig. 3   fig. 4

BATTEMENT SOUTENU

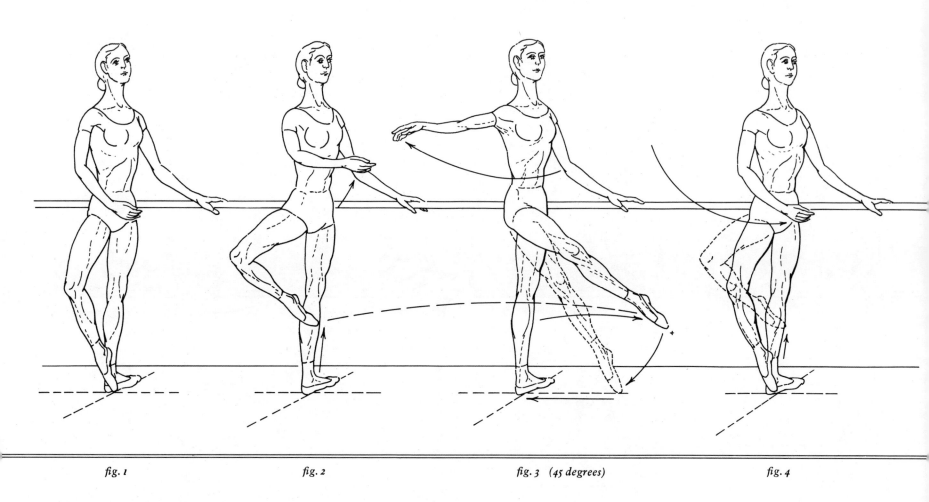

fig. 1   fig. 2   fig. 3 (45 degrees)   fig. 4

Plate 19. Battements Développés (at 45 and 90 degrees)

EXERCISE AT 45 DEGREES

From 5th position. Raise working foot to point in front of supporting ankle *(fig. 1)*, bring pointed toe in front of supporting calf *(fig. 2)* and extend working leg in air forward to 45 degrees *(fig. 3)*. Lower leg to point forward and close in 5th position *(fig. 3)*.

Repeat movement to side *(fig. 4)* and back.

[60]

EXERCISE AT 90 DEGREES

From 5th position. Raise working foot to point in front of supporting ankle *(fig. 5)*, bring pointed toe in front of supporting knee *(fig. 6)* and extend working leg in air forward to 90 degrees *(fig. 7)*. Lower leg to point forward and close in 5th position *(fig. 7)*.

Repeat movement to side and back.

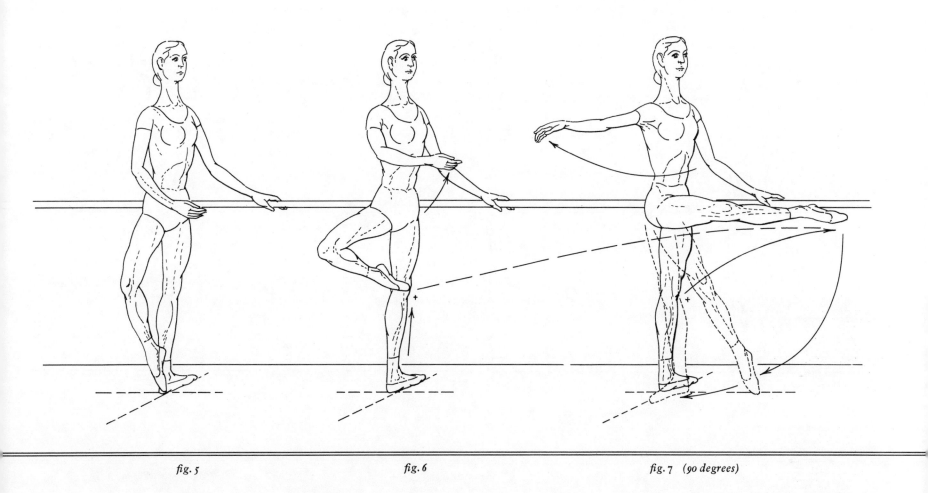

fig. 5   fig. 6   fig. 7 (90 degrees)

Working leg moves *evenly and continuously* until reaching 45 degrees or 90 degrees, and is momentarily sustained in this position before being lowered to point forward and back to 5th position.

This exercise may be executed with many variations, *e.g.*, with *relevé* on supporting leg as working leg extends each time.

Usually performed once at 45 degrees and once at 90 degrees in each direction.

POSTURE AND MUSCULAR CONTROL

1   Weight on supporting leg held straight and firm, torso erect.

2   Knee of working leg turned outward, calf and heel turned forward as leg extends.

3   Arm is extended to side as legs extend outward and returns to preparatory position as foot returns to 5th position.

[61]

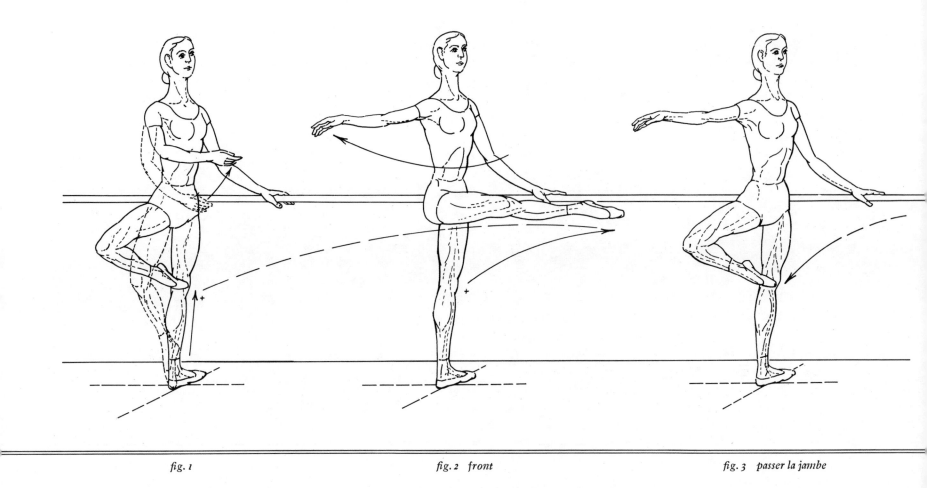

fig. 1   fig. 2   front   fig. 3   passer la jambe

Plate 20. Grands Battements Développés (passer la jambe)*

[Adagio at the bar]

Strengthens the torso and develops balance for Adagio movements.

*According to Cecchetti, *retiré*. According to Mme Nicolaeva-Legat, sometimes referred to as *tire-bouchon*.

[62]

Exercise

From 5th position. Raise working foot to knee of supporting leg, knee turned outward, toe pointing *(fig. 1)*, and without pause extend leg forward to 90 degrees *(fig. 2)*. Return extended leg, toe pointing, to supporting knee *(passer la jambe*) (fig. 3)*. Extend working leg to 2nd position 90 degrees *(fig. 4)*. Return extended leg, toe pointing,

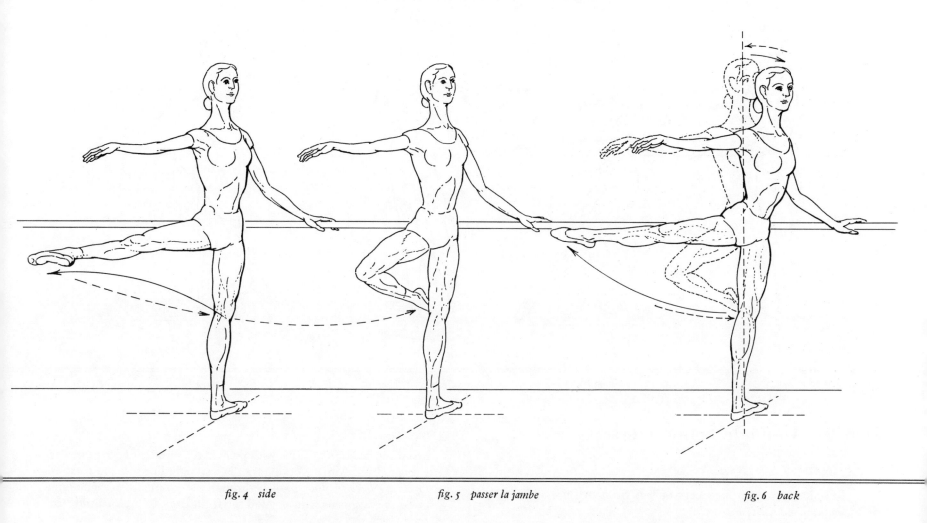

fig. 4 side   *fig. 5 passer la jambe*   *fig. 6 back*

to supporting knee *(fig. 5)*. Repeat movement to back *(fig. 6)* and side. Exercise may be executed with supporting foot on *demi-pointe*.

Working leg moves *evenly and continuously* until reaching 90 degrees and is *momentarily sustained* in this position, before returning to knee of supporting leg, again pausing before the next extension outward.

Usually performed once in each direction.

POSTURE AND MUSCULAR CONTROL

1   Weight on supporting leg held straight and firm, hold torso erect.

2   Extending working leg outward, draw abdomen in, lift diaphragm. Returning toe of extended leg to knee of supporting leg, turn working knee outward, bring calf and heel forward. Extending working leg to 2nd position, bring torso very slightly forward, hold shoulders down. Keep hips down and facing forward throughout exercise.

[63]

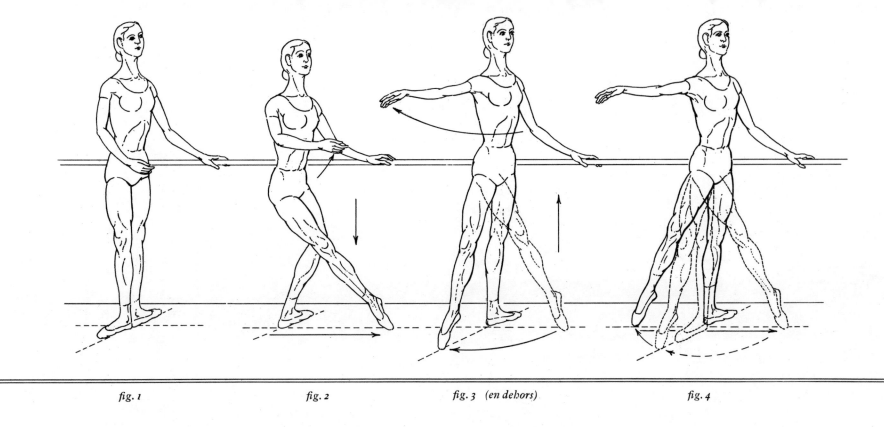

fig. 1 fig. 2 fig. 3 (en dehors) fig. 4

Plate 21. Rond de Jambe à terre

Facilitates rotary movement of legs from the hips and flexibility in ankles and insteps.

ROND DE JAMBE À TERRE EN DEHORS (outward)

Usually performed eight or sixteen times.

PREPARATION

From 1st position (*fig. 1*). Simultaneously execute *demi-plié* on supporting leg, extend working foot, toe keeping contact with floor, to point straight forward (*fig. 2*). Simultaneously straighten supporting leg and execute quarter circle to 2nd position with toe of working foot on floor (*fig. 3*).

EXERCISE: (*fig. 4*)

From 2nd position describe with pointed toe of extended leg a quarter circle to back. Move working foot in a straight line to point forward, *lowering heel to floor* passing through 1st position. Continue semi-circular movement with pointed toe from front to back *passing each time through 1st position.*

POSTURE AND MUSCULAR CONTROL

1 Hold torso erect. Weight on supporting leg throughout preparation and exercise. Keep working leg turned out, knee straight. *Keep pointed toe in contact with floor* throughout semi-circular movement.

2 Bring heel of straight working leg forward and *lower to floor* when passing each time through 1st position.

3 Accent semi-circular movement *outward to back*. Working leg moves continuously, toe sliding lightly over surface of floor.

[64]

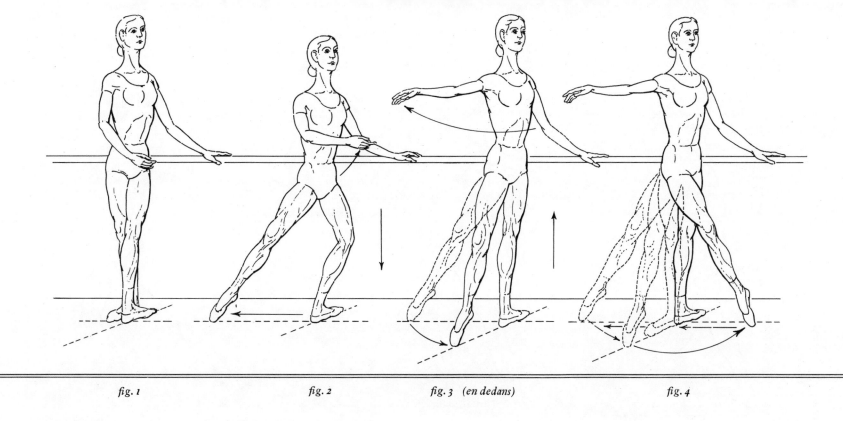

fig. 1   fig. 2   fig. 3 (en dedans)   fig. 4

ROND DE JAMBE À TERRE EN DEDANS (inward)

Usually performed eight or sixteen times.

PREPARATION

From 5th position (fig. 1). Simultaneously execute demi-plié on supporting leg, extend working foot, toe keeping contact with floor, to point straight back (fig. 2). Simultaneously straighten supporting leg and execute quarter circle to 2nd position with toe of working leg on floor (fig. 3).

EXERCISE: (fig. 4)

From 2nd position describe with pointed toe of extended leg a quarter circle to front. Move working foot in a straight line to point backward, lowering heel to floor passing through 1st position. Continue semi-circular movement with pointed toe from back to front passing each time through 1st position.

POSTURE AND MUSCULAR CONTROL

1   When extending working leg back for preparation en dedans, move erect torso slightly forward, hold shoulders down. Turn working leg out from thigh to toe.

2   Weight on supporting leg throughout preparation and exercise. Keep working leg turned out, knee straight. Keep pointed toe in contact with floor throughout semi-circular movement.

3   Bring heel of straight working leg forward and lower to floor when passing each time through 1st position.

4   Accent semi-circular movement inward to front. Working leg moves continuously, toe sliding lightly over surface of floor.

NOTE: Executing rond de jambe the working foot points directly in front and in back of the heel of the standing leg.

[65]

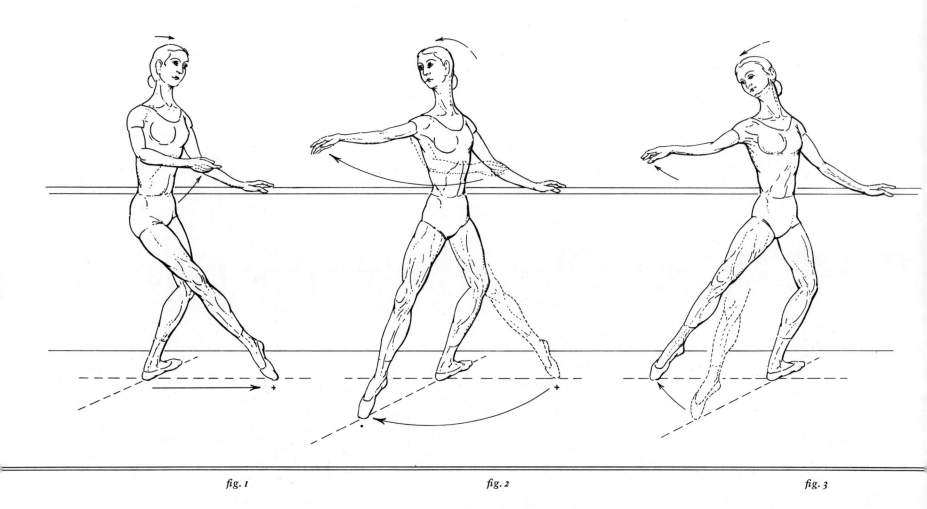

fig. 1   fig. 2   fig. 3

Plate 22. Grand Rond de Jambe à terre (a terminating movement)

(This is one of many terminating movements which may be executed after a series of *ronds de jambe à terre*.)

EXERCISE

From 5th position. Simultaneously execute *demi-plié* on supporting leg, extend working leg to maximum point forward on floor *(fig. 1)*. Supporting leg remains in *plié* for execution of large semi-circular movement to back *(figs. 2-3)* and front with working leg *(grand rond de jambe à terre) (fig. 4)*. Simultaneously rise on to half-toe of

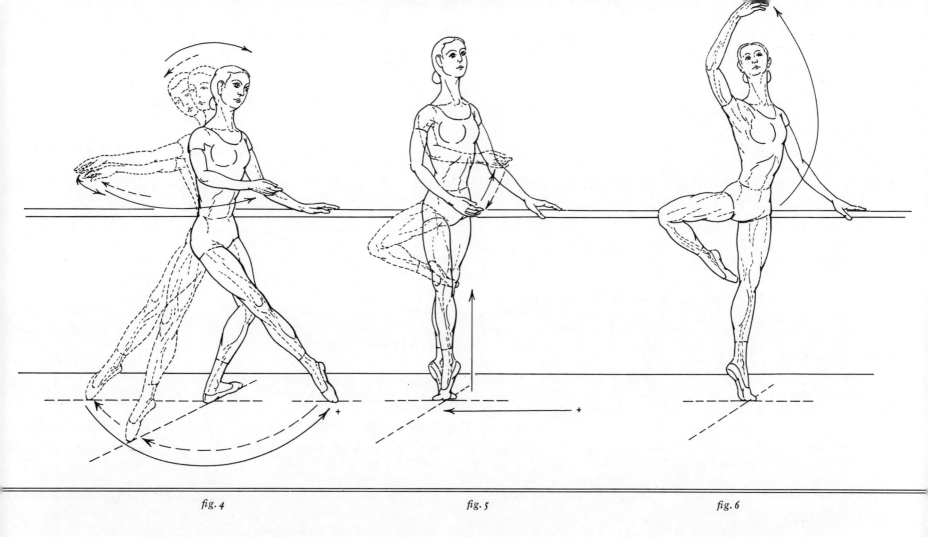

fig. 4   fig. 5   fig. 6

supporting leg and draw extended leg back to supporting leg (5th position *demi-pointes, battement soutenu*) *(fig. 5)*. Move working leg, toe pointed, up to knee of supporting leg (*passé*) *(fig. 6)*. Balance in this position before returning to 5th position.

POSTURE AND MUSCULAR CONTROL

1   Executing *grand rond de jambe* movement to back and front, weight on supporting leg. *Torso, head, and arm* accompany working leg, simultaneously moving outward as leg moves back, and inward as leg moves front.

2   When drawing legs together 5th position *demi-pointes (battement soutenu)*, straighten knees, tighten and turn thighs outward, hold legs straight and feet firmly together *(fig. 5)*.

3   When moving to *passé* position, simultaneously move. working leg, toe pointed, knee turned out, to knee of supporting leg, and carry arm above head in line of vision *(fig. 6)*.

Plate 23. Rond de Jambe en l'air (at 45 and 90 degrees)

(Circular movement of the leg in the air: *en dehors* [outward] and *en dedans* [inward].)

Strengthens entire leg, develops freedom of movement from knee to toe.

PREPARATION

From 5th position front, execute *battement* to 2nd position in the air 45 degrees.

EXERCISE

En dehors (outward) *(fig. 1)*: with pointed toe of working leg, describe *from knee downwards* a semi-circle, commencing with its backward arc, toe almost touching calf of supporting leg in passing to forward arc, *straightening in 2nd position* at conclusion of each circle.

En dedans (inward) *(fig. 2)*: from 5th position back, execute same exercise in reverse direction.

This exercise can also be executed with working leg at an angle of 90 degrees, and with varying speeds and rhythms. When executing double *rond de jambe* (two quick circles of the leg), full extension of leg takes place after second circle at 45 or 90 degrees in the air.

Usually performed eight times *en dehors* and eight times *en dedans*. *Rond de jambe en l'air* is also executed *relevé*.

ATTITUDE EN AVANT (forward)

(This is one of many terminating movements which may be executed after a series of *ronds de jambe en l'air*.)

EXERCISE: *(fig. 3)*

When terminating *rond de jambe en l'air*, bring pointed toe of extended leg from 2nd position in the air to position inside supporting knee. Move leg forward, *calf and heel turned outward (attitude en avant)*; simultaneously extended arm moves downward and upward to position above head in line of vision. Rise on to *demi-pointe* of supporting foot and hold balance.

POSTURE AND MUSCULAR CONTROL

1   Hold torso erect. Weight on supporting leg, knee straight and turned out throughout exercise.

2   Executing *rond de jambe, working leg from thigh to knee remains motionless* and *turned out* throughout exercise. Terminating each *rond de jambe, straighten knee*, bring heel of pointed toe forward, pausing momentarily in 2nd position *en l'air* before continuing movement.

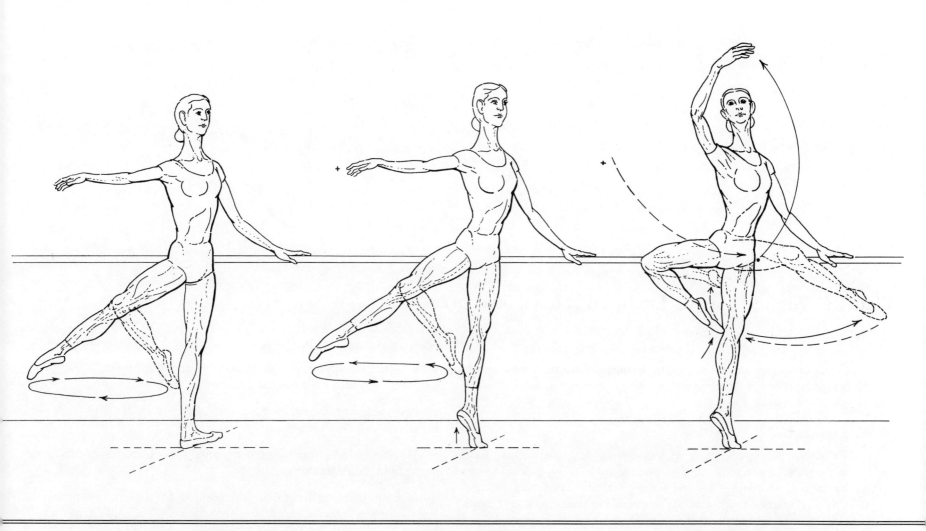

fig. 1   *en dehors*   fig. 2   *en dedans*   fig. 3   *attitude en avant*

ROND DE JAMBE EN L'AIR *(at 45 and 90 degrees)*

Plate 24. Grand Rond de Jambe en l'air (at 90 degrees)

Strengthens legs and torso, develops control for adagio movements. (This exercise is a slow and continous semi-circular movement in the air without pause.)

En dehors (outwards): From 5th position front, raise working foot, toe pointing down in front of supporting ankle. Move pointed toe up to knee of supporting leg and slowly extend working leg forward *(fig. 1)*. Describe a semi-circular movement in the air passing through 2nd position and terminating in *arabesque* back 90 degrees. Lower extended leg to 5th position back *(fig. 2)*.

En dedans (inward): From 5th position back, execute same exercise in reverse direction.

Usually performed once *en dehors* and once *en dedans*, and repeated on *demi-pointe*.

POSTURE AND MUSCULAR CONTROL

1   Weight on supporting leg, hold torso and head erect. Raising working foot, turn knee outward, point toe downward.

2   Extending working leg forward, draw abdomen in, lift diaphragm, bring calf and heel forward.

3   Moving to 2nd position in the air, bring erect torso slightly forward, hold shoulders down.

4   Moving working leg from 2nd position to back, carry torso slightly more forward, hold shoulders down. Gradually increase height of working leg, passing through 2nd position in the air to *arabesque* 90 degrees back. In reverse direction, gradually increase height of working leg passing through 2nd position in the air to 90 degrees forward.

5   Keep both legs straight and well turned out. Hold hips down and facing forward throughout movement.

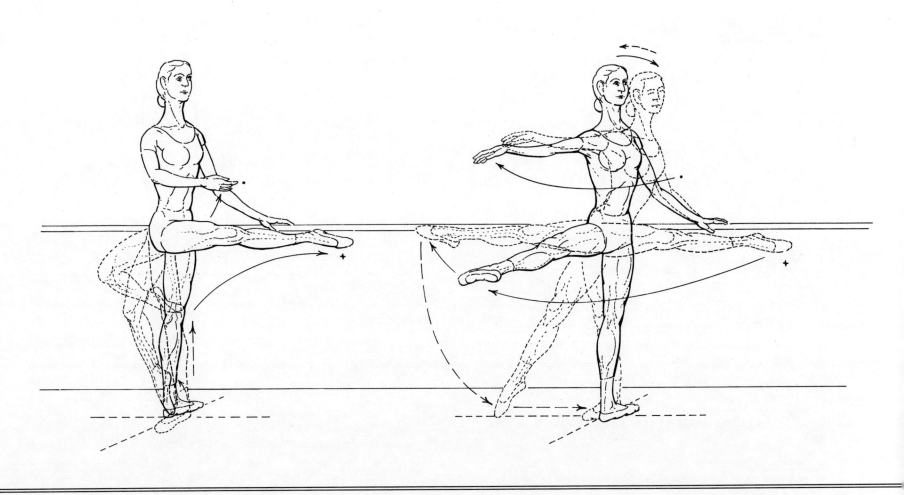

fig. 1

fig. 2

GRAND ROND DE JAMBE EN L'AIR *(90 degrees)*

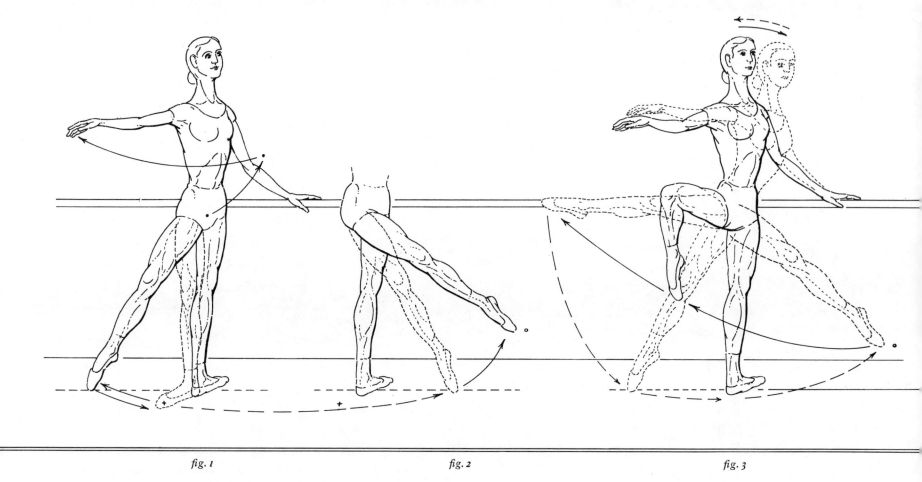

fig. 1   fig. 2   fig. 3

Plate 25. Grand Rond de Jambe Jeté

Develops legs from thigh to toe and gives freedom for rotary movement in hips.

(*Jeté*—throwing leg into the air.)

(Usually executed in conjunction with *rond de jambe à terre*.)

---

*According to Cecchetti, *grand battement en rond*.

EXERCISE

En dehors (bending working leg as it is thrown into the air) *(Pl. 25a):* point working foot 4th position back *(fig. 1)*. Swing leg forward, lowering heel to floor, *passing through 1st position*, to 45 degrees *(figs. 1-2)*. Bend knee outward and energetically carry leg upward and around to back, passing through 2nd position *en l'air*, through *attitude croisée* back, terminating in *arabesque* 90 degrees. Return working leg to 4th position to continue movement *(fig. 3)*.

En dehors (with straight working leg thrown into the air)* *(Pl. 25b):* Point working foot 4th position back *(fig. 1)*. Swing leg forward, lowering heel to floor, passing through 1st position to 45 degrees

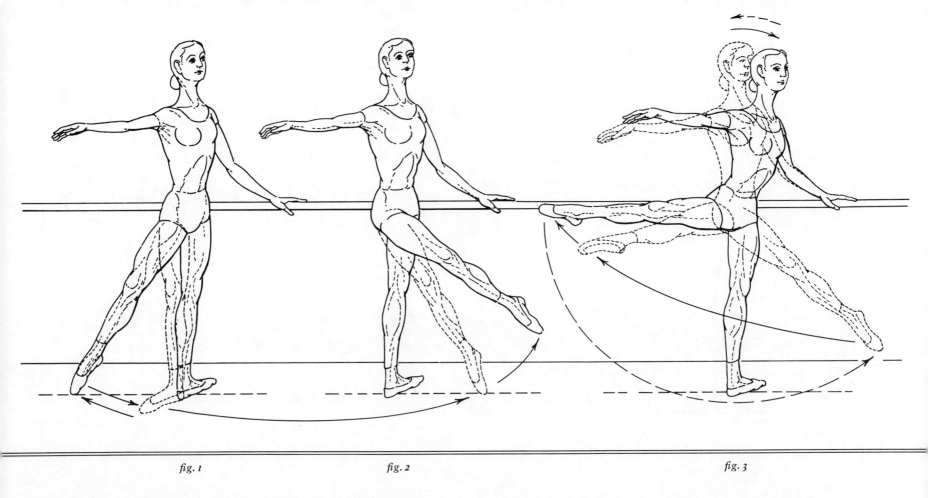

fig. 1   *fig. 2*   *fig. 3*

(figs. 1-2), and without pause, working leg held straight, energetically describe a semi-circular movement *en l'air* passing through 2nd position and terminating in *arabesque* 90 degrees *(fig. 3)*. Return to 4th position back to continue movement *(fig. 1)*.

En dedans: Point working foot 4th front. Execute both exercises in reverse direction.

POSTURE AND MUSCULAR CONTROL

1 Weight on supporting leg held straight and firm throughout movement. *Bring heel of working foot forward* when lowering it to floor, passing each time through 1st position.

2 *Torso leans slightly forward,* as working leg is carried back to 90 degrees *(fig. 3)*. When passing working leg through 2nd position to *arabesque* back, hold shoulders down.

3 *(Pl. 25a, fig. 3)* Lift knee high, passing through 2nd position to back, knee turned out, toe pointed.

4 *(Pl. 25b, fig. 3)* The working leg describes a large semi-circle, beginning at 45 degrees front, gradually increasing in height, passing through 2nd position in the air to *arabesque* 90 degrees back.

[73]

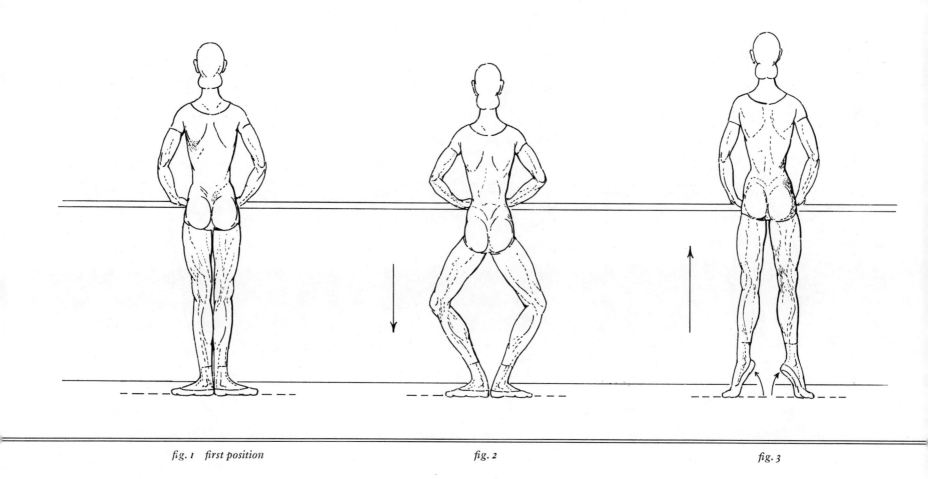

fig. 1   first position   fig. 2   fig. 3

Plate 26. Relevés (facing bar—first and second positions)

Strengthens Achilles tendon, insteps, knees, and thighs.

EXERCISE

From 1st position (fig. 1): Heels together, execute *demi-plié*, heels remaining on floor, knees bending outward in direct line over center of feet *(fig. 2)*; rise on to *demi-pointes*, simultaneously straightening both knees *(fig. 3)*. Return heels to floor, execute *demi-plié*, and repeat movement *(fig. 2)*.

Usually performed eight times in each position.

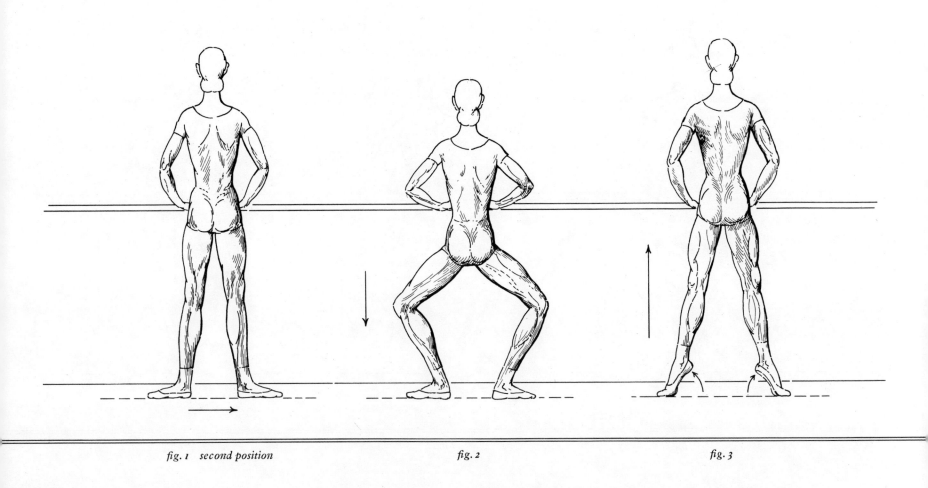

fig. 1   second position   fig. 2   fig. 3

From 2nd position (fig. 1): Heels separated by a distance of one foot, execute *demi-plié (fig. 2)*; rise on to *demi-pointes*, simultaneously straightening both knees *(fig. 3)*. Return heels to floor, execute *demi-plié*, and repeat movement *(fig. 2)*.

POSTURE AND MUSCULAR CONTROL

1   When executing *demi-plié* in 1st position, distribute weight equally between the feet, draw abdomen in, hold shoulders down, hands holding bar lightly. Knees move outward in direct line over center of feet, *heels remain on floor.*

2   Return heels to floor *lightly and quickly* before repeating each *plié*.

3   Executing *relevé*, simultaneously tighten buttocks and straighten knees. Turn thighs outward, bring heels *forward and together* in 1st position.

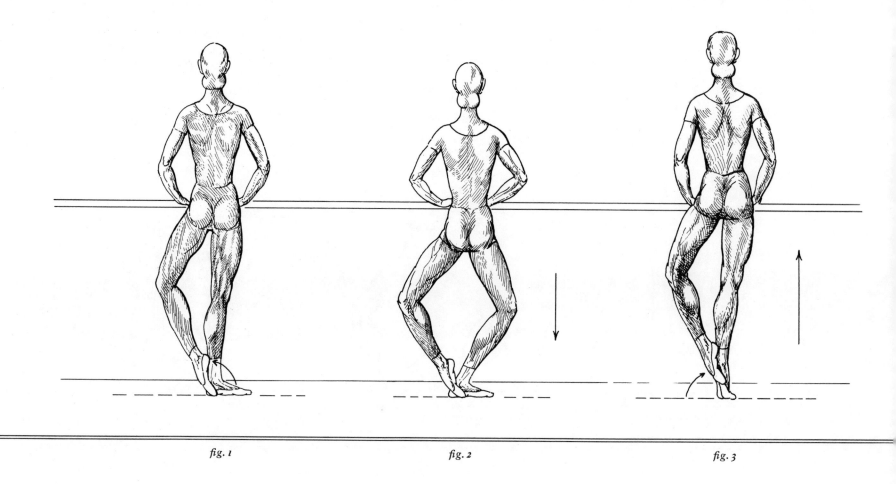

Plate 27. Relevés (sur le cou-de-pied)

Usually performed eight times on right or left foot.

From 5th position, working foot *sur le cou-de-pied (fig. 1)*: Execute *demi-plié (fig. 2)* and *relevé* on to *demi-pointe* of supporting foot, simultaneously straightening supporting knee, raising working foot to position *sur le cou-de-pied back*, toe pointing down *(fig. 3)*. Repeat the *demi-plié* on supporting leg, holding foot of raised leg in position *sur le cou-de-pied* back *during movement*. Repeat exercise with the other foot in position *sur le cou-de-pied* back.

This movement may be executed with working foot *sur le cou-de-pied* in front of supporting ankle.

POSTURE AND MUSCULAR CONTROL

1   When executing *relevé* on one leg, hold torso and head erect; center weight on supporting foot.

[76]

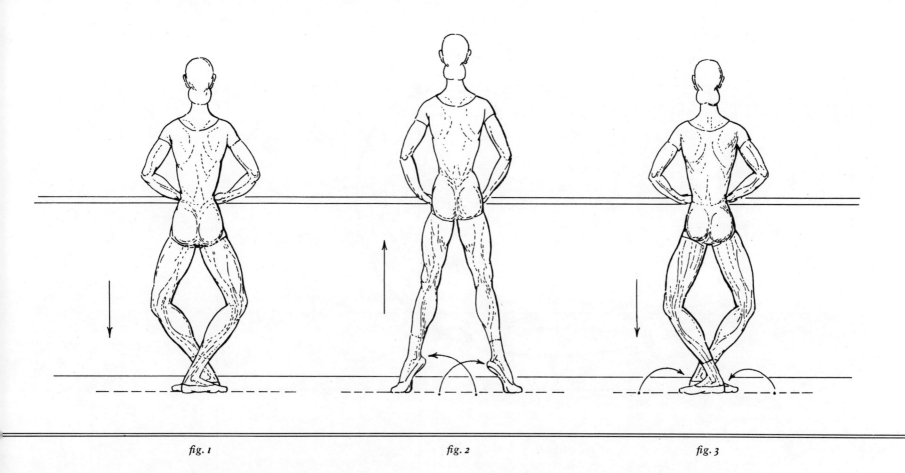

fig. 1　　　　　　　*fig. 2*　　　　　　　*fig. 3*

Plate 28. Échappés (facing the bar)

Strengthens Achilles tendon, insteps, knees and thighs.

EXERCISE

From 5th position left foot front, execute *demi-plié* (fig. 1), energetically slide both feet outward to 2nd position on to *demi-pointes* (fig. 2). Return to *demi-plié* in 5th position left foot *back* (fig. 3). Repeat exercise alternating position of feet in 5th position.

Usually performed eight or sixteen times.

POSTURE AND MUSCULAR CONTROL

1 Executing *demi-plié*, hold torso and head erect, shoulders down, distribute weight equally between both feet in firm 5th position, heels remaining on floor.

2 Sliding on to *demi-pointes* in 2nd position, simultaneously tighten buttocks, thighs, and knees, draw abdomen in, hold shoulders down. Turn legs outward, bring heels forward.

3 Upon each return of feet to 5th position, lower heels to floor *lightly and quickly* before repeating each *plié*, preparatory to sliding on to *demi-pointes* in 2nd position (*échappé*).

The Arabesque Spiral

Part II: Exercises at the Center

Introduction to Center Practice and Adagio

Center work begins with various combinations of exercises previously executed at the bar: for example, *battements tendus*, *grands battements*, *développés*, and *ronds de jambe*.

When the student leaves the bar and moves into the center, *port de bras* and carriage of the head and torso are of paramount importance. The student is made aware of the conception of *épaulement* (see pp. 80-81) and the basic directions of the body (see pp. 82-87). *Port de bras* should be performed slowly and distinctly, each position being assumed accurately before proceeding to the next; at a later stage of training the exercises may be performed with a flowing and continuous movement of the arms and body. Of the many possible exercises in *port de bras*, only a few examples are given here.

According to Vaganova, there are three fundamental positions of the arms, with a *preparatory position*, when the arms are held down and rounded, slightly forward from the body; in *1st position*, the arms are raised in front of the body on a level with the diaphragm; in *2nd position* the arms are extended to the side, rounded, palms held inward in line of vision; in *3rd position* the arms are rounded and held above the head in line of vision.

According to Cecchetti, there are five fundamental positions of the arms, which approximate to the positions of the feet: in *1st position*, arms are held down and rounded, the tips of the fingers barely touching the thighs; in *2nd position* the arms are extended to the side; in *3rd position* one arm is held down in front of the body and the other is extended slightly to the side; in *4th position* one arm is extended to the side and the other held either above the head *(en haut)* or in front of the body on a level with the diaphragm *(en avant)*; in *5th position* the arms are held rounded and down in front of the body *(en bas)*, or on a level with the diaphragm *(en avant)*, or above the head *(en haut)*.

According to Mme Nicolaeva-Legat, there are again five fundamental positions of the arms: in *1st position* the arms are lowered and rounded, slightly advanced from the body; in *2nd position* the arms are rounded and raised in front to level of chest; in *3rd position* the arms are rounded and raised above the head in line of vision; in *4th position* the arms are extended to the side, palms held inward, in line of vision; in *5th position* the arms are outstretched behind the body.

A very important part of center practice is the adagio, a generic term for a combination of slow and sustained movements designed to develop line and balance. It may consist of a series of *battements développés* in each of the basic directions of the body (see pp. 82-87), with *relevé* and balance on the supporting leg, slow rotation on the supporting leg with working leg extended in various positions *en l'air*; other movements may also be introduced, *e.g.*, *grand fouetté en tournant*, *renversé en dehors*, and various *pirouettes*.

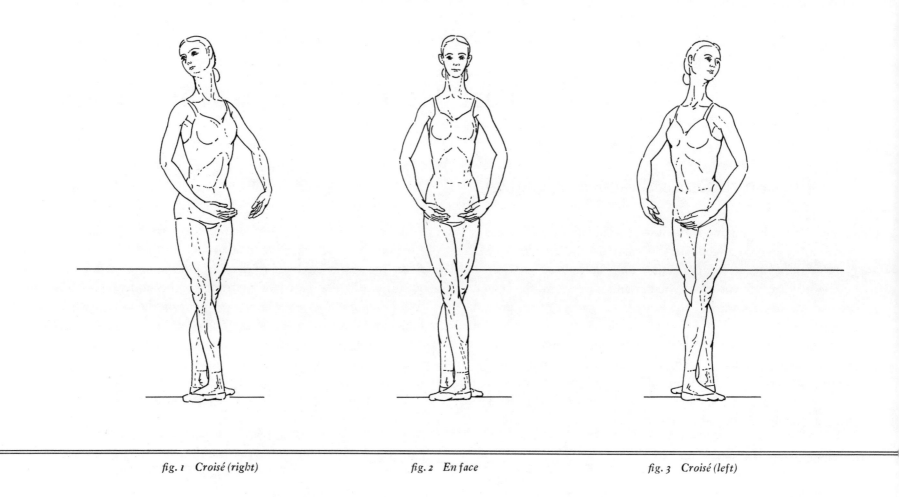

fig. 1   Croisé (right)   *fig. 2   En face*   *fig. 3   Croisé (left)*

Plate 29. Épaulement (croisé-effacé, basic positions in the center)

Position of the shoulders in relation to head and legs is an established rule of the classic dance. The two fundamental positions are *croisé* and *effacé*. These positions are in contrast to the center figure facing straight forward, *en face (fig. 2)*.

ÉPAULEMENT CROISÉ (5th position)

Croisé right foot front, *right shoulder forward*, head inclining right, body at slightly oblique angle, facing front. Arms held down and rounded, slightly advanced from body (preparatory position) *(fig. 1)*.

Croisé left foot front, *left shoulder forward*, head inclining left *(fig. 3)*.

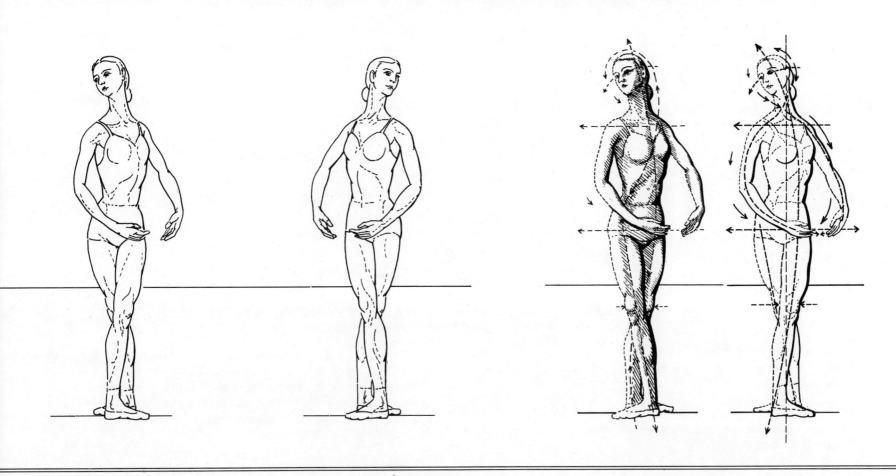

fig. 4   Éffacé (right)   *fig. 5   Éffacé (left)*   *fig. 6   Theory of design*

ÉPAULEMENT ÉFFACÉ (5th position)

Effacé left foot front, *right shoulder forward*, head inclining to right *(fig. 4)*.

Effacé right foot front, *left shoulder forward*, head inclining left, body at slightly oblique angle, facing front. Arms held down and rounded, slightly advanced from body *(fig. 5)*.

POSTURE AND MUSCULAR CONTROL

Hold torso erect, draw abdomen in, and tighten buttocks to facilitate stability and balance; turn out legs from thighs to feet. Hold shoulders down, lift diaphragm, hold arms rounded and free from strain. Relax neck.

[81]

Plate 30. Basic Positions of the Body

To achieve the classic line and symmetrical relationship of head, shoulders, torso, and legs, the following positions are of the utmost importance.

Arms move from preparatory position *through 1st position* to positions described.

All these positions are also executed standing on the right leg, and with the working leg *en l'air* at 45 or 90 degrees. *Écarté devant en l'air* (forward) may be executed with torso held erect or leaning away from extended leg as far back as possible.

POSTURE AND MUSCULAR CONTROL IN ALL POSITIONS

1 Weight on supporting leg and *centered on supporting foot*, preventing rolling forward.

2 Draw abdomen in, lift diaphragm, hold shoulders down, keep neck, arms, and hands free of tension and strain.

3 Bring heel of pointed foot well forward in each position.

[82]

CROISÉ DEVANT POINTE TENDUE [Crossed 4th position front] *(fig. 1)*

Stand on straight supporting left leg, right leg held straight, toe pointing on floor *croisé* forward to left side, *thigh to heel turned forward*. Torso and hips at an oblique angle to audience, with *right shoulder front*, incline torso slightly back and to the right, incline head to right. Raise left arm above head in line of vision. Extend right arm to right side, both palms held inward.

QUATRIÈME DEVANT [Forward] *(fig. 2)*

Standing on straight supporting left leg, right leg held straight, toe pointing on floor straight front. Head, torso, and hips face directly forward. Extend both arms to sides, rounded, palms held inward, slightly forward in line of vision.

ÉCARTÉ DEVANT *(fig. 3)*

Standing on straight supporting left leg, right leg held straight, toe pointing on floor diagonally to right side, *thigh to heel turned forward*; turn torso and hips at an oblique angle to audience with *right shoulder front*, hold torso erect. Head inclines to right. Raise right arm above head in line of vision, extend left arm to left side, both palms turned inward.

fig. 1 *Croisé devant point tendue*   fig. 2 *Quatrième devant*   fig. 3 *Écarté devant*

BASIC POSITIONS OF THE BODY

Plate 31a. Basic Positions of the Body (continued)

EFFACÉ DEVANT [Open 4th position front] *(fig. 4)*

Standing on straight supporting left leg, right leg held straight, toe pointing on floor diagonally to right side, *thigh to heel turned forward*. Torso and hips at an oblique angle to audience, with *left shoulder front*, incline body slightly back and head to the left. Raise left arm above head in line of vision, extend right arm to right side, both palms held inward.

À LA SECONDE [2nd position] *(fig. 5)*

Standing on straight supporting left leg, right leg held straight, toe pointing on floor to right side, *thigh to heel turned forward*; head, torso, and hips face directly forward. Extend both arms to sides, slightly forward in line of vision, rounded, and elbows slightly raised, palms held inward.

EFFACÉ DERRIÈRE [Open 4th position back] *(fig. 6)*

Standing on straight supporting left leg, right leg held straight, toe pointing on floor diagonally back, *thigh to heel turned forward*; torso and hips at an oblique angle to the audience, *right shoulder front*, inclining torso forward and to the left. Raise right arm above head in line of vision, palm held inward, head facing palm of right hand, extend left arm to left side, palm turned inward.

fig. 4 *Effacé devant*   fig. 5 *À la seconde*   fig. 6 *Effacé derrière*

BASIC POSITIONS OF THE BODY *(continued)*

Plate 31b. Basic Positions of the Body (continued)

ÉCARTÉ DERRIÈRE [Diagonally back] *(fig. 7)*

Standing on straight supporting left leg, right leg held straight, toe pointing on floor diagonally back, *thigh to heel turned forward*; torso and hips at oblique angle to audience with *left shoulder forward*, head inclining to right shoulder. Raise left arm above head in line of vision, extend right arm to right side, palms held inward.

QUATRIÈME DERRIÈRE [Straight in back] *(fig. 8)*

Standing on straight supporting left leg, right leg held straight, toe pointing on floor, straight back, *turned out from thigh to heel*; head, torso, and hips face directly forward. Extend both arms to side, rounded, palms held inward, slightly forward in line of vision.

CROISÉ DERRIÈRE [Crossed 4th position back] *(fig. 9)*

Standing on straight supporting left leg, right leg held straight, toe pointing on floor *croisé* back to left side, thigh to heel turned forward; torso and hips at oblique angle to audience with *left shoulder front*. Hold torso erect, incline head and body to the left. Raise right arm above head in line of vision, extend left arm to left side.

fig. 7   *Écarté derrière*   fig. 8   *Quatrième derrière*   fig. 9   *Croisé derrière*

BASIC POSITIONS OF THE BODY *(continued)*

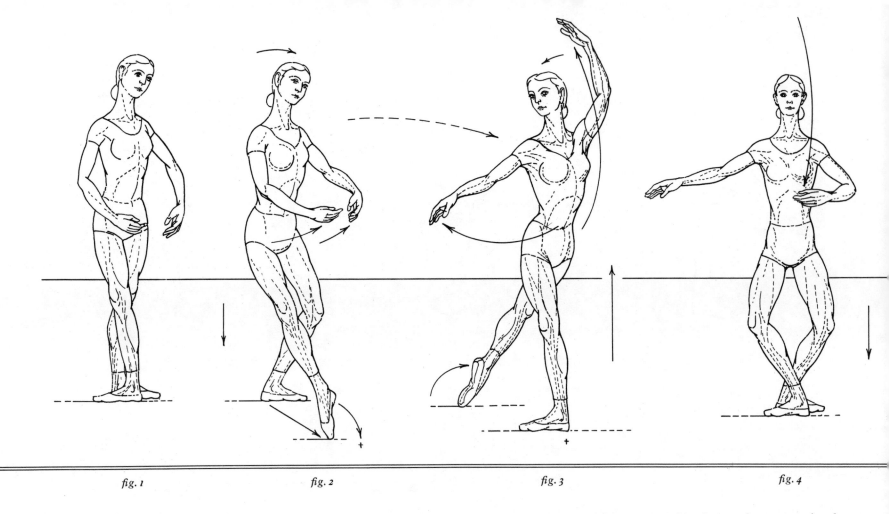

fig. 1   fig. 2   fig. 3   fig. 4

Plate 32. Petit Temps Lié (en avant—forward)

A combination of leg and arm movements based on three fundamental positions of the feet, the 4th, 5th, and 2nd.

Temps lié may be executed in the same manner moving backwards. *Temps lié* may be executed stepping each time on to *demi-pointes* before *demi-plié* in 5th position.

The exercise is executed very smoothly, legs and arms moving harmoniously in co-ordination.

PREPARATION
5th position, right foot front, right shoulder forward, arms in preparatory position *(fig. 1)*.

EXERCISE
Execute *demi-plié*, sliding right foot on floor to point *croisé* forward, raising arms to 1st position *(fig. 2)*; simultaneously transfer weight on to right foot, straightening both legs, pointing left foot *croisé* back, carrying left arm above head and right arm to right side *(fig. 3)*. Simultaneously left foot closes in back of right foot 5th position *demi-*

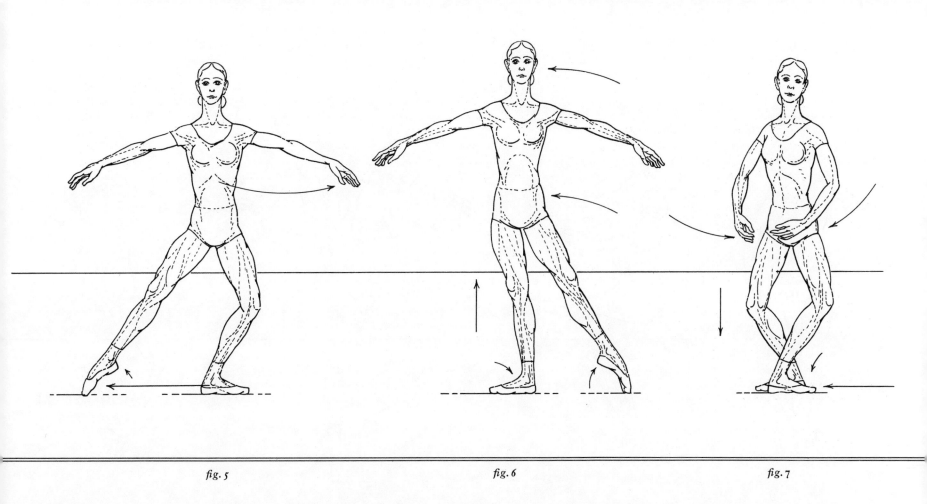

plié, lower left arm to chest level *(fig. 4)*. Right foot slides on floor to point 2nd position (left leg in *demi-plié*), left arm opens to 2nd position *(fig. 5)*. Transfer weight to right foot, simultaneously pointing left foot 2nd position, straightening both legs *(fig. 6)*. Left foot closes in 5th position *demi-plié*, arms returning to preparatory position *(fig. 7)*, and movement is repeated, sliding left foot *croisé* forward, *etc.*

POSTURE AND MUSCULAR CONTROL

1   Weight on left foot *demi-plié* sliding right foot *croisé* forward, incline torso forward to left; arms rounded, raised to chest level.

2   Transferring weight to right foot, *croisé* forward, draw abdomen in.

3   Position *croisé* forward, hold torso erect, inclining torso and head slightly to right, weight on right foot.

4   5th position *demi-plié*, draw abdomen in, distribute weight equally between the feet.

5   Extending right leg to 2nd position, draw abdomen in, weight centered on left foot *demi-plié*.

6   Transferring weight to right foot, hold torso erect.

[89]

fig. 1   fig. 2   fig. 3   fig. 4

Plate 33. Grand Temps Lié (at 90 degrees)

PREPARATION

5th position right foot front, right shoulder forward, arms in preparatory position *(fig. 1)*.

fig. 5

fig. 6

fig. 7

EXERCISE

Simultaneously execute *demi-plié* on left leg, developing right leg *croisé* forward 90 degrees, raising arms to 1st position *(fig. 2)*. Step on to right *demi-pointe (posé en avant) en attitude croisée en l'air*. Execute *coupé* on to left foot *demi-plié*, right foot pointing *sur le cou-de-pied* in front of left ankle, simultaneously lowering left arm to level of diaphragm *(fig. 4)*. Develop right leg to 2nd position, simultaneously opening left arm to side *(fig. 5)*. Step on to right *demi-pointe* raising left leg to 2nd position *en l'air* 90 degrees *(fig. 6)*. Close in 5th position *demi-plié* left foot front, arms returning to preparatory position *(fig. 7)*

Grand temps lié at 90 degrees, *temps lié sauté*, is also executed with a jump each time from 5th position, executing *posé en avant* or *à la seconde*, etc.

[91]

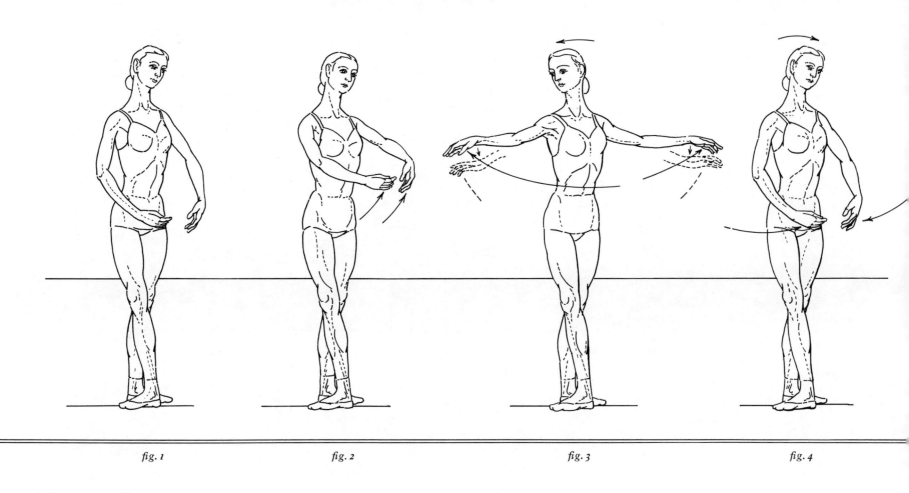

fig. 1   fig. 2   fig. 3   fig. 4

Plate 34. Port de Bras (I)

Move arms slowly and continuously through each position.

PREPARATION

5th position *croisé*, right foot front, arms in preparatory position.

---

*In the Cecchetti method the palms remain facing the audience.

[92]

EXERCISE

1st Movement (fig. 1): From preparatory position arms are raised to a position slightly more advanced from the body. Incline head and torso left.

2nd Movement (fig. 2): Raise arms to chest level, fingers in line with center of body; head and torso remain inclined to left.

3rd Movement (fig. 3): Simultaneously extend both arms to sides, palms facing inward, head and torso lean to right.

Returning to 1st Movement (fig. 3-4): Raise arms slightly, turning palms downward;* as arms are lowered, hands are raised gently from the wrists. Incline torso to left, and lower arms.

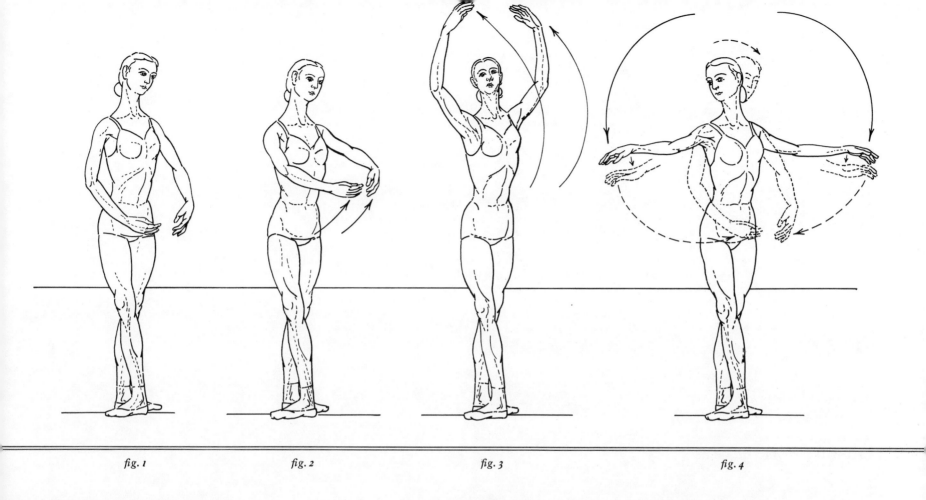

fig. 1   fig. 2   fig. 3   fig. 4

Plate 35. Port de Bras (II)

PREPARATION

5th position *croisé*, right foot front, arms in preparatory position.

EXERCISE

1st Movement (fig. 1): From preparatory position arms are raised to a position slightly more advanced from the body. Incline head and torso to left.

2nd Movement (fig. 2): Raise arms to chest level, fingers in line with center of body; head and torso remain inclined to left.

3rd Movement (fig. 3): Simultaneously move torso erect, carry arms above head in line of vision, *turn head upward* towards palm of right hand.

4th Movement (fig. 4): Simultaneously lower arms with palms held inward to extended position at sides, incline head and torso to right.

Returning to preparatory position (fig. 4): Raise arms slightly, turning palms downward. As arms are lowered, hands are raised gently from the wrists. Incline head and torso to left and lower arms to preparatory position.

[93]

Plate 36. Port de Bras (III)

5th position *croisé*, right foot front, arms in preparatory position.

EXERCISE

1st Movement (fig. 1): From preparatory position rounded arms are raised to a position slightly more advanced from the body. Incline head and torso to left.

2nd Movement (fig. 2): Raise arms to chest level, fingers in line with center of body; head and torso remain inclined to left.

3rd Movement (fig. 2): Simultaneously carry right arm above head in line of vision, move left arm to left side, turn head upward toward palm of right hand.

4th Movement (fig. 3): Lower right arm with palm held inward to extended position at side. Simultaneously incline head and torso to right.

Returning to preparatory position (figs. 3-4): Raise arms slightly, turning palms downward. As arms are lowered, hands are raised gently from the wrists. Simultaneously incline head and torso to left and lower arms to preparatory position.

PORT DE BRAS III

Plate 37. Port de Bras (IV)

PREPARATION

5th position *croisé*, right foot front, arms in preparatory position.

EXERCISE

1st Movement (fig. 1): From preparatory position rounded arms are raised to a position slightly more advanced from the body. Simultaneously incline head and torso to left.

2nd Movement (fig. 1): Raise arms to chest level, fingers in line with center of body. Head and torso remain inclined to left.

3rd Movement (fig.1): Simultaneously extend both arms to side, palms facing inward, incline head and torso slightly to right.

4th Movement (figs. 1-2): Raise arms slightly, turning palms downward. Arms are lowered, hands raised gently from the wrists. Bend torso downward from the waist. Arms accompany movement of torso; neck is relaxed and head inclined toward the knees. Keep both arms rounded in lowered position.

5th Movement (fig. 3): As body rises to upright position, carry arms forward and upward, rounded and extended, fingers in line with center of body, to chest level.

6th and 7th Movements (figs. 3-4): Simultaneously carry right arm above head, move left arm to left side, bring right shoulder forward. Continue bending torso, head, and right arm backwards, inclined to right side. Bring torso erect, simultaneously lowering right arm to extended position at right side *(fig. 1)* Repeat *port de bras* or return to preparatory position.

POSTURE AND MUSCULAR CONTROL

1 As body bends forward draw abdomen in. Hold knees straight, turned outward and firmly together. Neck is relaxed as head drops forward.

2 When returning body to upright position, raise right arm above head, lift diaphragm, hold shoulders down.

3 When bending torso back and to the right, thrust hips slightly forward, bring right shoulder forward.

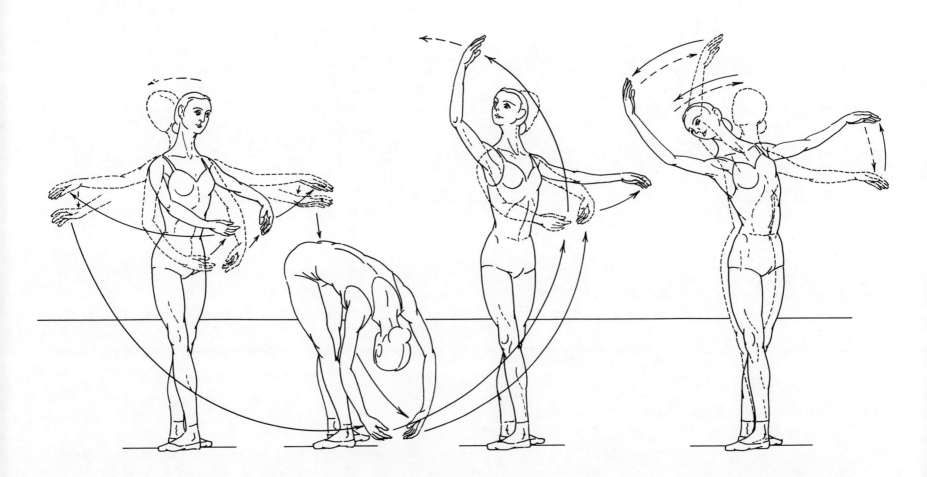

fig. 1   fig. 2   fig. 3   fig. 4

PORT DE BRAS IV

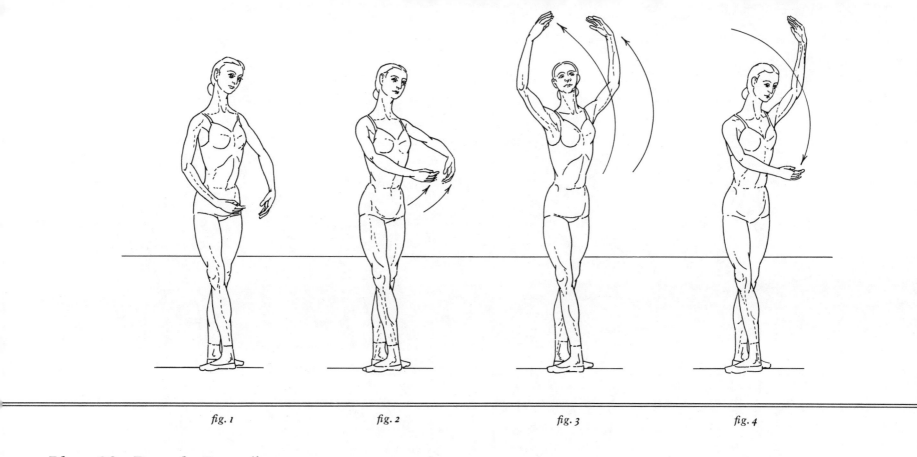

fig. 1   fig. 2   fig. 3   fig. 4

Plate 38. Port de Bras (in seven movements)

Execute all torso, arm, and head movements distinctly and pause momentarily in each position.

PREPARATION

5th position *croisé*, right foot front, arms in preparatory position.

[98]

EXERCISE

1st Movement (fig. 1): From preparatory position arms are raised to a position slightly more advanced from the body. Incline head and torso to *left*.

2nd Movement (fig. 2): Raise arms to chest level, fingers in line with center of body; head and torso remain inclined to left.

3rd Movement (fig. 3): Simultaneously move torso erect, carry arms above head in line of vision, turn head upward towards palm of right hand.

4th Movement (fig. 4): Simultaneously lower *right* arm to chest level, follow the movement downward with head, eyes directed to fingers in line with center of body.

fig. 5   fig. 6   fig. 7

5th Movement (fig. 5): Simultaneously extend right arm to right side, incline head and torso to right.

6th Movement (fig. 6): Lower left arm to chest level, fingers in line with center of body. Head remains inclined to right.

7th Movement (fig. 7): Extend left arm to left side. Head remains inclined to right. Returning to preparatory position, raise arms slightly, turning palms downward; as arms are lowered hands are raised gently from the wrists. Incline torso to left and lower arms to preparatory position *(fig. 1)*.

POSTURE AND MUSCULAR CONTROL

1st Movement: Hold shoulders down, draw abdomen in. Hold slight tension at base of shoulders, arms rounded and fingers relaxed.

2nd Movement: Raising arms to chest level, and inclining torso to left, *hold abdomen concave,* effecting quality of roundness in movement of body and arms.

3rd Movement: Moving torso erect, lift diaphragm. Raising arms above head, *hold shoulders down.*

4th Movement: Lowering right arm, draw abdomen in.

5th Movement: Extending right arm to side and inclining head and torso to right, *lift diaphragm.*

6th Movement: When left arm descends to chest level, *diaphragm remains lifted.*

7th Movement: Arms are extended to maximum within line of vision, shoulders down, elbows lifted, palms held inward. Arms return to preparatory position before repeating movement.

[99]

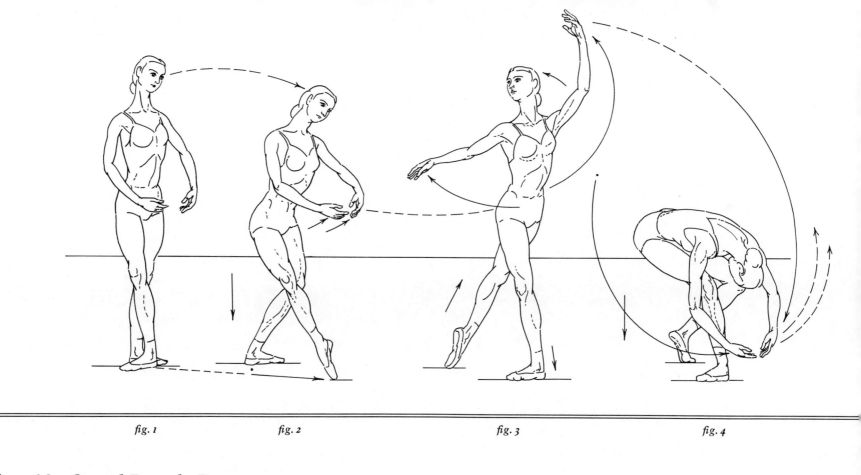

fig. 1   fig. 2   fig. 3   fig. 4

Plate 39. Grand Port de Bras

PREPARATION

5th position *croisé*, right foot front, arms in preparatory position (fig. 1).

EXERCISE

1st Movement (fig. 2): Simultaneously execute *demi-plié* on left leg, slide right toe on floor to 4th position *croisé* forward, incline torso forward and head to left, carry rounded arms forward and upward to diaphragm level.

[100]

2nd Movement (fig. 3): Simultaneously lower right heel to floor, transferring weight to right leg through *demi-plié*. Point left toe *croisé* back, straightening both knees. Raise left arm from chest level above head, right arm to right side, bring torso erect, head and torso inclining slightly right.

3rd Movement (fig. 4): Simultaneously lower pointed toe to *demi-pointe, demi-plié* on both legs, centering weight, bending torso and head forward and downward until top of head almost touches floor; rounded left arm accompanies torso downward to lowered position, right arm is carried down to meet left arm in lowered position.

fig. 5   fig. 6

4th Movement (fig. 5): Simultaneously lower left heel to floor, transferring weight to left foot, rise upward with circular movement to left, turning torso, head, and arms to left and bending back; right arm is raised to position above head, left arm is extended to left side; point right foot *croisé* forward.

5th Movement (fig. 6): Simultaneously straighten torso and complete circular movement by turning to right into position *croisé* forward. Move right arm to extended position right side, move left arm to position above head, incline torso and head to right.

POSTURE AND MUSCULAR CONTROL

1st Movement: Execute *demi-plié* with weight on left supporting leg, heel on floor; slide right toe lightly on floor, bringing heel forward, to 4th position *croisé* front.

2nd Movement: Weight is transferred from the back foot to both feet, and on to the front foot. Lowering heel of right foot to floor, bring heel forward (4th position *croisé*). Pointing *croisé* back, turn out left leg. As torso moves erect and arms are carried into position, lift diaphragm, hold shoulders down, tighten buttocks.

3rd Movement: Executing *plié* and bending torso down, draw abdomen in, keep weight on forward foot. Head drops downward during the movement and inclines toward the knees.

4th and 5th Movements: Weight is transferred from front foot to both feet, and on to back foot. The circular motion upward of torso, head and arms is a swinging movement into final position without pause. As torso swings upward and around *(fig. 5)*, hold shoulders down, turning forward into final position. Point right foot *croisé* front, turn leg out, and bring heel forward.

Plate 40. Attitudes (en avant—en face—en arrière)

All these positions can be executed with the heel of the supporting foot on the ground, *plié, demi-pointe (relevé)*, and by the *danseuse* on *pointe*.

ATTITUDE CROISÉE DEVANT *(fig. 1)*

Standing on left foot, the torso is held erect, inclining slightly to right, shoulders held down. Extended right leg is lifted forward, knee bent, with *calf and heel brought forward*. Left arm raised above head in line of vision, right arm at side. Head inclines to right.

ATTITUDE EFFACÉE EN L'AIR *(fig. 2)*

Standing on left foot, the body is at an oblique angle to audience, back well arched, with *right shoulder forward*. Right leg, knee bent, is thrust diagonally back into the air, bringing *calf and heel forward*, knee held higher than foot. Torso and head incline to right, right arm above head in line of vision, palm held inward, left arm at left side, palm held downward.

ATTITUDE CROISÉE DERRIÈRE *(fig. 3)*

Standing on left foot, the torso is carried forward from the waist line, back well arched, and shoulders held down. Extended right leg is thrust behind body with knee held higher than foot. Right arm is raised above head in line of vision, left arm at left side. Torso and head inclined to left.

POSTURE AND MUSCULAR CONTROL

1 To maintain balance, hold supporting leg straight and firm, turned out. To hold balance when rising on *demi-pointe*, increase muscular tension in buttocks, thighs, and abdomen, lift diaphragm.

2 Free neck and arms from strain, hold shoulders down.

3 In *attitude effacée en l'air*, with right leg raised, thrust hips slightly forward and lean into right hip.

[102]

fig. 1   *Attitude croisée devant*   fig. 2   *Attitude effacée en l'air*   fig. 3   *Attitude croisée derrière*

ATTITUDES

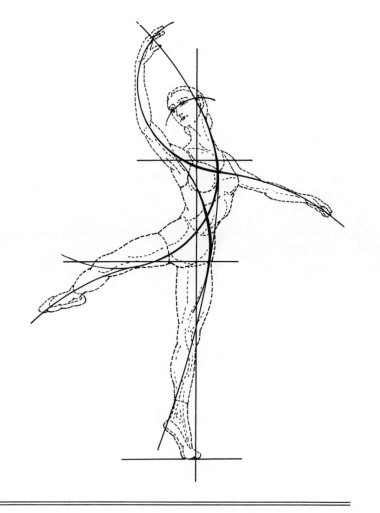

Theory of design (41a)

Plate 41. Attitudes (examples of variations)

Attitude croisée devant may also be executed as follows: with both arms above head in line of vision, torso held erect, and with right arm above head and left arm extended to side, inclining torso to left *(fig. 1)*.

Croisée devant executed with *plié:* extended right leg is lifted and pointed *straight* forward. Left arm is raised to level of diaphragm. Head and torso incline to left *(fig. 2)*.

Attitude croisée derrière may also be executed as follows: with both arms above head in line of vision, torso held erect *(fig. 3)*, and with left arm above head and right arm extended to right side, inclining torso to the right.

Attitude effacée en diagonale is executed, standing on left foot *demi-plié*, back arched, with *right shoulder forward*. Right leg is thrust diagonally back into the air, leg *straight*, pointed toe level with bent knee of supporting leg. Torso and head incline to left, right arm above head in line of vision, palm held inward, left arm at left side, palm held downward *(fig. 4)*.

fig. 1   *Attitude croisée devant (var.)*   fig. 2   *Attitude croisée devant (var.)*   fig. 3   *Attitude croisée derrière (var.)*   fig. 4   *Attitude effacée en diagonale*

ATTITUDES *(variations)*

[105]

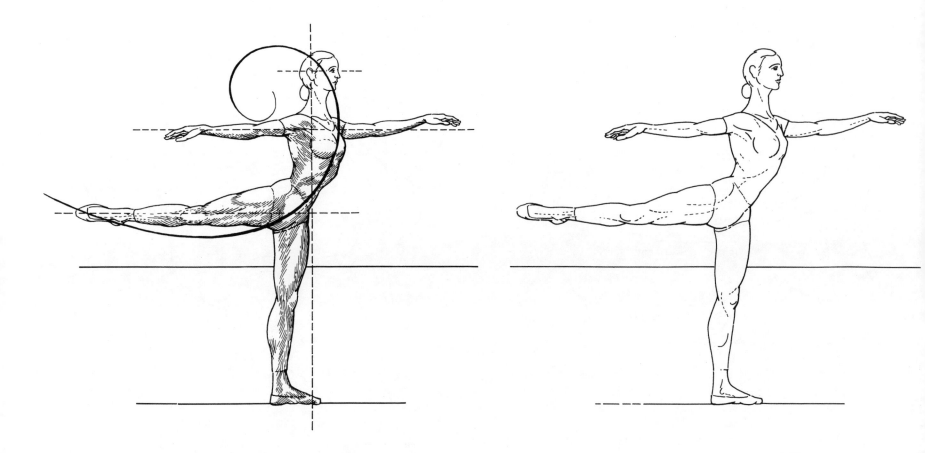

Theory of design (42a)

fig. b   First Arabesque

Plate 42. Arabesques (Cecchetti Method)*

All these positions can be executed with the heel of the supporting foot on the ground, *plié*, on *demi-pointe (relevé)* and by the *danseuse* on *pointe*.

*(Numbers according to the Cecchetti system)

[106]

1st ARABESQUE *(fig. b)*

Standing on left leg, with right leg extended straight back in the air 90 degrees, hold torso forward from the waist with back well arched, hips and shoulders in one line, facing forward, shoulders held down. Head faces extended left arm. Right arm is extended back parallel with and above right leg.

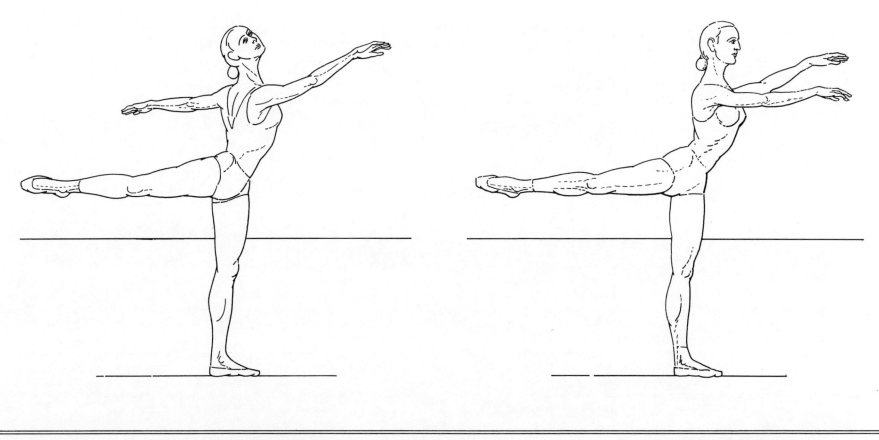

fig. c   Second Arabesque   *fig. d   Third Arabesque*

2nd ARABESQUE (*Croisée*) (*fig. c*)

Standing on left leg, right leg extended straight back in the air at 90 degrees, incline torso forward, back well arched, shoulders held down, right shoulder forward, inclining head to the right. The left arm is extended behind the body, right arm extended forward, palms held downward.

3rd ARABESQUE (*fig. d*)

Standing on left leg, with right leg extended straight back in the air at 90 degrees, incline torso forward, back well arched, hips and shoulders in one line, facing forward, head in profile. Extend both arms forward, palms held downward, left arm slightly higher.

[107]

Plate 43. Arabesques (continued)

4th ARABESQUE *(fig. a)*

Standing on left leg, body facing forward at an oblique angle to audience, extended right leg held straight and thrust backward. Torso is carried forward from the waist line, back well arched, hips and shoulders in one line, facing forward, head facing forward. Right arm is extended forward, left arm extended back, palms facing downward.

5th ARABESQUE *(fig. b)*

Standing on left leg, body facing forward at an oblique angle to audience, extended right leg held straight and thrust backward. Incline torso forward, back well arched, hips and shoulders in one line, facing forward, head facing forward. Extend both arms forward to the right side, palms held downward.

[108]

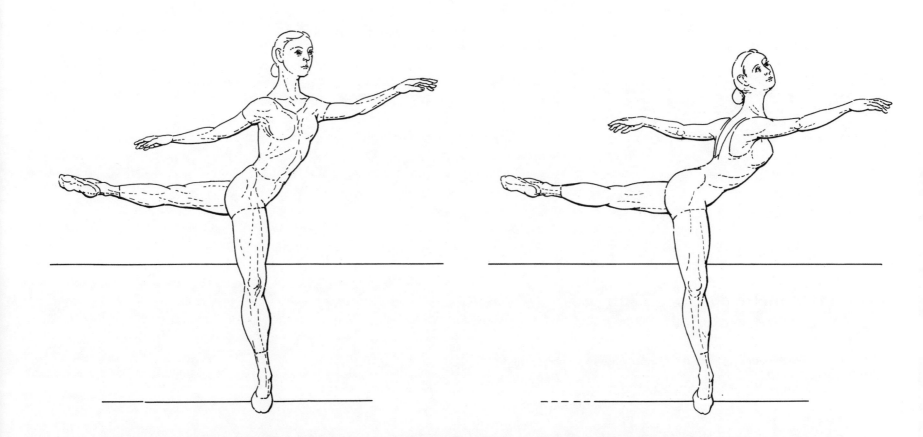

fig. a Third Arabesque (Vaganova)

fig. b Fourth Arabesque (Vaganova)

Plate 44. Arabesques (continued)

ARABESQUE CROISÉE

(3rd *arabesque* according to Vaganova) *(fig. a)*

Standing on right leg, body facing forward at an oblique angle to the audience, with left leg extended straight back in the air at an angle slightly higher than 90 degrees, hold torso forward from the waist with back well arched, hips and shoulders in one line, facing forward. Head faces extended left arm. Right arm extended back, both palms held downward.

(4th *arabesque* according to Vaganova) *(fig. b)*

Standing on right leg, with left leg extended back in the air at an angle slightly higher than 90 degrees, hold torso forward from the waist with back well arched, right shoulder forward, inclining head to the right. The left arm is extended behind the body, right arm extended forward, palms held downward.

[109]

Plate 45. Fouetté en face en l'air

Entire movement is executed without pause from preparation to final position *(arabesque)*.

PREPARATION

From 5th position right front *(fig. 1)*, simultaneously step on to right foot *demi-plié croisé* forward, transferring weight on to right foot from 5th to 4th position, bending torso and head right; raising arms slightly from preparatory position *(fig. 2)*.

EXERCISE

Simultaneously rise on to *demi-pointe* of supporting foot *(relevé)*, swinging working leg through 1st position on floor up to 2nd position in the air; moving both arms, rounded, upward to chest level and above head without pause *(fig. 3)*. Turning on *demi-pointe* of supporting leg, *simultaneously* turning torso and head to right, opening right arm extended forward facing right, left arm stretched back above and parallel to working leg thrust back 90 degrees in the air *(arabesque)*, *demi-plié* on supporting leg *(fig. 4)*.

This movement may be executed springing into the air as the body moves from 2nd position into *arabesque*. It may also be executed in the reverse direction, starting in *arabesque* and finishing *effacé* forward.

POSTURE AND MUSCULAR CONTROL

1 Moving from preparatory position to 4th position *croisé*, body is controlled but moves easily.

2 Rising on to *demi-pointe* of supporting leg, press supporting foot into floor and tense knee. Working leg swinging to 2nd position held straight and turned out.

3 Turning to *arabesque* position carry torso slightly forward, with back well arched. Hold shoulders down, tighten buttocks and abdomen until reaching final position with supporting leg *demi-plié*.

fig. 1   fig. 2   fig. 3   fig. 4

FOUETTÉ EN FACE EN L'AIR

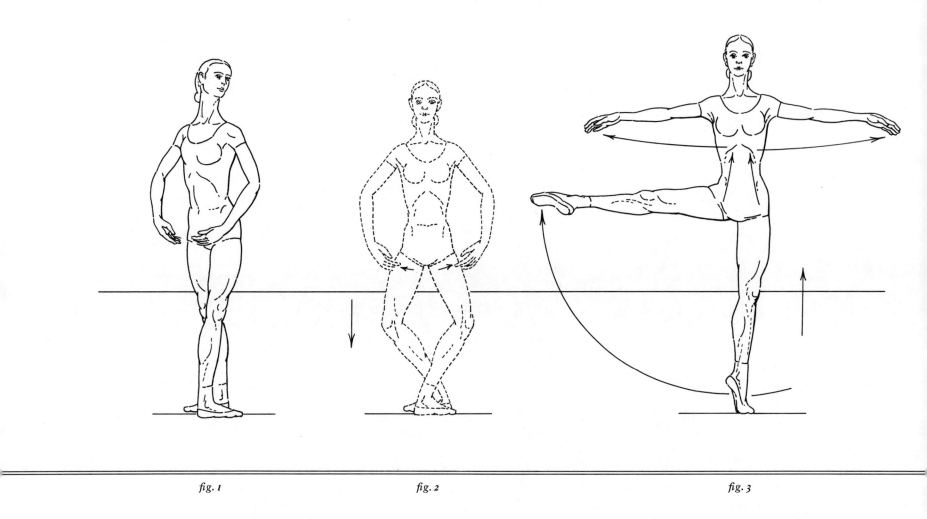

fig. 1

fig. 2

fig. 3

Plate 46. Grand Fouetté en tournant

Entire movement is executed without pause from preparation to final position *(arabesque)*.

EXERCISE

5th position, left foot front, arms in preparatory position *(fig. 1)*. Execute *demi-plié*, open arms slightly to side *(fig. 2)*. Simultaneously *relevé* on supporting leg, swing right leg to second position *en l'air*,

and open arms through 1st to 2nd position *(fig 3)*. *Demi-plié* on supporting leg, bringing working leg and both arms down to pass through 1st position *(fig. 4)*; execute quarter-turn to left back, simultaneously rising on to *demi-pointe* of supporting foot, turning body to left and swinging working leg forward and up to 90 degrees, moving both arms up to position above head *(fig. 5)*. Swing torso around to face forward, right shoulder front, back well arched, working leg remaining thrust back and turned outward in the air at 90 degrees (4th *ara-*

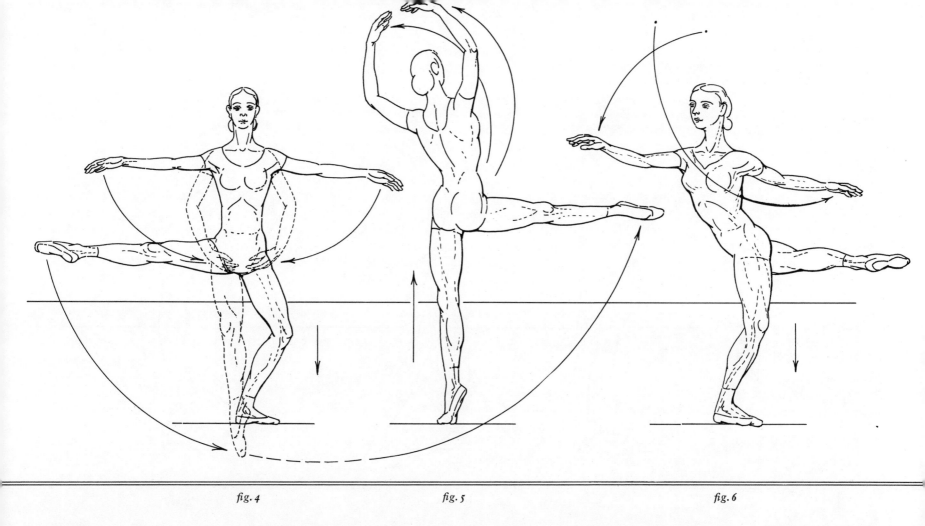

fig. 4   fig. 5   fig. 6

besque). Plié on supporting leg, opening right arm forward, left arm extended to left side *(fig. 6).*

This movement may be executed springing into the air as right leg swings to 2nd position and as body executes quarter-turn to left back, instead of rising on to *demi-pointe.*

POSTURE AND MUSCULAR CONTROL

1   Rising on to *demi-pointe* of supporting leg *(relevé),* press foot into floor and tense supporting knee. Working leg swinging to 2nd position is held straight and turned outward; hold shoulders down, tighten buttocks and abdomen to secure balance.

2   From 2nd position *en l'air* move easily into *plié* before swinging working leg energetically forward and upward to 90 degrees and completing turn into final position.

3   Swinging torso around to face forward and opening arms, tighten buttocks to maintain balance, hold shoulders down, and free neck and arms from strain.

[113]

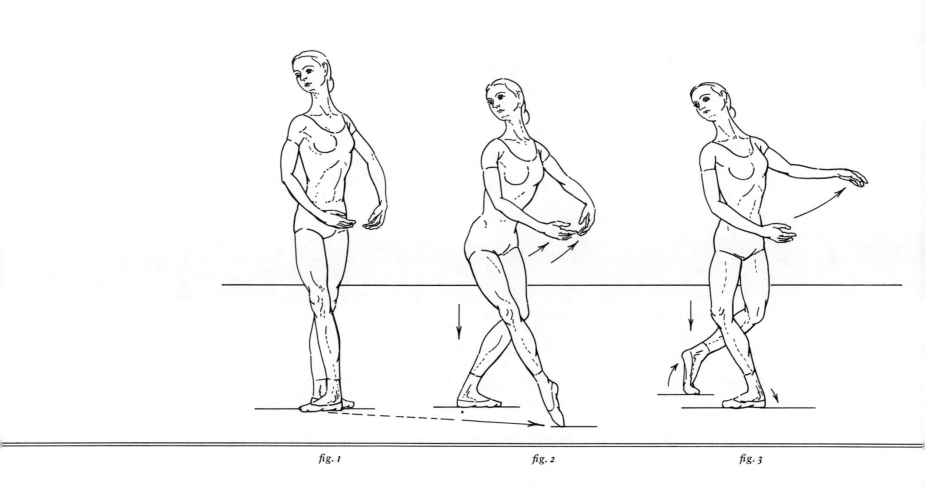

fig. 1 *fig. 2* *fig. 3*

Plate 47. Grand Rond de Jambe en l'air (terminating with renversé en dehors)

Entire movement is executed without pause from preparatory position to final position, *croisé* forward.

Renversé en dehors may be executed *sauté* (jumped) instead of *relevé*, and also *sur les pointes*. There are also various other preparatory steps which may lead into *renversé*.

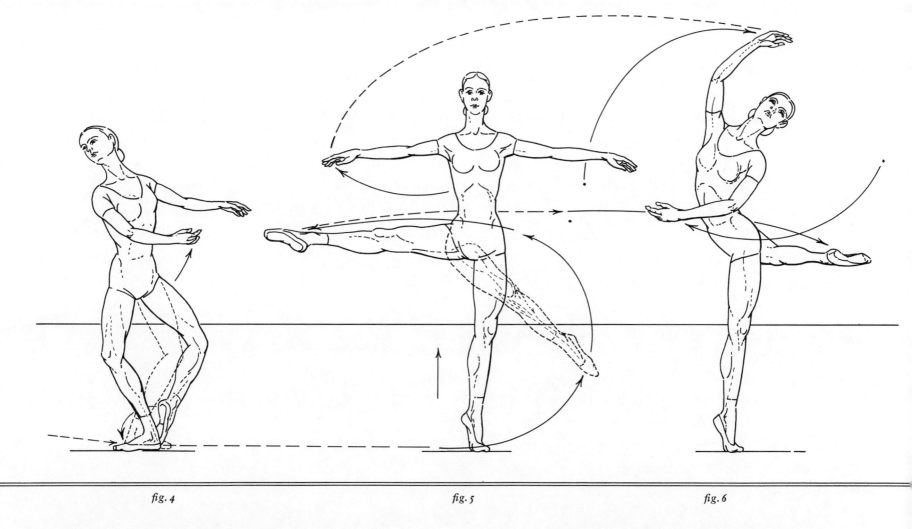

(Illustration and text continued on following page 116)

fig. 4   fig. 5   fig. 6

GRAND ROND DE JAMBE EN L'AIR

EXERCISE

From 5th position right front *(fig. 1)*, step on to right foot in *plié croisé* forward, move left foot *sur le cou-de-pied* back, bending torso and head to right, extending left arm to left side, right arm remaining in preparatory position *(figs. 2, 3, 4)*. Without pause, *plié* on left supporting foot *(fig. 4)*, left arm returning to preparatory position; rise on to left *demi-pointe (relevé)* executing a semi-circular movement to the back in the air with working leg from 45 degrees front to position *attitude croisée* back 90 degrees; arms move from preparatory position to chest level, opening slightly sideways, right arm moves above head and left arm to preparatory position *(figs. 5, 6)*.

RENVERSÉ EN DEHORS

Renversé en dehors: simultaneously plié on supporting leg, moving torso and head forward, *bending vigorously to the left and back* *(fig. 7)* forcing legs to execute movement *pas de bourrée en tournant; turning,* bring torso erect, return arms to preparatory position,

[115]

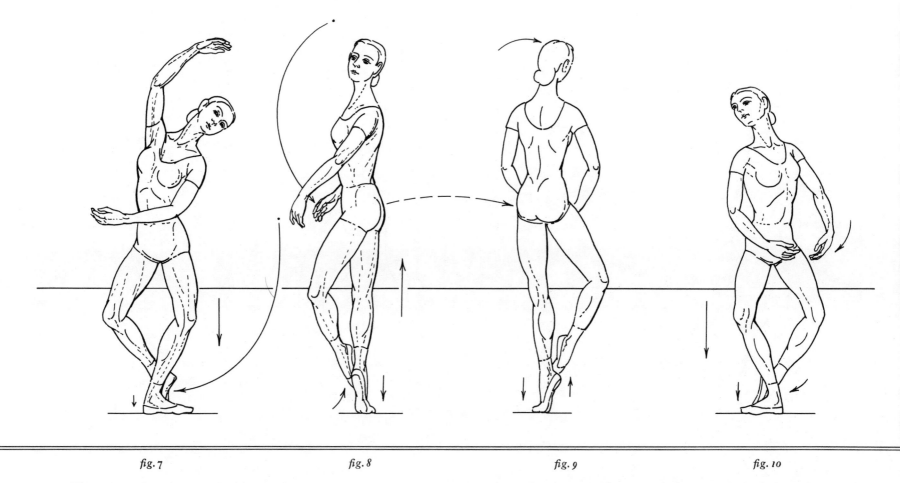

fig. 7   fig. 8   fig. 9   fig. 10

(Illustration and text continued from preceding page 115)

step on to *demi-pointe* of right foot, lifting left foot *sur le cou-de-pied* front (fig. 8), step on to *demi-pointe* of left foot, lifting right foot *sur le cou-de-pied* front (fig. 9); fall on to right foot *plié croisé* forward, bending torso and head to right, left foot in position *sur le cou-de-pied* back (fig. 10).

POSTURE AND MUSCULAR CONTROL

1   Moving from 5th to 4th position, the body is controlled but moves easily.

2   Swinging working leg into *attitude croisée* back, move torso forward with back well arched, hold shoulders down; bend and swing torso forward and backward energetically to give dynamic force to *renversé*.

3   Body remains facing forward until first step of *pas de bourrée*.

4   Executing *pas de bourrée en tournant*, lift left and right foot with precise, *staccato* movements to position *sur le cou-de-pied* front, pointing toes downward.

5   Arm movement in *renversé* must be broad and free, with rounded arms.

[116]

Pirouettes, Turns and Linking Movements

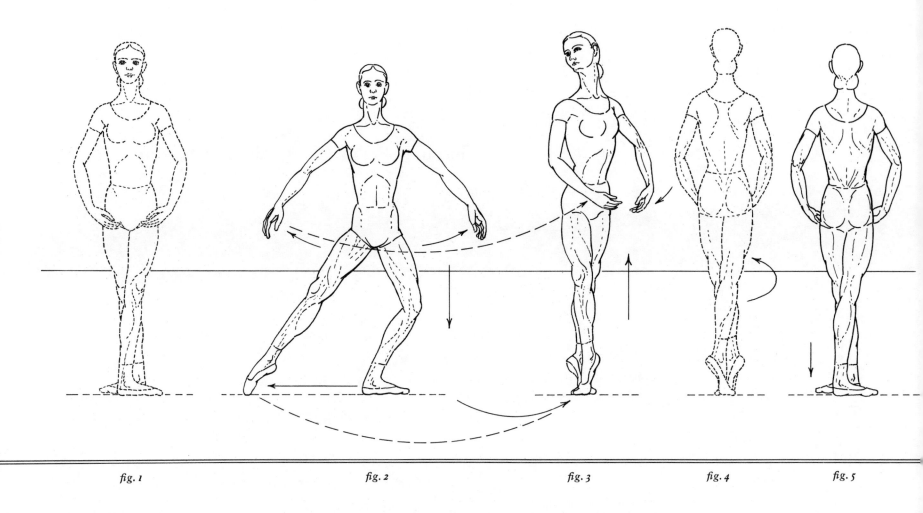

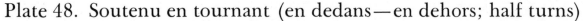

fig. 1   fig. 2   fig. 3   fig. 4   fig. 5

Plate 48. Soutenu en tournant (en dedans—en dehors; half turns)

EXERCISE
From 5th position left front *(fig. 1)*. Simultaneously execute *demi-plié* on left supporting leg, slide and point right working foot to 2nd position, opening arms from preparatory position to the sides *(fig. 2)*.

[118]

Half turn to face back: draw extended right foot in *front* of supporting foot, rising to 5th position *demi-pointes*, bringing arms together in 1st position *(fig. 3)*; turn on demi-pointes to face back *(fig. 4)*; return heels to floor, left foot 5th position front *(fig. 5)*.

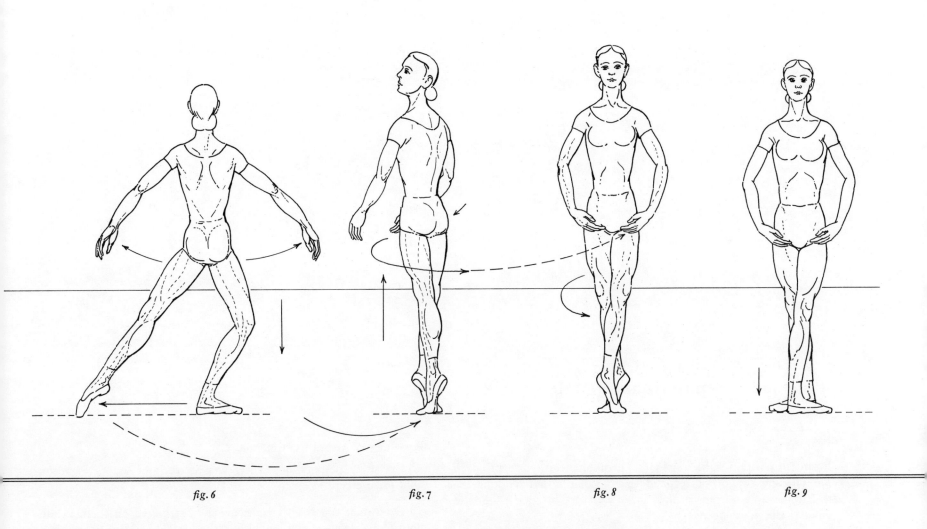

fig. 6   fig. 7   fig. 8   fig. 9

Half turn to face front: simultaneously *demi-plié* on right supporting leg, slide and point left foot to 2nd position *(fig. 6)*, opening arms to the sides, draw extended foot in *back* of supporting foot, rising to 5th position *demi-pointes;* bring arms together in 1st position *(fig. 7);* turn on *demi-pointes* to face front *(fig. 8);* return heels to floor in 5th position left foot front *(fig. 9).*

POSTURE AND MUSCULAR CONTROL

1   Executing preparations, center weight on supporting foot in *demi-plié.*

2   Executing half turns, tighten thighs and hold shoulders down to give stability and maintain balance. Straighten both knees and press feet on *demi-pointes* into the floor.

Plate 49. Soutenu en tournant (en dedans)

From 5th position right front *(fig. 1)*, simultaneously execute *demi-plié* on right supporting leg, sliding and pointing left working foot to 2nd position, opening arms from preparatory position a short distance to the sides *(fig. 2)*.

Exercise

Simultaneously draw extended left foot in front of supporting foot, rising to 5th position *demi-pointes*, bringing arms together in 1st position *(fig. 3)*. Turn inside on *demi-pointes*, moving arms upward to a position above head in line of vision, feet 5th position *demi-pointes*, right front foot *(fig. 4)*.

[120]

Posture and Muscular Control

1 Executing preparation, center weight on right supporting foot, hold torso erect.

2 Draw feet together, weight evenly distributed on them in 5th position on *demi-pointes*, hold both legs straight and firmly together, turned out from thigh to heel, incline head to left shoulder.

3 Turning, press feet into floor, move torso slightly forward from waistline, hold shoulders down, tighten thighs for stability and balance. On completion of turn, head inclines to right.

4 Move arms easily throughout exercise.

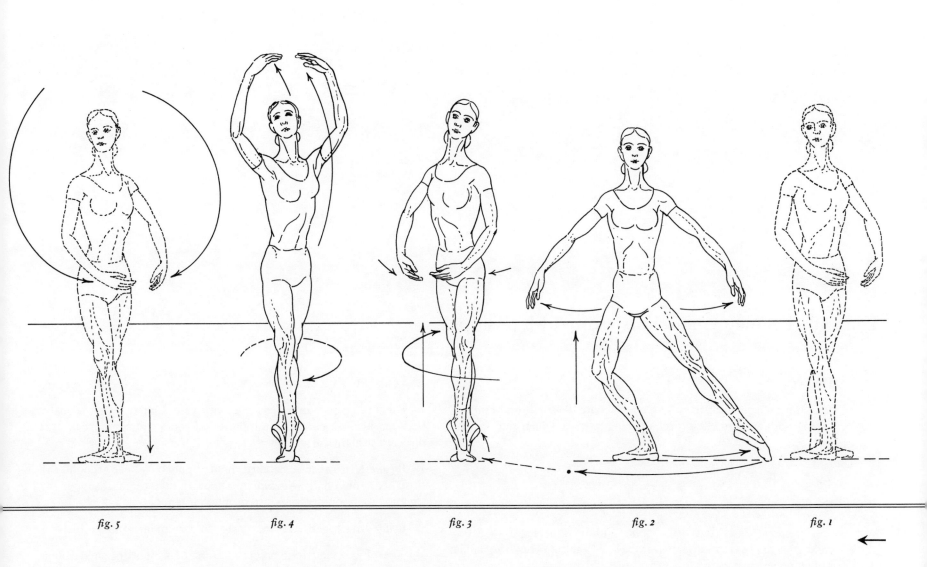

SOUTENU EN TOURNANT *(en dedans)*

Plate 50. Pirouette en dehors (from fifth position)

5th position right foot front *(fig. 1)*. Execute *demi-plié* on both feet, raising both arms to chest level, opening left arm to left side *(fig. 2)*.

EXERCISE

Turning, *relevé* swiftly to *demi-pointe* of left supporting foot, lifting right foot to position *sur le cou-de-pied* in front of supporting ankle; simultaneously swinging left arm forcefully back to meet right arm in 1st position *(figs. 3, 4)*, remain momentarily on *demi-pointe* of supporting foot before passing right foot from position *sur le cou-de-pied front* to 5th position *back* in *demi-plié (fig. 5)*.

POSTURE AND MUSCULAR CONTROL

1 Execute preparatory *demi-plié* with ease. Center weight equally between both feet in 5th position. Hold torso and head erect, eyes directed straight forward.

2 *Pirouette:* to secure stability, hold supporting knee straight and firm, press foot on *demi-pointe* into floor, tighten thigh of supporting leg and hold shoulders down to maintain balance.

3 Bring arms together energetically to give momentum to turn.

4 Toe of working foot points in front of supporting ankle, knee turned out, calf and heel brought forward.

5 At completion of turn, hold torso and head erect, eyes directed straight forward. This rule applies to all *pirouettes*.

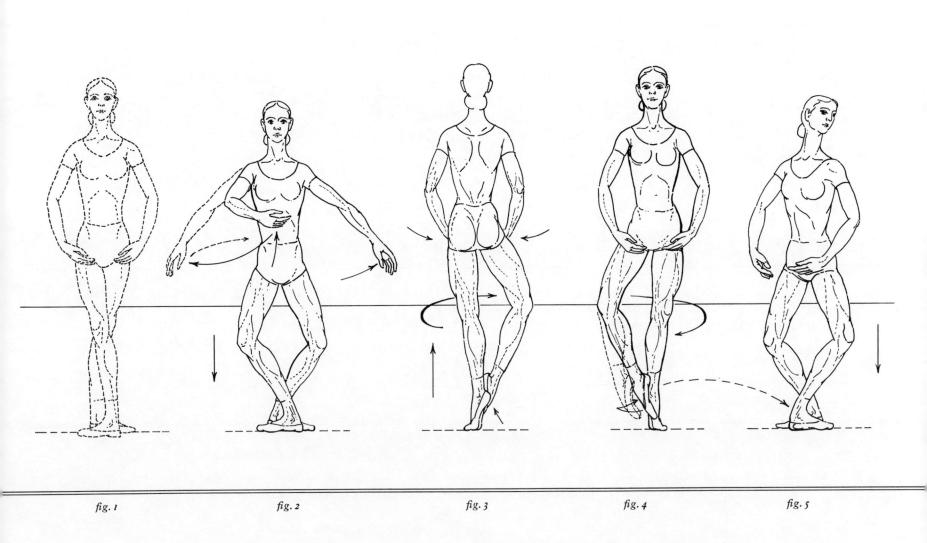

fig. 1   fig. 2   fig. 3   fig. 4   fig. 5

PIROUETTE EN DEHORS *(from 5th position)*

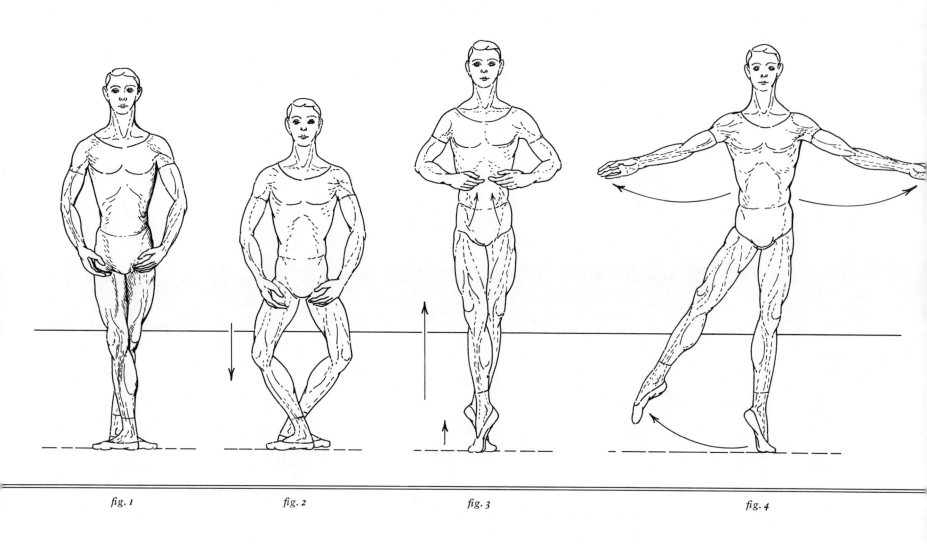

fig. 1 fig. 2   fig. 3   fig. 4

Plate 51. Pirouette en dehors (from second position)

PREPARATION

From 5th position right front *(fig. 1)*, execute *demi-plié (fig. 2)*, rising on to 5th position *demi-pointes*, raising both arms to chest level *(fig. 3)*. Simultaneously open both arms and right leg into 2nd position *(fig. 4)*.

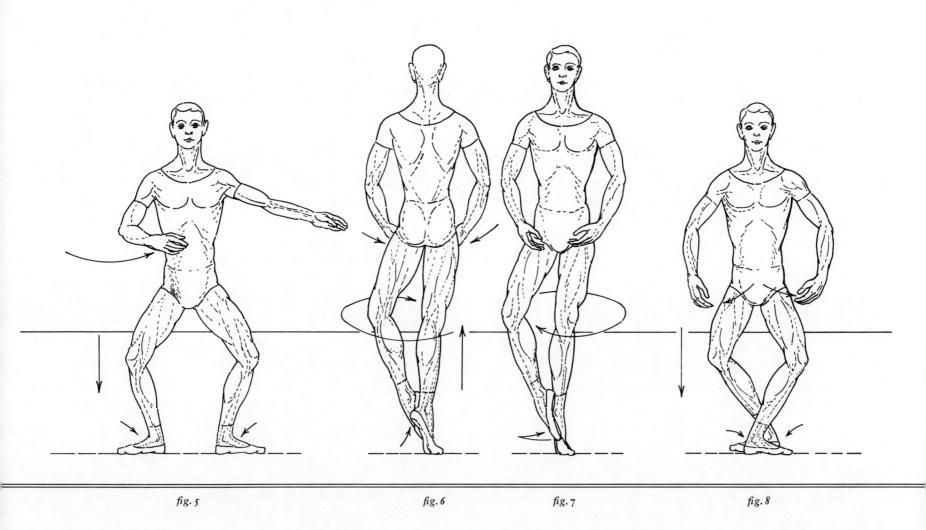

fig. 5   fig. 6   fig. 7   fig. 8

EXERCISE

Execute *demi-plié* in 2nd position, swing right arm back to 1st position chest level *(fig. 5)*; execute *pirouette en dehors (figs. 6, 7)*, terminating in 5th position *right foot back (fig. 8)*.

This movement may be executed without *relevé* in preparation, sliding right foot to point in 2nd position.

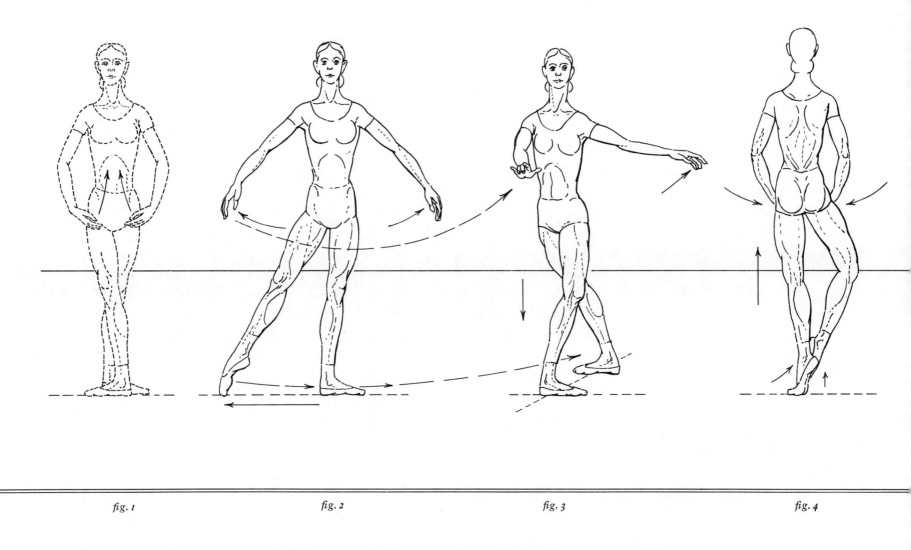

Plate 52. Pirouette en dehors (croisé en arrière—from fourth position)

There are two preparations for *pirouette en dehors* from 4th position:

PREPARATION

From 5th position right front, raise both arms to chest level, slide right foot to point in 2nd position opening both arms sideways, holding both knees straight *(fig. 2)*. Simultaneously bend left knee and

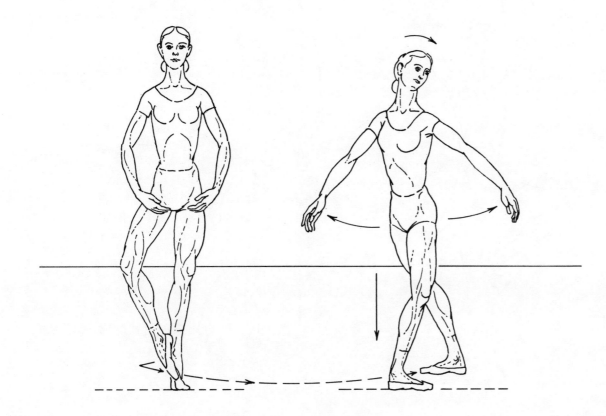

fig. 5   fig. 6   *(See Illustration for 2nd preparation on following page 128)*

slide straight right leg back to 4th position *croisé* back (passing through 1st position on floor); swing right arm back to 1st position chest level *(fig. 3)*, palm of right hand facing forward.

EXERCISE

From this position execute *pirouette en dehors (figs. 4, 5)*, terminating in 4th position *croisé* back, opening both arms to sides *(fig. 6)*.

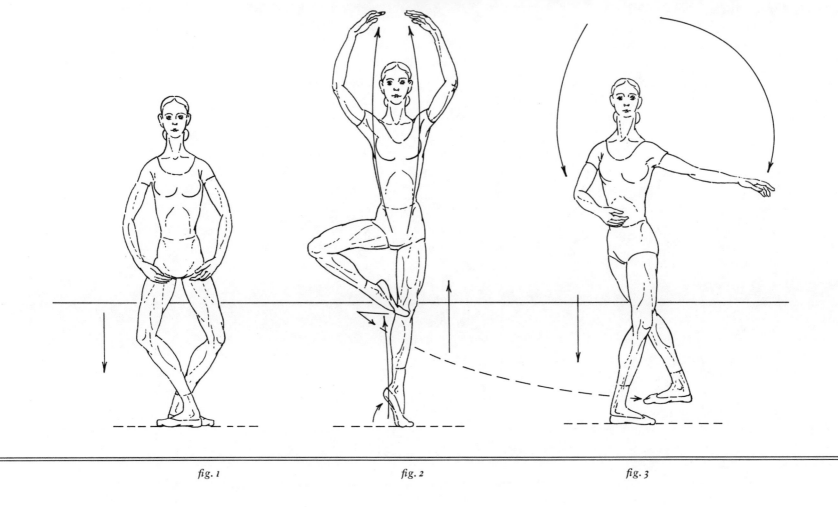

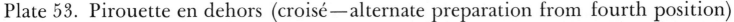

fig. 1   fig. 2   fig. 3

Plate 53. Pirouette en dehors (croisé—alternate preparation from fourth position)

PREPARATION

From 5th position right front, execute *relevé passé derrière**: rise on *demi-pointe* of supporting foot, raising right leg, toe pointing in front of supporting knee, moving both arms upward from prepara-

*This movement, called *relevé passé derrière* by Cecchetti, is called by Vaganova *sissonne simple*, and in the Legat system *sissonne passer la jambe*.

[128]

tory position to 3rd position *(fig. 2)*; simultaneously passing right leg back to 4th position, bend supporting leg; lower right arm to chest level, open left arm to left side *(fig. 3)*.

EXERCISE

Execute *pirouette en dehors* from 4th position *croisé* back.

When executing *pirouette* from 4th position *croisé* back, weight is forward over supporting leg, back leg is held *straight*.

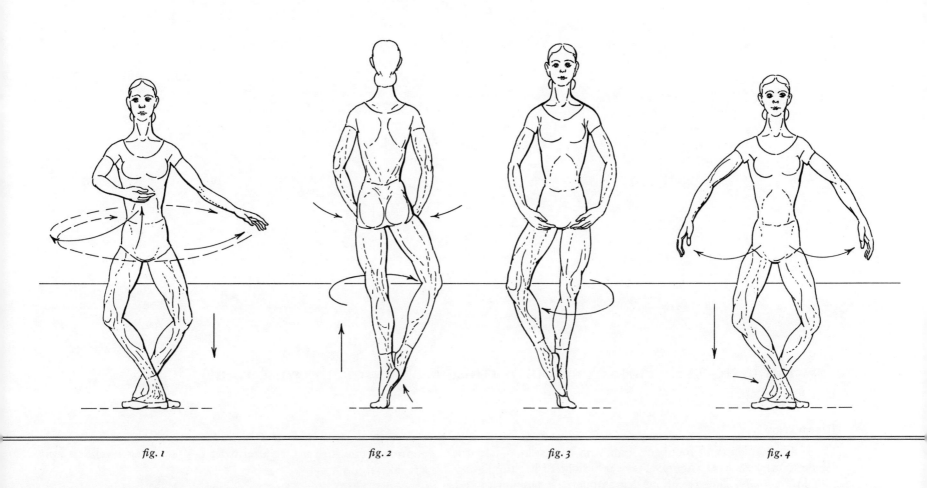

fig. 1   fig. 2   fig. 3   fig. 4

Plate 54. Pirouette en dehors (from fifth to fifth position without change of feet)

Executing a continuous series of *pirouettes* from 5th position to 5th position.

The essential impetus for this *pirouette* is gained by the movement of the arms, opening easily to the sides with each *demi-plié* in 5th position and closing forcefully in 1st position when turning.

PREPARATION

From 5th position right front, execute *demi-plié*, raising arms to chest level and moving left arm to left side *(fig. 1)*.

EXERCISE

Execute *pirouette en dehors (figs. 2, 3)*, terminating in *demi-plié* 5th position right foot front, opening both arms to sides *(fig. 4)*. Continue series of *pirouettes*; at the termination of each turn execute *demi-plié* in 5th position right front, opening arms to the sides.

[129]

Plate 55. Pirouette en dedans (from fourth croisé back to fourth croisé front)

Croisé 4th position right foot back, right arm 2nd position, left arm 1st position chest level *(fig. 1)*. Transfer weight to left supporting foot in *demi-plié*, sliding working leg through 1st position to 2nd position, opening left arm to 2nd position *(fig. 2)*.

Exercise

Turning *inwards*, rise on to *demi-pointe* of supporting foot, whipping working foot inward to position *sur le cou-de-pied* in front of supporting ankle, swinging arms forcefully together in 1st position *(fig. 3)*. Pause momentarily on *demi-pointe* with working foot *sur le cou-de-pied* front, before transferring weight on to right foot 4th

position *croisé* forward, right arm 1st position chest level, left arm left side *(figs. 4, 5)*.

Posture and Muscular Control

1   Preparation: weight centered on front supporting foot, with bent knee turned out, working leg held straight *croisé* back. Hold torso erect, forward over supporting knee, back well arched, head inclining to left.

2   Executing *pirouette en dedans*, working leg moves briskly out to 2nd position and back *sur le cou-de-pied*, knee turned outward, calf and heel brought forward, toe pointing down in front of supporting ankle. Tighten thigh of straight supporting leg, press foot on *demi-pointe* into floor.

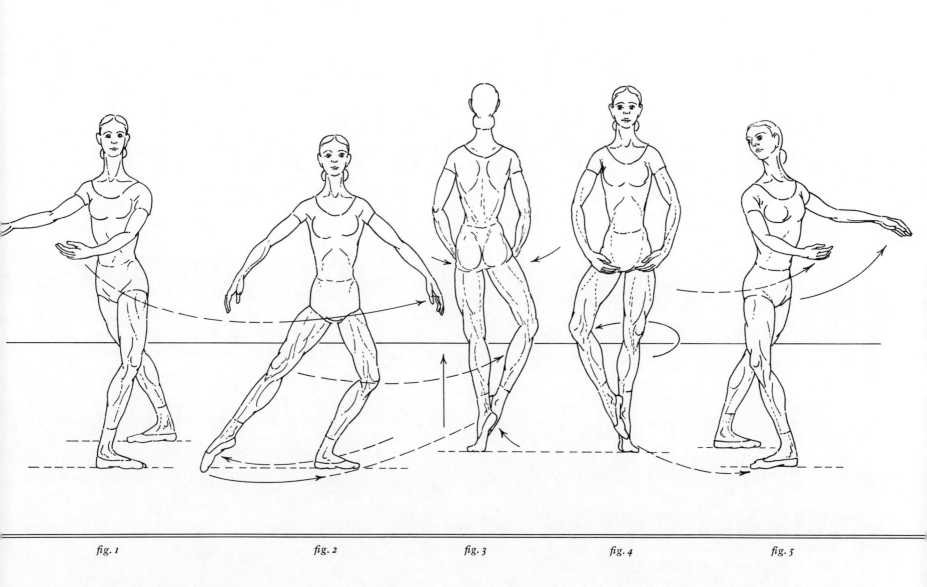

PIROUETTE EN DEDANS *(from 4th croisé back to 4th croisé front)*

fig. 1   fig. 2   fig. 3   fig. 4   fig. 5

Plate 56. Tour à la seconde (at 90 degrees, en dedans)*

PREPARATION

Croisé 4th position left foot front *(fig. 1)*.

EXERCISE

Turning inward, rise on to *demi-pointe* of supporting foot, energetically swinging working leg up to 2nd position in the air 90 degrees, simultaneously moving arms up to chest level and above head *(fig. 2)*. As extended leg descends, open arms and transfer weight from supporting leg on to working leg position *croisé* forward, right arm descending to 1st position chest level, left arm to left side *(figs. 3, 4)*.

---

*According to Mme Nicolaeva-Legat, *grande pirouette à la seconde*.

POSTURE AND MUSCULAR CONTROL

1 Preparation: weight centered on front supporting foot, bent knee turned out. Hold torso erect, forward over supporting knee, back well arched, head inclining to left.

2 Turning, swing both arms and working leg forcefully upward, hold supporting leg straight and firm, press supporting foot on *demi-pointe* into floor.

3 When turning with leg *à la seconde en l'air*, tighten thighs, buttocks and abdomen, shoulders down, torso held erect and slightly forward over hips.

4 As working leg descends, bend torso and head to right.

5 At beginning and completion of turn, eyes are directed straight forward.

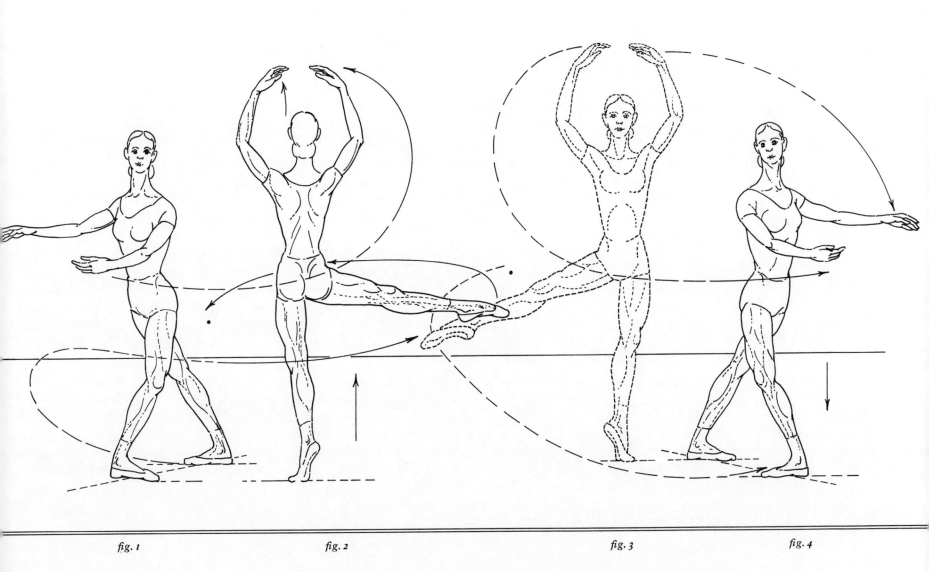

fig. 1   fig. 2   fig. 3   fig. 4

TOUR À LA SECONDE *(at 90 degrees en dedans)**

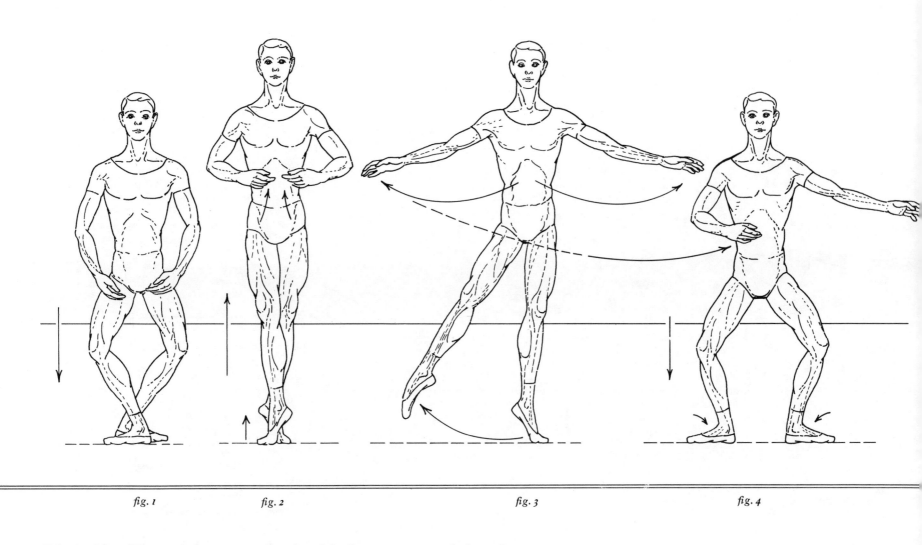

fig. 1   fig. 2   fig. 3   fig. 4

Plate 57. Tour à la seconde (at 90 degrees, en dehors)*

PREPARATION

From 5th position right front, execute *demi-plié*, *relevé* to 5th position *demi-pointes* (*figs. 1, 2*), working leg moves briskly to 2nd position a short distance from floor; raise arms to chest level and out to the sides (*fig. 3*). Execute *demi-plié* in 2nd position swinging right arm back to chest level (*fig. 4*).

---

*According to Mme Nicolaeva-Legat, *grande pirouette à la seconde*.

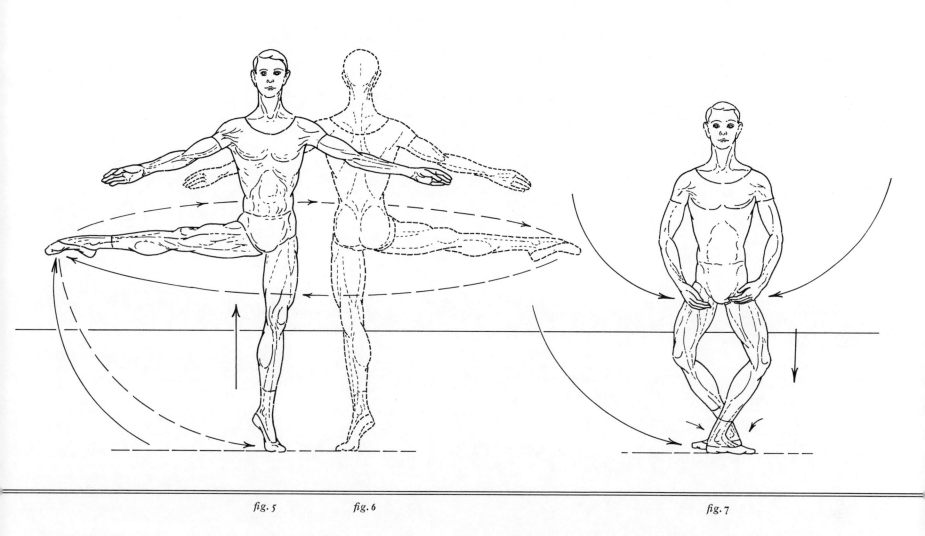

fig. 5   fig. 6   fig. 7

EXERCISE

Pirouette en l'air en dehors (turning back): rise swiftly on to *demi-pointe* of supporting foot, thrusting straight working leg to 2nd position in the air, opening right arm forcefully to the side *(figs. 5, 6)*; extended working leg is momentarily held in 2nd position before descending to 5th position back in *demi-plié*; arms returned to preparatory position *(fig. 7)*.

POSTURE AND MUSCULAR CONTROL

1 Hold torso and head erect, weight on *supporting leg* when moving working leg briskly to 2nd position. Move easily into *demi-plié* in 2nd position distributing weight *equally between both feet*.

2 Swing into turn forcefully, holding supporting leg straight and firm, press foot on *demi-pointe* into floor. When turning, hold shoulders down, tighten thighs and buttocks to maintain balance.

[135]

Plate 58. Tour en Attitude (en dedans)*

EXERCISE

From *croisé* 4th position left front *(fig. 1)*. *Relevé* on to *demi-pointe* of front supporting foot, turning forcefully inward *(en dedans)*, thrusting bent working leg back in the air at 90 degrees *(attitude croisée* back). Arms swing together in 1st position, then left arm opens to left side, right arm swings above head in line of vision *(figs. 2, 3)*. On completion of turn, slide working foot through 1st position to 4th position *croisé* front, right arm accompanying right leg forward *(fig. 4)*.

This *pirouette* may also be executed *en dehors*.

POSTURE AND MUSCULAR CONTROL

1 Preparation: weight centered on front supporting foot, move torso forward from the waistline directly over bent supporting knee, left shoulder front, head inclining to left.

2 Swing forcefully into turn, moving torso forward from the waistline *over supporting leg*, back well arched. When turning, hold shoulders down, tighten buttocks and thighs for balance and to maintain position of leg thrust into the air *en attitude*.

---

*According to Mme Nicolaeva-Legat, *pirouette en attitude*.

fig. 1   fig. 2   fig. 3   fig. 4

TOUR EN ATTITUDE *(en dedans)**

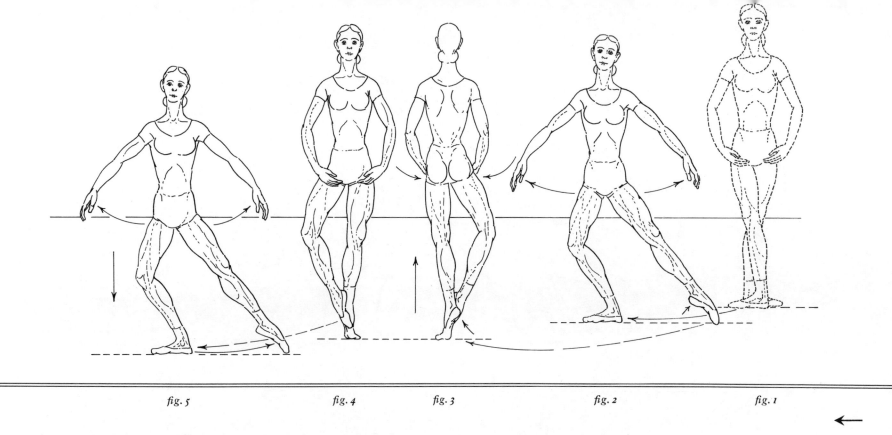

Plate 59. Tours (from preparation dégagé; en dehors—en dedans)*

A series of turns executed diagonally, around or straight across the room.

En Dehors

From 5th position right front: extend right foot to right, execute *demi-plié* on right foot, opening arms a short distance to the sides *(fig. 2)*. Immediately swing left leg in a semi-circle inward; step on to left foot *demi-pointe* turning to the right, lifting right foot to position *sur le cou-de-pied* in front of left ankle. Swing arms together in 1st position *(figs. 3, 4)*. Extend right foot to right, executing *demi-plié* and continue movement *(fig. 5)*.

*According to Vaganova. Sometimes known as *tours piqués*.
According to Cecchetti, *posés tours en dehors*.

Posture and Muscular Control

1 Step easily on to right foot in *plié*, holding torso erect, left shoulder front, inclining head to left.

2 Turning, swing rounded arms forcefully together in 1st position, hold torso and head erect, hold shoulders down, hold supporting leg straight and firm, press foot on *demi-pointe* into floor. Eyes directed straight forward at start and completion of each turn.

3 Hold working foot *sur le cou-de-pied* in *front* of supporting ankle, turn knee outward, bring calf and heel forward and point toe down.

[138]

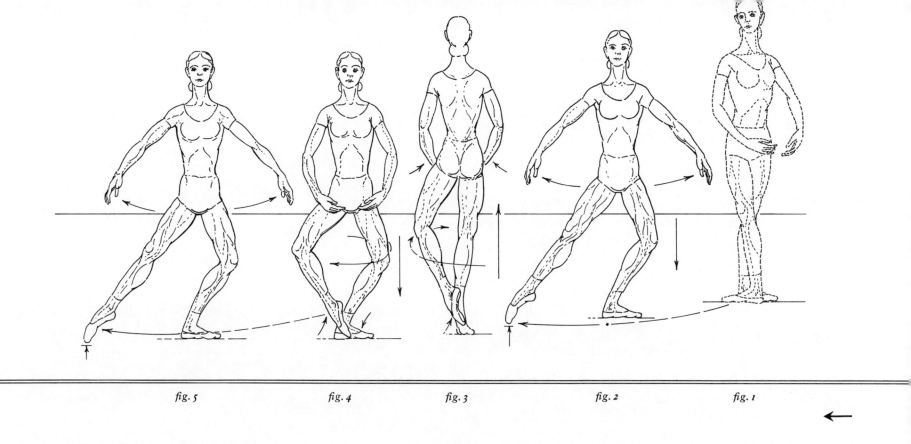

| fig. 5 | fig. 4 | fig. 3 | fig. 2 | fig. 1 |

←

En Dedans*

From 5th position right front, execute *demi-plié* on left leg, simultaneously opening arms a short distance to the sides *(figs. 1, 2)*. Step and turn to right on *demi-pointe* of right foot, lift left foot *sur le cou-de-pied* behind supporting ankle; swing arms together in 1st position *(fig. 3)*.

To continue movement, transfer weight on to left foot in *demi-plié*, right foot *sur le cou-de-pied* front *(fig. 4)* of left ankle.

This may be executed with left foot *sur le cou-de-pied* front.

---

*Sometimes known as *tours piqués*; according to Cecchetti, *posés tours en dedans*.

Posture and Muscular Control

1 Preparation: hold torso erect, right shoulder front, incline head slightly to right.

2 Before turning, stepping on to right *demi-pointe*, incline head slightly to left shoulder, eyes directed straight forward.

3 Turning, hold torso and head erect, swing rounded arms forcefully together, hold shoulders down, tighten buttocks, thighs and abdomen, hold supporting leg straight and firm, press foot on *demi-pointe* into floor, working foot *sur le cou-de-pied* back (or front) of supporting ankle, knee turned outward, calf and heel brought forward, toe pointing down.

Plate 60. Tours Chaînés Déboulés (en dedans)*

Fast turns executed on *demi-pointes* or *pointes*, straight across the room, diagonally or in a circle.

Exercise

From 5th position right front: step diagonally forward and turn on right *demi-pointe* to right, opening arms a short distance to the sides *(fig. 1)*. Continue turning by stepping on left *demi-pointe* in front of right, bring arms together in 1st position *(figs. 2, 3)*. To continue movement, thrust right leg forward each time in line of direction *(fig. 4)*.

Posture and Muscular Control

1   Hold torso erect and slightly forward from the waist line, shoulders and hips in line, stepping each time on to right *demi-pointe*.

2   In shifting from right to left foot on *demi-pointes*, keep feet together, legs turned out from thigh to heel. Open and close arms to a lesser degree as speed of turn increases.

---

*According to Cecchetti, *petits tours*.

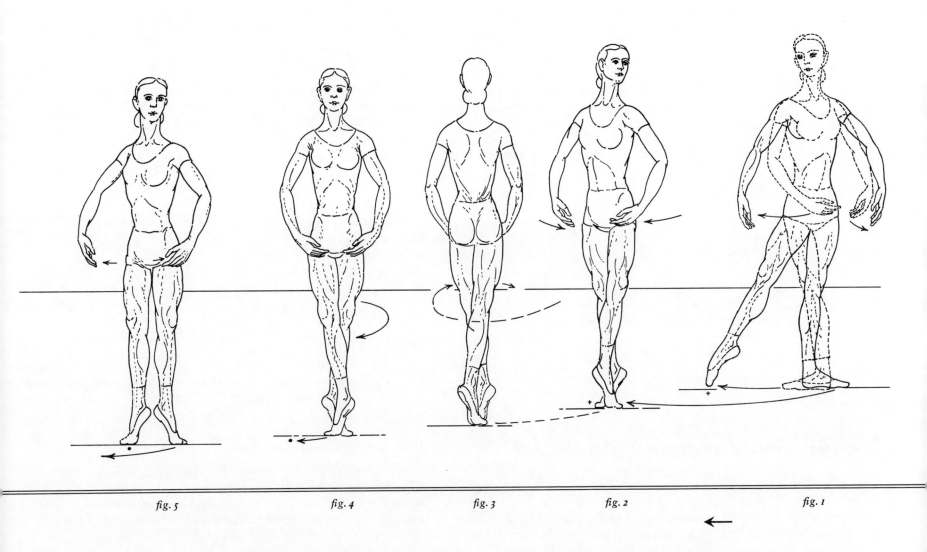

fig. 5   fig. 4   fig. 3   fig. 2   fig. 1

TOURS CHÂINÉS DÉBOULÉS *(en dedans)**

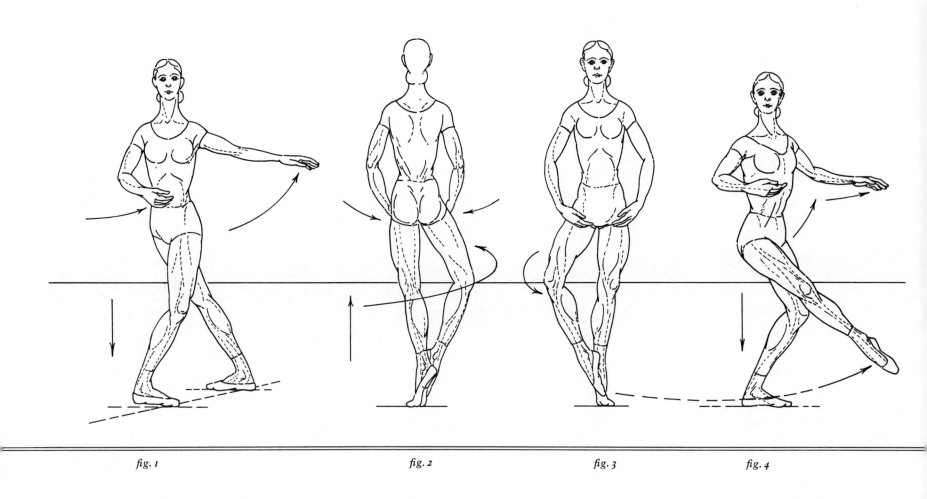

Plate 61. Fouetté en tournant (en dehors)

A series of turns on supporting leg, whipping working leg in a quarter-circle while turning, thrusting working leg *croisé* forward and simultaneously executing *demi-plié* on supporting leg at the termination of each turn.

PREPARATION: *Pirouette en dehors*

4th position facing *croisé* forward left front *(fig. 1)*. Execute *pirouette en dehors* on left supporting leg *(fig. 2)*, then thrust working leg energetically *croisé* forward 45 degrees, executing *demi-plié* on supporting leg; right arm chest level, left arm swinging out to left side *(figs. 3, 4)*.

EXERCISE: *Fouetté en dehors*

Swing working leg and right arm to 2nd position in the air, rising and turning on *demi-pointe* of supporting foot; whip working leg inward,

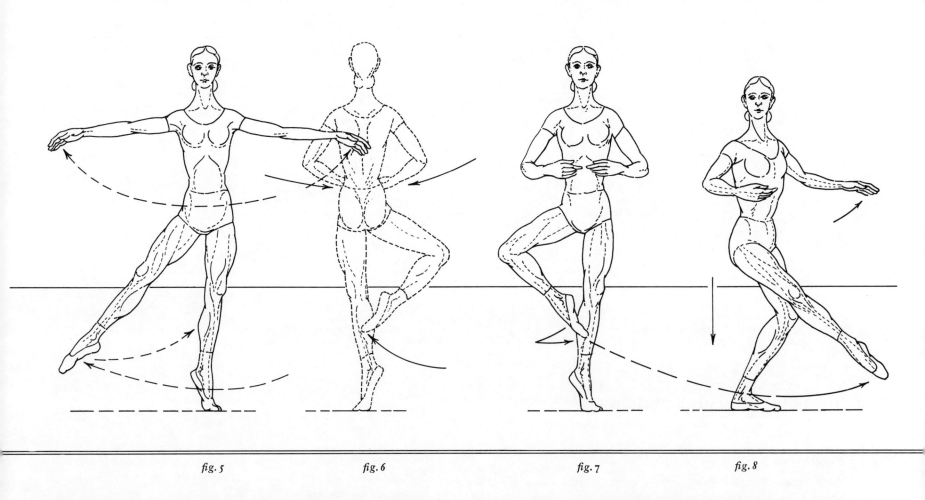

fig. 5   fig. 6   fig. 7   fig. 8

passing toe quickly from back to front of supporting knee, swinging rounded arms forcefully together *(figs. 5, 6)*. To continue a series of *fouettés en tournant*, thrust working leg energetically *croisé* forward at 45 degrees and execute *demi-plié* on supporting leg, opening arms to 2nd position *(figs. 7, 8)*.

This exercise may also be executed *en dedans*.

POSTURE AND MUSCULAR CONTROL

1   Preparation: hold torso and head erect, slightly forward over front bent supporting knee. Center weight on front foot.

2   When executing *fouetté*, tighten thigh of straight supporting leg and press foot on *demi-pointe* into floor. As working leg passes in back of supporting knee, simultaneously swing rounded arms forcefully together, hold shoulders down, tighten buttocks and thighs to give stability and keep working knee turned out.

3   Descend easily each time into *demi-plié* on supporting leg, simultaneously opening arms to 2nd position at the termination of each turn thrusting working leg *croisé* forward.

4   At completion of each turn, hold torso and head erect, eyes directed straight forward.

Plate 62. Tour en l'air (en dehors)

PREPARATION

5th position right foot front, arms in preparatory position. Raise both arms to chest level. Execute *demi-plié*, opening left arm to 2nd position *(fig. 1)*.

EXERCISE

Jump vigorously upward, turning *en dehors* and bringing left arm to meet right arm in 1st position *(fig. 2)*; feet change position in the air, landing in 5th position *demi-plié* left foot front, arms in preparatory position *(figs. 3, 4)*.

The *double tour en l'air* is a most important technical feat for the male dancer. There are various terminations that may be used: in 2nd position, on one foot with the other leg extended *en l'air à la seconde*, in *attitude allongée, etc.;* and on one knee (a frequent termination of classic male variations).

POSTURE AND MUSCULAR CONTROL

1 Hold torso erect, move easily into *demi-plié*, knees turned outward, heels remaining on floor.

2 Springing into the air, both feet push away from the floor, and the left arm is brought forcefully inward to meet the right, giving impetus to the turn.

3 The torso is held erect and slightly forward from the hip-line; both legs held straight from thighs to pointed toes in the air.

[144]

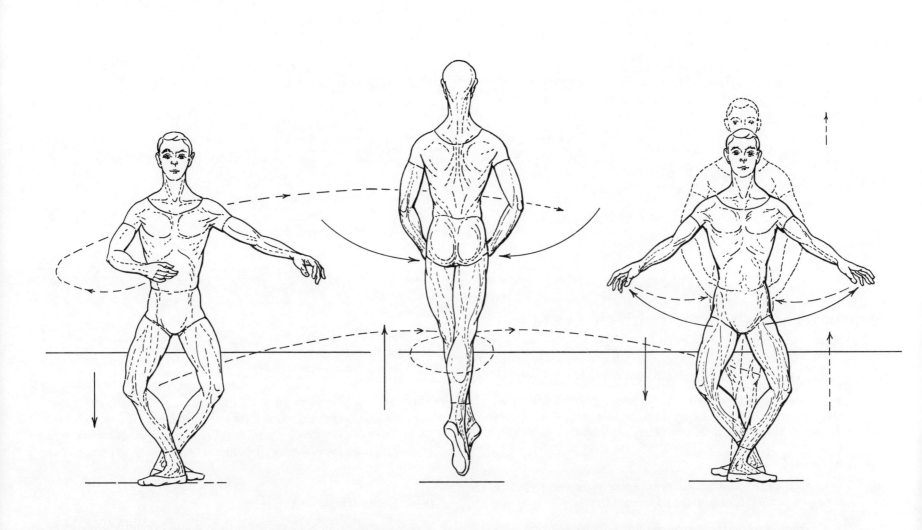

fig. 1   fig. 2   figs. 3-4

TOUR EN L'AIR *(en dehors)*

Plate 63. Pas de Bourrée (with change of feet)*

5th position right foot front, arms in preparatory position. Simultaneously execute *demi-plié croisé* on right foot, lift left foot *sur le cou-de-pied* behind right ankle, extend left arm slightly to left side *(fig. 2)*.

EXERCISE

(a)   Step on to left *demi-pointe*, opening right arm to 2nd position, lift right pointed foot in front of left ankle *(fig. 3)*;

(b)   Step on to right *demi-pointe*, lift left pointed foot in front of right ankle *(fig. 4)*;

(c)   Step on to left foot *demi-plié croisé* forward, right foot *sur le cou-de-pied* in back of left ankle, left arm in preparatory position, right arm slightly open to right side *(fig. 5)*.

---

*According to Cecchetti, *pas de bourrée dessous*.

[146]

There are many varieties of *pas de bourrée*, e.g. without change of feet, terminating position *effacé* forward and back *(see pp. 148-49)*, *pas de bourrée dessus et dessous.(see pp. 150-1)*, *pas de bourrée couru* (running on *demi-pointes* in 1st position, usually as a preparation for a jump), etc.

POSTURE AND MUSCULAR CONTROL

1   Executing *demi-plié croisé* on right foot, bring right shoulder front, incline head to right.

2   Executing *pas de bourrée*, lift feet precisely and distinctly, toes pointing in front of ankles, straightening supporting leg and moving a short distance to the right.

3   Executing *demi-plié croisé* on left foot, bring left shoulder front, incline head to left.

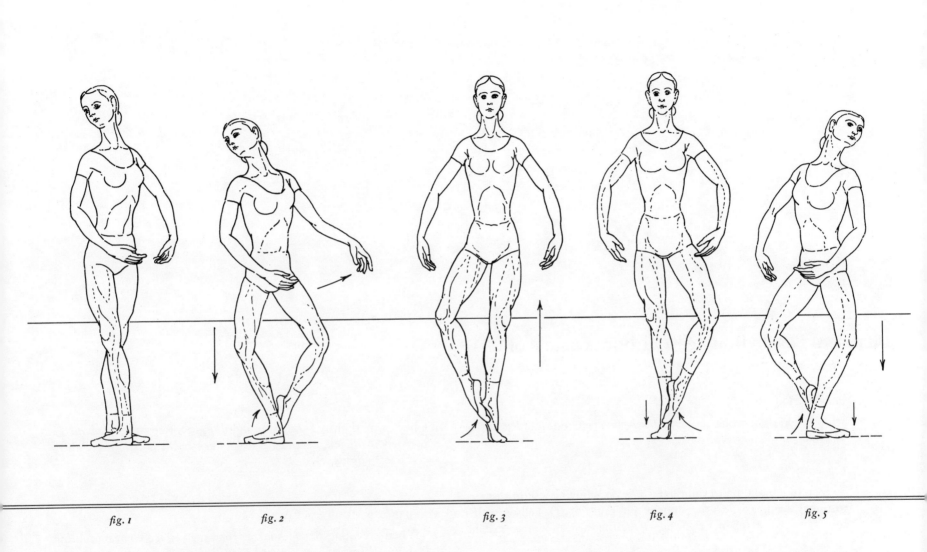

fig. 1   fig. 2   fig. 3   fig. 4   fig. 5

PAS DE BOURRÉE *(with change of feet)**

Plate 64. Pas de Bourrée (without change of feet)*

PREPARATION

5th position right front: execute *demi-plié croisé* on right leg, lifting left foot *sur le cou-de-pied* back *(fig. 1)*.

EXERCISE

Step on to left and on to right *demi-pointes* (moving a short distance to right), bring arms to preparatory position *(fig. 2)*. Fall on to left foot *demi-plié*, extending right leg *effacé* forward 45 degrees, extend-ing both arms slightly forward to right *(fig. 3)*. Repeat *pas de bourrée* movements to back, extend left leg *effacé* back, both arms slightly back to left *(figs. 4, 5)*.

POSTURE AND MUSCULAR CONTROL

1   When executing *pas de bourrée* forward *(effacé en avant)*, bring left shoulder forward and incline head slightly to left. Executing *pas de bourrée* to back *(effacé en arrière)*, bring right shoulder forward and incline head slightly to right.

2   Straighten both knees when executing *pas de bourrée*.

---

*According to Cecchetti, *pas de bourrée en avant* and *en arrière*.
According to Mme. Nicolaeva-Legat, *pas de bourrée ballotté en avant* and *en arrière*.

[148]

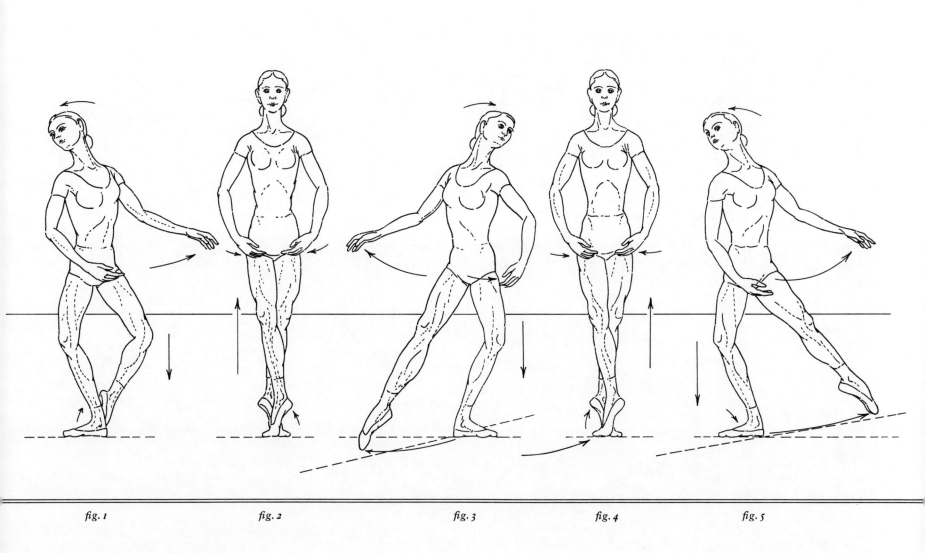

PAS DE BOURRÉE *(without change of feet)**

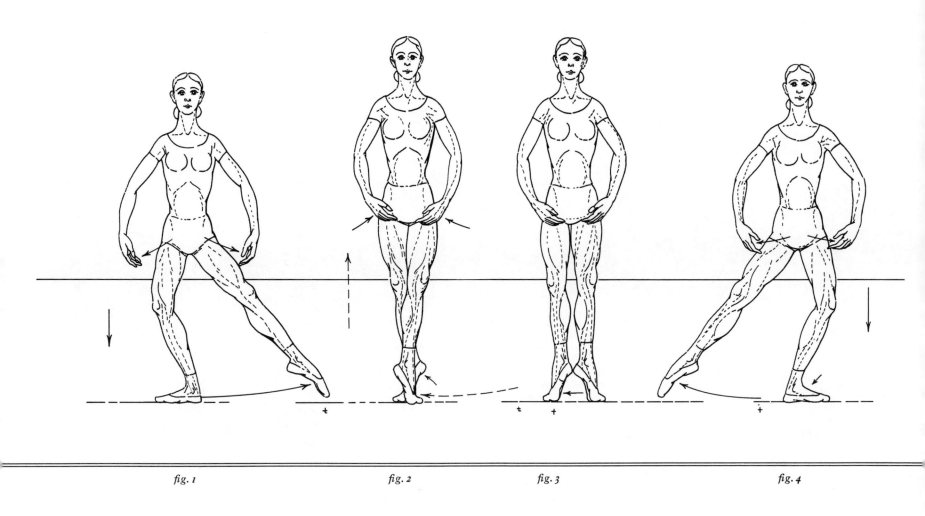

fig. 1   fig. 2   fig. 3   fig. 4

Plate 65. Pas de Bourrée (dessus et dessous—under and over)

EXERCISE

Dessus (Over, *i.e.*, extended leg passes in front, "over" supporting leg) 5th position right front; execute *demi-plié* on right leg, extending left leg to 2nd position a slight distance from the floor. Open arms sideways *(fig. 1)*. Draw extended (left) leg in front of right 5th posi-

tion *demi-pointes*, bring arms together in 1st position *(fig. 2)*, step on to right *demi-pointe* a short distance to the right *(fig. 3)*, descend on to left foot *demi-plié*, extending right leg to 2nd position, opening arms sideways *(fig. 4)*.

[150]

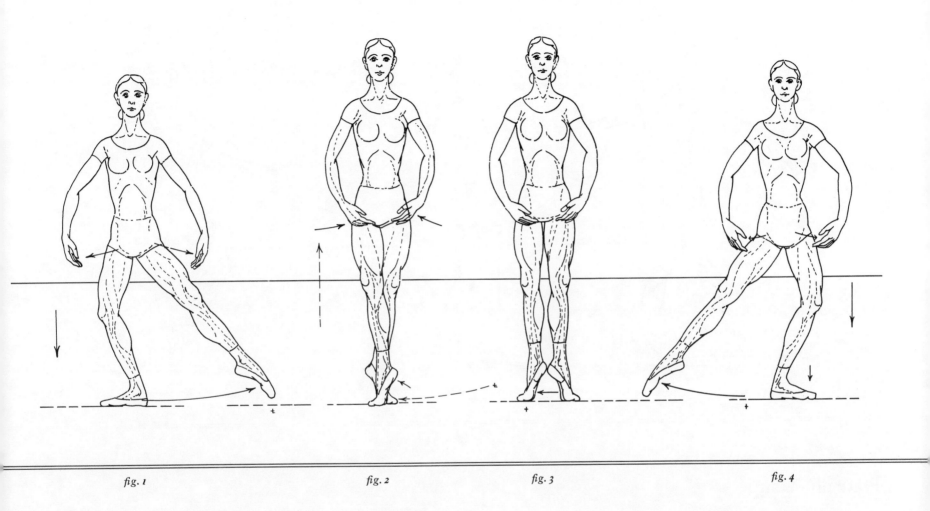

fig. 1   fig. 2   fig. 3   fig. 4

Dessous (Under, *i.e.*, extended leg passes in back, under supporting leg) 5th position left front; execute *demi-plié* on right leg, extending left leg to 2nd position a slight distance from the floor. Open arms sideways *(fig. 1)*. Draw extended (left) leg in back of right 5th position *demi-pointes*, bring arms together in 1st position *(fig. 2)*, step on to right *demi-pointe* a short distance to the right *(fig. 3)*, descend on to left foot *demi-plié*, extending right leg to 2nd position, opening arms sideways *(fig. 4)*.

This movement is usually executed as a combination, moving over to the right, then under to the left, or *vice versa*. Leg should be extended to exact 2nd position each time. Move easily into *demi-plié* on supporting leg, bringing extended leg back to 5th position *demi-pointes* in a straight line each time. This *pas de bourrée* may be executed *en tournant—dessus* (over) *en dedans*, *dessous* (under) *en dehors*.

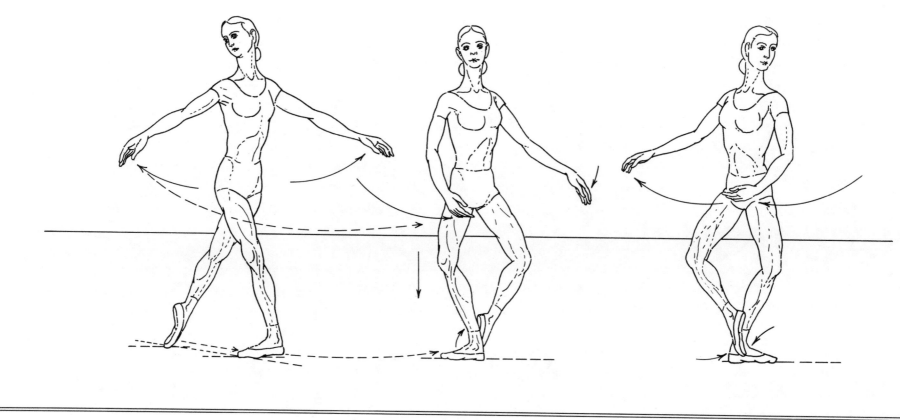

Plate 66. Coupé

A small intermediary step, generally a preparation for *pas de bourrée, ballonné, etc.*

PREPARATION

4th position *croisé* back, right front, left pointing back *(fig. 1)*.

[152]

EXERCISE

Coupé en avant (forward): execute *demi-plié* on supporting leg, bringing working foot *sur le cou-de-pied* back; move right arm to preparatory position, left arm to left side *(fig. 2)*. Working foot replaces supporting foot by quickly executing *demi-plié* and lifting right foot *sur le cou-de-pied* in front of left ankle. Left arm to preparatory position, right arm out at right side *(fig. 3)*.

Coupé en arrière (backward): execute exercise in reverse direction.

Coupé may also be executed stepping on to *demi-pointe* instead of into *demi-plié*.

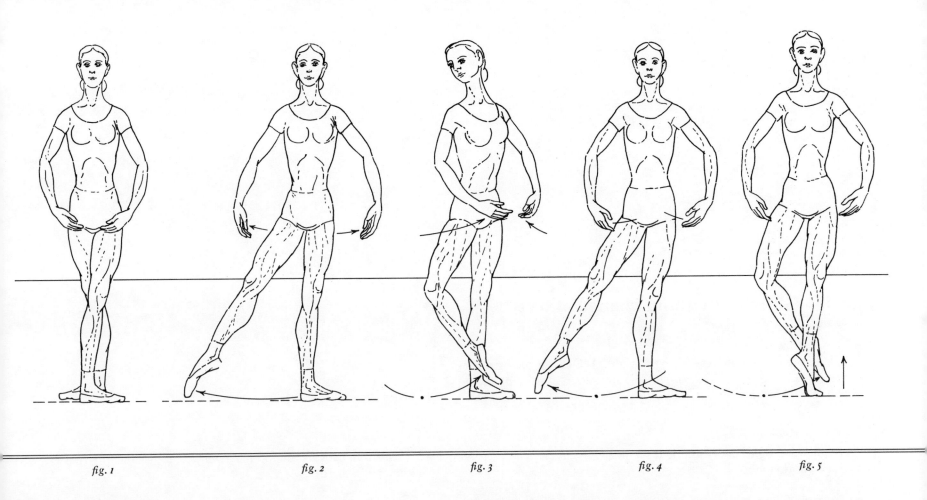

fig. 1   *fig. 2*   *fig. 3*   *fig. 4*   *fig. 5*

Plate 67. Flic-Flac*

EXERCISE

1st movement: 5th position left front: slide right working foot sideways to 2nd position a short distance from the floor, opening both arms sideways *(fig. 2)*, swing working leg inward, striking the floor

*According to Cecchetti, *fouetté* movement of the foot *à terre*.

with toe of working foot before it passes in front of supporting ankle, simultaneously bringing arms to 1st position *(fig. 3)*.

2nd movement: extend working foot sideways to 2nd position a short distance from floor, opening both arms sideways, digging sharply with *demi-pointe* of working foot into floor before bringing *sur le cou-de-pied* back, executing *relevé* on supporting foot *(figs. 4, 5)*. Pause momentarily on *demi-pointe* of supporting foot before returning to 5th position *demi-plié*.

Flic-flac may be executed turning *(en dedans* and *en dehors)*, with *relevé* on second movement only.

[153]

Plate 68. Glissade (without change of feet)*

(Without change of feet moving to right.*) This is a gliding movement with the accent in *demi-plié* in 5th position, usually preceding jumps and leaps.

PREPARATION

5th position right foot front, right shoulder forward, arms in preparatory position *(fig. 1)*.

EXERCISE

(a)   Execute *demi-plié*, sliding right foot on floor until reaching 2nd position, toe fully pointed, opening arms a short distance to the sides *(fig. 2)*;

(b)   Push away from floor with left foot, momentarily straightening knees, and transfer weight of body on to right foot *demi-plié*; stretch left leg to maximum, pointing toe on floor 2nd position *(fig. 3)*;

(c)   Slide foot back to 5th position *demi-plié*, returning arms to preparatory position *(figs. 4, 5)*.

Glissade may be executed in the reverse direction, or alternating feet each time in *demi-plié* 5th position, *i.e.*, left front left shoulder forward, right front right shoulder forward†. It may also be executed in all directions and *en tournant*.

POSTURE AND MUSCULAR CONTROL

1   At moment of transition from left foot to right, both legs are stretched to maximum from thighs to pointed toes, just off the ground.

2   When executing *demi-plié* in 5th position there must be a slight counter-pull upward; both heels on the ground.

---

*According to Cecchetti, *glissade devant*.

†According to Cecchetti, *glissade changée*.

[154]

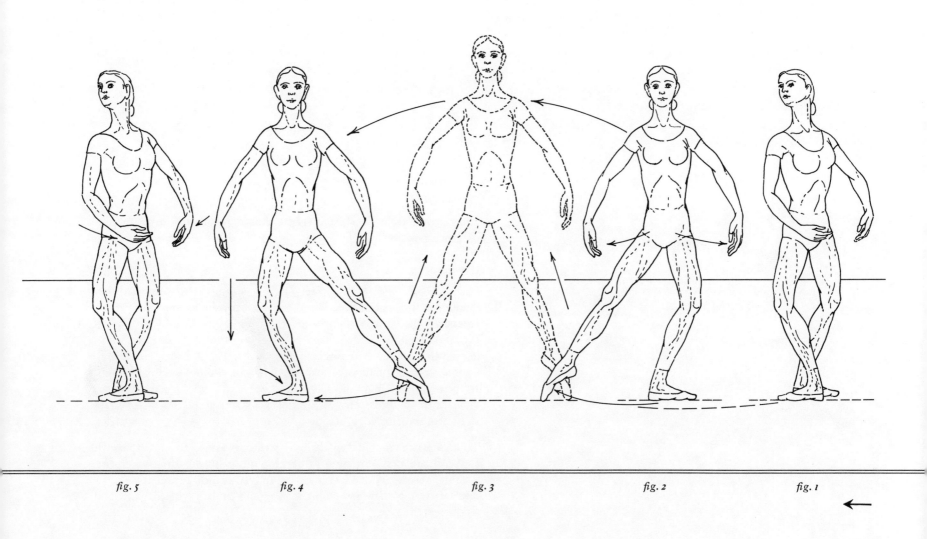

fig. 5   fig. 4   fig. 3   fig. 2   fig. 1

GLISSADE *(without change of feet)**

Plate 69. Pas Failli*

PREPARATION

5th position right foot front, right shoulder forward, arms in preparatory position.

EXERCISE

Execute *demi-plié* on both feet *(fig. 1)*, spring lightly upward, extending both legs 5th position in the air, arms in 1st position, simultaneously turn torso slightly to the right, left shoulder forward *(effacé)*, opening left leg diagonally back in the air 45 degrees, moving arms easily to 2nd position *(figs. 2, 3)*. Right foot descends to floor *demi-plié*, quickly followed by left foot, sliding on floor through 1st position to 4th position *croisé*, knee and heel turned outward; incline head and torso to left, left arm accompanies left leg forward, right arm remains at right side *(figs. 4, 5)*.

This step is executed swiftly and without pause, from 5th to 4th *croisé*. Arms move softly and harmoniously during the movement. *Pas failli* may be used as a connecting movement, or as preparation for *pirouettes*, in which case right arm would be brought forward and left arm at the side.

---

*According to Cecchetti, *demi-contretemps (temps levé* and *chassé croisé)*, with the *temps levé* taken *sur le cou-de-pied* back.

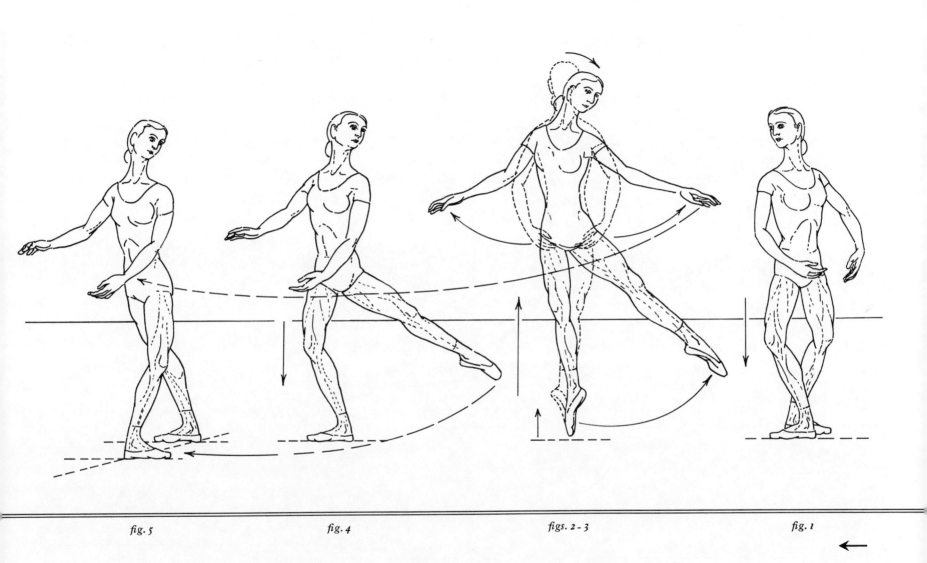

fig. 5   fig. 4   figs. 2-3   fig. 1

PAS FAILLI*

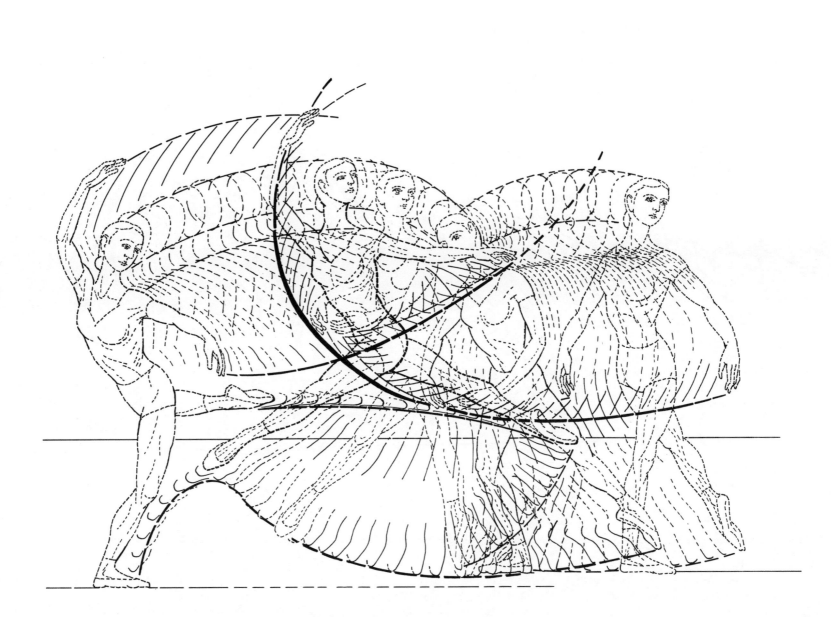

Space Pattern of the Grand Jeté en avant

Part III: Allegro

Introduction to Allegro

Allegro follows the adagio and consists of jumping steps. These may be divided into the following categories (according to Mme Nicolaeva-Legat):

1 From both feet on to both feet;
2 From both feet, finishing on one foot;
3 From one foot, finishing on both feet;
4 From one foot on to the other;
5 Consecutive jumping on one foot.

Elevation is developed gradually: the first movements in jumping are simple—from both feet to both feet in the 1st and 2nd positions (*temps levé, changement de pieds, échappé*). Care must be taken to perfect all small jumping steps before attempting to execute the larger. The dancer must control her body in the air and avoid all convulsive movements of the torso and neck: the effect must be effortless. Every jump begins with *demi-plié*, both heels remaining on the ground, before pushing away from the floor with both feet and springing upward into the air with legs stretched to maximum from thighs to pointed toes. In the early stages of training, the arms remain in the preparatory position, or low 2nd, before any attempt is made to combine and co-ordinate the movement of the legs with its accompanying movement of the arms. At a further stage of development the larger jumps are practised, combinations introduced, and sequences linked together.

Ballon (literally, bouncing), the smooth falling and rising of the feet in the passage from step to step, is the ideal achievement of the classic ballet technique. The most important elements in *ballon* are the light ascent and the soft descent to the floor, first with the toes, then through the foot to the heel, into *demi-plié*. (This is only possible for the *danseuse* if pliable ballet shoes are worn.)

Beating Steps (Batterie)

Exercises at the bar, such as *battements frappés* and *petits battements sur le cou-de-pied*, are a preparation for the execution of beating steps in the center. Almost all jumping steps may be embellished with a beat: this introduces an added element of virtuosity and brilliance. The student must first master the simple beating steps, or *petite batterie: royale, entrechat quatre, entrechat trois, entrechat cinq*, and *brisés*. All these are executed with the feet barely leaving the floor. To achieve clean and distinct beats, the beat must be made with the calves, both legs stretched to maximum and turned out from thighs to pointed toes, opening slightly sideways in the air before and after each beat.

At a later stage in development the dancer progresses to *grande batterie (entrechat six, entrechat six de volée, entrechat sept, cabrioles)* and *pas battus (e.g., sissonne, saut de basque, grand jeté en tournant entrelacé*, when performed with a beat). These movements necessitate a vigorous springing into the air.

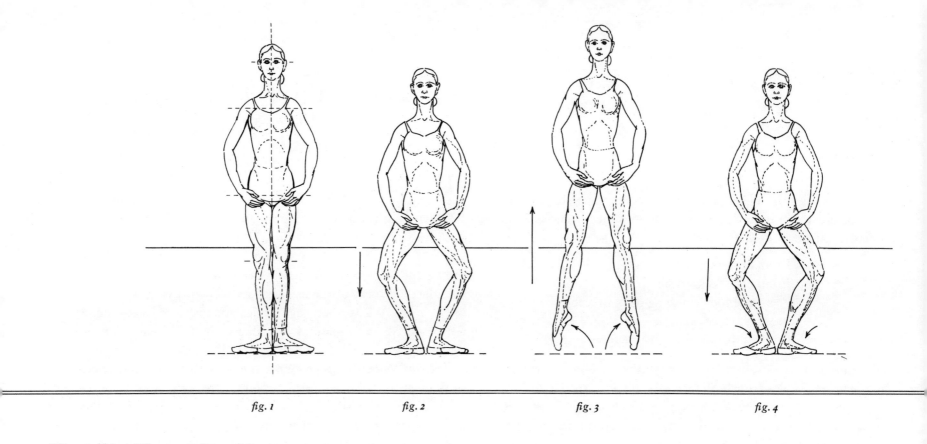

fig. 1   fig. 2   fig. 3   fig. 4

Plate 70. Temps Levé*

Temps levé is executed from 2nd and 4th positions, each series of jumps completed by straightening knees.

Jumping from both feet on to both feet.

PREPARATION

Standing in 1st position, arms in preparatory position throughout movement (*fig. 1*).

EXERCISE

Execute *demi-plié* (*fig. 2*), jump upward straightening both legs, toes pointed to maximum in the air in 1st position (*fig. 3*). Descending to floor, toes reach the ground first before lowering heels in 1st position *demi-plié* (*fig. 4*).

---

*According to Cecchetti, small springs in 1st position.

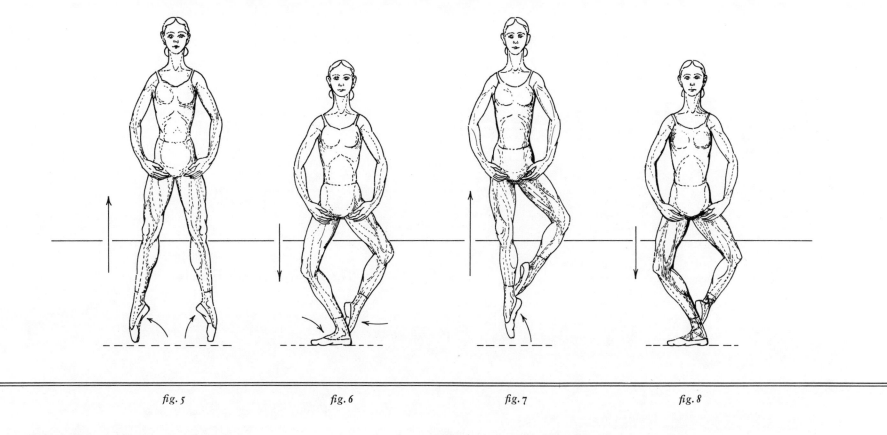

Jumping from both feet on to one foot.

PREPARATION

1st position, arms in preparatory position *(fig. 4)*.

EXERCISE

Execute *demi-plié*, jump upward, straightening both legs, toes pointed to maximum in the air in 1st position *(fig. 5)*; right foot descends to floor *demi-plié*, left foot pointing *sur le cou-de-pied* behind right ankle *(fig. 6)*.

Jumping from one foot on to one foot *(fig. 6)*.

EXERCISE

Jump upward from right foot *demi-plié*, straightening right leg from thigh to toe in the air *(fig. 7)*, left foot pointing *sur le cou-de-pied*

behind right ankle; right foot descends to floor *demi-plié*, left foot pointing *sur le cou-de-pied* behind right ankle *(fig. 8)*.

POSTURE AND MUSCULAR CONTROL

1 Standing in 1st position, hold torso erect, shoulders down, both arms in preparatory position, softly rounded from shoulders to finger-tips, neck and arms completely free from strain, legs turned outward from thighs to heels.

2 Heels remain on floor when executing *demi-pliés* preparatory to jumping.

3 Jumping upward, both feet push away from floor, legs stretched to maximum from thighs to toes in the air.

4 Descending to floor, slight muscular tension in buttocks and thighs effects a light and soft descent to floor *demi-plié* (toes reach floor before heels).

Plate 71. Petit Changement de Pieds

PREPARATION

5th position right foot front, arms in preparatory position.

EXERCISE

Execute *demi-plié*, distributing weight equally between the feet *(fig. 2)*; jump upward, straightening both legs from thighs to toes, 5th position in the air *(fig. 3)*; descending to floor, feet change position, toes strike the floor first before lowering heels in 5th position *demi-plié* left foot front *(fig. 4)*.

Changement de pieds may be executed with the toes barely leaving the floor. *Grand changement de pieds*, as the name implies, is executed in the same manner with a higher jump upward into the air.

POSTURE AND MUSCULAR CONTROL

1 Executing *demi-plié*, hold torso erect, draw abdomen in.

2 Jumping, feet push away from the floor, legs are stretched to maximum from thighs to pointed toes.

3 Descending to floor, slight muscular tension in buttocks and thighs effects a light and soft descent to floor 5th position *demi-plié* (toes reach floor before heels).

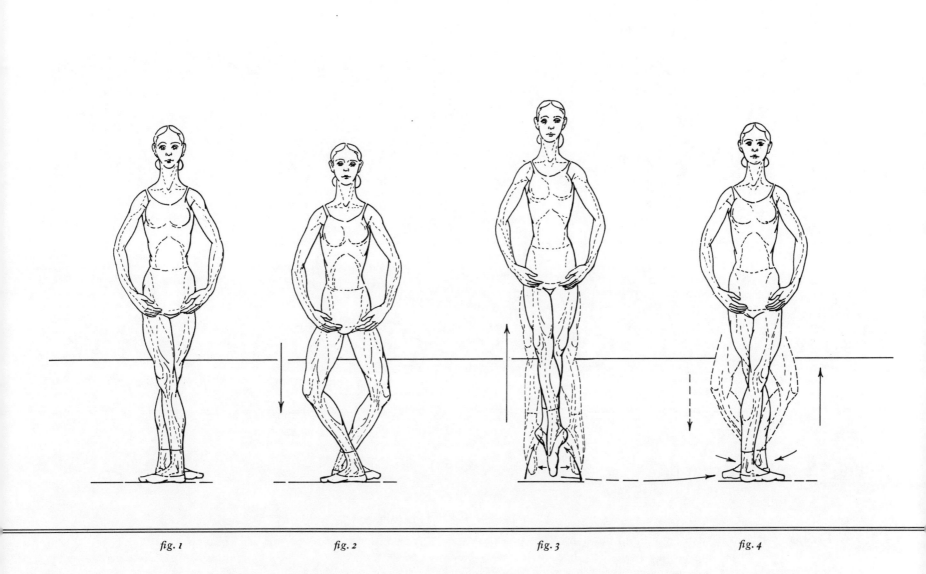

fig. 1   fig. 2   fig. 3   fig. 4

PETIT CHANGEMENT DE PIEDS

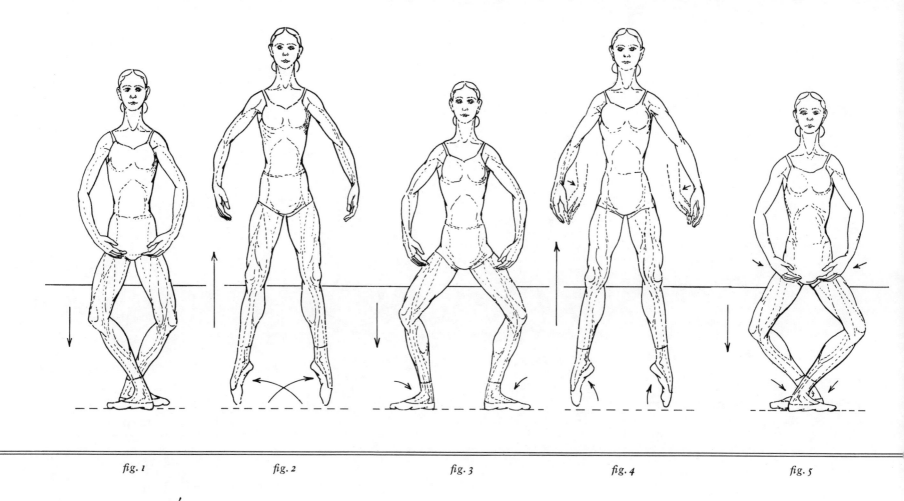

fig. 1   fig. 2   fig. 3   fig. 4   fig. 5

Plate 72 a. Petit Échappé

Echappé may be executed jumping to positions *croisé* or *effacé*, and may be finished landing on one foot, the other *sur le cou-de-pied*, front or back. Arms move harmoniously with legs, from preparatory position passing through 1st position to low 2nd position and back to preparatory position. Arms move harmoniously with legs from preparatory position out to low 2nd position and back again.

[164]

5th position right foot front, arms in preparatory position.

EXERCISE

Execute *demi-plié*, distributing weight equally between both feet; jump, straightening both legs from thighs to toes, to 2nd position *demi-plié* (figs. 2, 3); jump, straightening both legs from thighs to toes, back to 5th position *demi-plié*, bringing left foot front (figs. 4, 5).

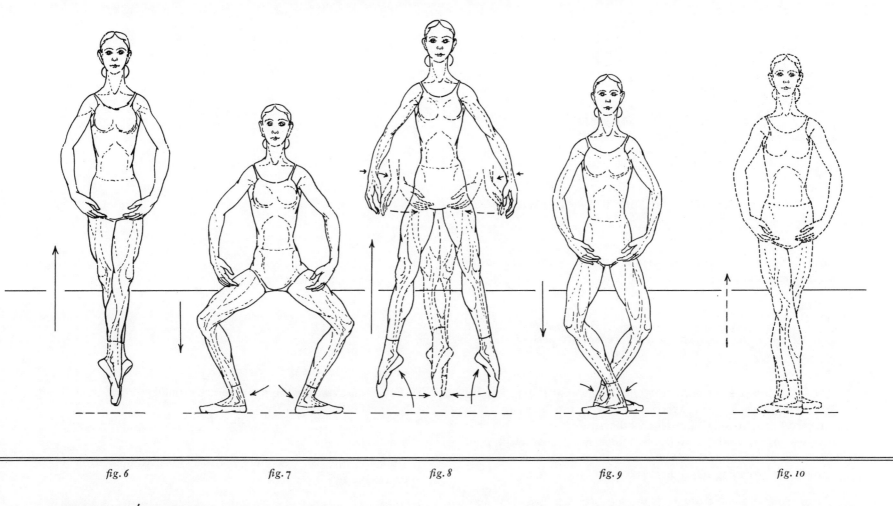

fig. 6   fig. 7   fig. 8   fig. 9   fig. 10

b. Grand Échappé

PREPARATION

From 5th position *demi-plié (fig. 5)*.

EXERCISE

Jump vigorously upward straightening both legs, toes pointed to maximum, 5th position in the air *(fig. 6)*; both feet descend to floor 2nd position *demi-plié (fig. 7)*; jump upward, bringing legs and feet together 5th position in the air, right foot front *(fig. 8)*; descend to floor 5th position *demi-plié (figs. 9, 10)*.

POSTURE AND MUSCULAR CONTROL

1 Executing *demi-plié*, hold torso erect, draw abdomen in, keep both heels on floor.

2 Jumping upward, both feet push away from the floor, legs straightened to maximum in the air from thighs to toes.

3 Descending to floor, slight muscular tension in buttocks and thighs effects a light and soft descent into *demi-plié* (toes reach floor before heels).

[165]

Plate 73. Pas Assemblé (en avant—forward)*

The correct execution of *assemblé* is essential as a foundation for all subsequent jumping steps.

PREPARATION

5th position right foot front, arms in preparatory position.

EXERCISE

Execute *demi-plié* on both feet *(fig. 1)*, quickly sliding left leg to exact 2nd position, pointed toe barely leaving the floor *(fig. 2)*; jump upward, straightening both legs in the air, left leg 2nd position 45 degrees *(fig. 3)*; both feet descend to floor simultaneously 5th position *demi-plié* left foot front *(fig. 4)*; straighten both knees and repeat movement extending the right leg to point 2nd position.

Arms move harmoniously with the legs, from preparatory position passing through 1st position to 2nd, and back to preparatory position.

Assemblé may be executed *en arrière* (backwards)†, also in positions *croisé* and *effacé*.

Assemblé de volée: assemblé travelling in any direction.

Assemblé en tournant: during the *assemblé* the body turns in the air. This movement necessitates a larger jump, the leg extended at 90 degrees.

The above two variations of *assemblé* necessitate a preparatory movement, such as *pas de bourrée couru, glissade, pas de basque*, etc.

POSTURE AND MUSCULAR CONTROL

1 Executing *demi-plié*, hold torso erect, shoulders down, abdomen in.

2 Sliding left leg to 2nd position, center weight on right foot *demi-plié*.

3 Jumping upward, straighten both legs to maximum from thighs to toes in the air.

4 Both feet descend to floor simultaneously; a slight muscular tension in buttocks and thighs effects a light, soft descent into *demi-plié* (toes reach floor before heels).

---

*According to Cecchetti, *assemblé dessus*.
In the Cecchetti method an *assemblé* is said to be *soutenu* when the knees are straightened and another *demi-plié* is made before executing the next movement. *Assemblé de suite* is the name given to this movement when it is executed in a series, without straightening the knees at the conclusion of each *assemblé*.

†According to Cecchetti, *assemblé dessous*.

fig. 1   fig. 2   fig. 3   fig. 4

PAS ASSEMBLÉ* *(en avant—forward)*

Plate 74. Pas Jeté (en avant—forward)*

A jump, transferring weight from one foot on to the other.

PREPARATION

5th position right foot front, arms in preparatory position *(fig. 1)*.

EXERCISE

Execute *demi-plié*, simultaneously sliding left foot on floor to exact 2nd position, pointed toes barely leaving the floor *(fig. 2)*; jump upward from right foot, straightening both legs from thighs to toes in the air *(fig. 3)*; left foot descends to floor, replacing right foot, *demi-plié*, right foot points *sur le cou-de-pied* in back of left ankle *(fig. 4)*.

To progress forward repeat movement, extending right leg to 2nd position.

Pas jeté en arrière (backwards)† is executed in the reverse direction, with feet pointing *sur le cou-de-pied* in front of ankles.

Pas jeté may be executed moving in all directions.

POSTURE AND MUSCULAR CONTROL

1 Preparation: hold torso erect, slightly forward from waistline, back slightly arched.

2 Sliding left leg to 2nd position, center weight on right foot *demi-plié*.

3 Jumping, right foot pushes away from floor into the air.

4 Descending on to left foot, slight muscular tension in buttocks and thighs effects a light and soft descent into *demi-plié* (toes reach floor before heel). Both knees turned outward throughout movement.

---

*According to Cecchetti, *jeté devant*. According to Mme Nicolaeva-Legat, *jeté simple* or *jeté fondu*.

†According to Cecchetti, *jeté derrière*.

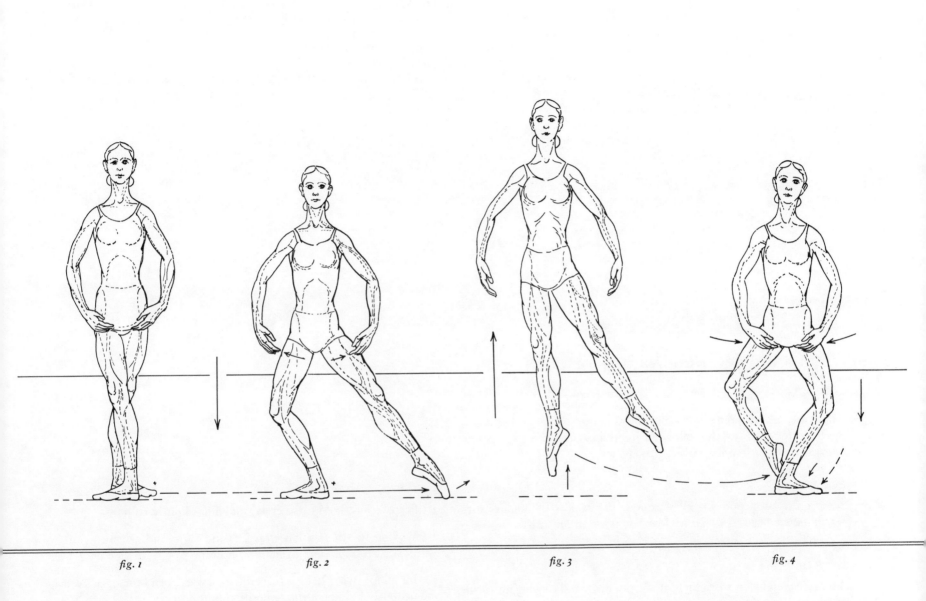

fig. 1   fig. 2   fig. 3   fig. 4

PAS JETÉ *(en avant—forward)**

Plate 75. Grand Jeté (en avant—forward)

There are various preparatory movements to give impetus for bending torso forward and the following jump into the air, such as *pas de bourrée couru, sissonne tombée, glissade, etc.*

PREPARATION

Stand on left leg, pointing right foot *croisé* back, left shoulder forward, incline head to left; arms low 2nd position *(fig. 1)*.

EXERCISE

Transfer weight on to right foot by simultaneously swinging torso, arms and right leg forward to right into deep *plié* position *effacé (fig. 2)*; immediately jump upward, simultaneously swinging left leg and arms forward into the air *en attitude (fig. 3)*; jump diagonally forward on to left foot *demi-plié en attitude croisée en avant (fig. 4)*.

[170]

POSTURE AND MUSCULAR CONTROL

1 Preparation: hold torso erect, inclining slightly to left.

2 Moving to 4th position *effacé:* swing torso and arms easily forward, right foot passing through 1st position to 4th position deep *plié*.

3 Jumping: swing left leg forcefully forward, bend torso backward, momentarily holding *attitude* position in the air.

4 Descending on to left foot, tighten buttocks and thighs to effect a light, soft descent on to left foot *demi-plié* (toes reach floor before heel).

GRAND JETÉ *(en avant—forward)*

Plate 76. Jeté Fermé (closed)

Jeté fermé may be executed moving forward, backward, *effacé*, *croisé* and *écarté*. This movement may terminate on one leg with the other *sur le cou-de-pied* front or back, when it is called *jeté fondu*.

PREPARATION

5th position right foot front, right shoulder front, head inclining to right, arms in preparatory position *(fig. 1)*.

EXERCISE

Execute *demi-plié*, simultaneously sliding and extending left leg to 2nd position 45 degrees *(fig. 2)*; jump from right foot on to left foot, moving to left *(figs. 3, 4)*, transferring weight on to left foot *demi-plié* and extending right leg 2nd position 45 degrees; close right foot 5th position in front, *demi-plié*, inclining torso and head left; straighten knees, bring torso erect *(figs. 4, 5)*.

Arms move harmoniously with legs during exercise from preparatory position through 1st to low 2nd position, and back to preparatory position.

POSTURE AND MUSCULAR CONTROL

1 Executing *demi-plié* and extending left leg to 2nd position, draw abdomen in, keep weight on right foot *demi-plié*.

2 Jumping, straighten both legs, pointing toes to maximum in the air. Transfer weight on to left foot *demi-plié*, before closing right foot 5th position *demi-plié*.

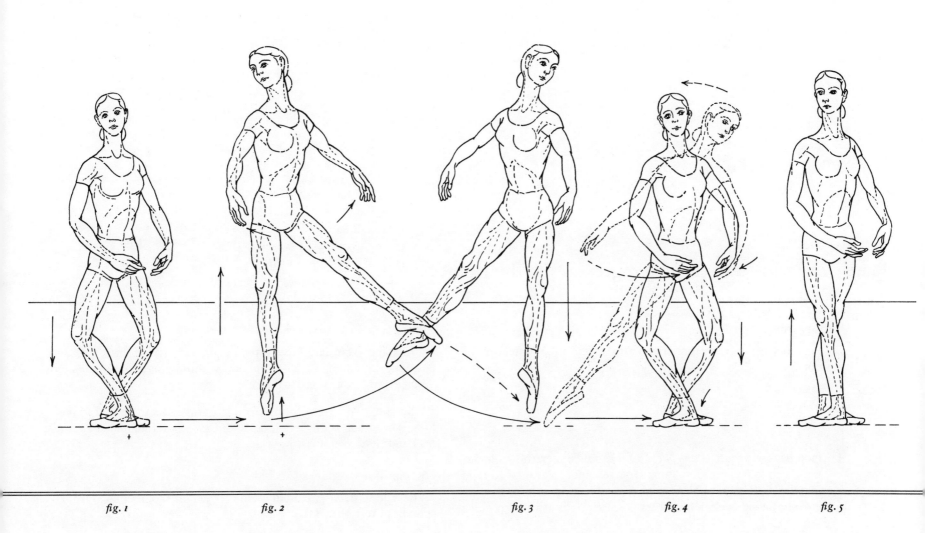

fig. 1   fig. 2   fig. 3   fig. 4   fig. 5

JETÉ FERMÉ *(closed)*

[173]

Plate 77. Jetés (half-turns, progressing to the right)

5th position, right foot front, right arm 1st position, left arm 2nd position.

EXERCISE

To face back: execute *demi-plié (fig. 1)*, quickly extend right leg and right arm to 2nd position, jump from left foot *(fig. 2)* on to right foot *demi-plié*, left foot pointing *sur le cou-de-pied* in front of right ankle, body facing back, left arm 1st position, right arm 2nd position *(fig. 3)*.

To face front: extend left leg and left arm to 2nd position, jump from right foot on to left foot *demi-plié*, right foot pointing *sur le cou-de-pied* in front of left ankle, body facing front, right arm 1st position, left arm 2nd position *(fig. 5)*.

COORDINATION OF ARM AND LEG MOVEMENTS

1 Jumping from left foot, extend right arm and right leg to 2nd position; descending on to right foot, withdraw left foot *sur le cou-de-pied* and left arm in 1st position.

2 Jumping from right foot, extend left arm and left leg to 2nd position; descending on to left foot, withdraw right foot *sur le cou-de-pied* and right arm in 1st position.

POSTURE AND MUSCULAR CONTROL

1 Executing *demi-plié*, hold torso erect, right shoulder forward, incline head to right.

2 Swing arms and extend legs easily to 2nd position.

3 Descending on to right or left foot *demi-plié*, a slight muscular tension in the buttocks and thighs effects a light, soft descent into *demi-plié* (toes reach floor before heels).

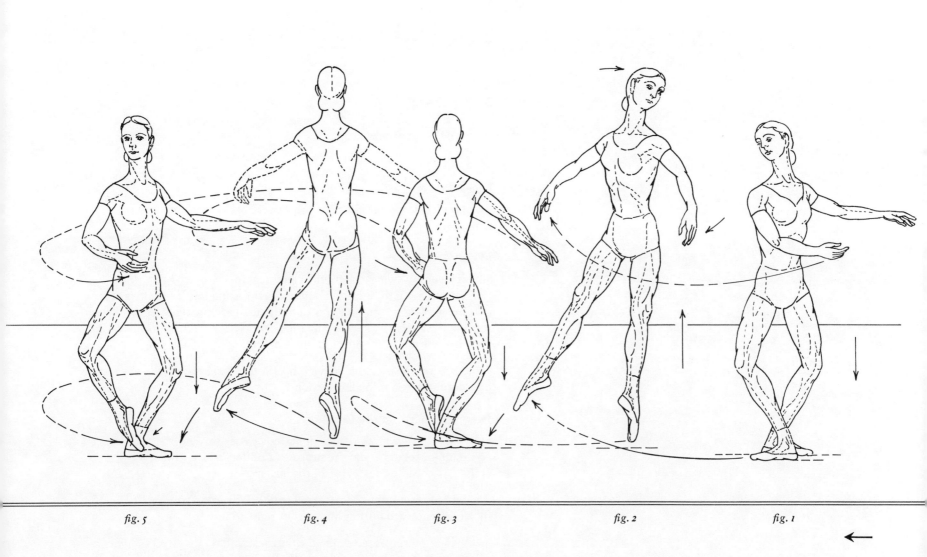

fig. 5   fig. 4   fig. 3   fig. 2   fig. 1

JETÉS *(progressing to the right)*

Plate 78. Jeté Passé*

Stand on left leg, pointing right foot *croisé* back, arms low 2nd position *(fig. 1)*.

EXERCISE

Simultaneously swing torso and right leg forward to right, transferring weight on to right foot *demi-plié*, thrusting left leg backwards into the air *(fig. 2)*; jump from right foot, thrusting right leg backward in the air *(fig. 3)*, on to left foot *demi-plié*, bending torso back, right leg remains in the air position *en attitude croisé* back *(fig. 4)*.

Jeté passé may be executed moving backwards and horizontally across or around the room in all directions.

POSTURE AND MUSCULAR CONTROL

1 From position *croisé* back, right foot passes through 1st position on the floor, torso bending forward to position *effacé;* thrust left leg as high as possible backwards in the air.

2 Jumping from right foot, torso bends backwards. Arms move harmoniously upward during jump from right to left foot.

3 A slight muscular tension in the buttocks and thighs effects a light, soft descent on to left foot *demi-plié* (toes reach floor before heels).

---

*Sometimes called *temps de flèche*.

fig. 4   fig. 3   fig. 2   fig. 1

JETÉ PASSÉ*

Plate 79. Jeté en tournant (à terre en avant — forward)*

This movement is usually executed a number of times moving horizontally across, or round the room.

PREPARATION

5th position right foot front, right shoulder forward *(fig. 1)*.

EXERCISE

Execute *demi-plié*, sliding right foot on the floor forward *effacé* *(fig. 2)*; dart on to right foot *demi-plié* in 1st *arabesque (fig. 3)*. Executing a turn in the air to the right, jump lightly upward from right foot, drawing left leg in front of right in 5th position in the air *(fig. 4)*. Left foot descends to floor *demi-plié*, right foot *sur le cou-de-pied* in front of left ankle *(fig. 5)*.

---

*According to Cecchetti, *élancé tour en arabesque*.

POSTURE AND MUSCULAR CONTROL

1   Preparation and executing *demi-plié* on left leg, hold torso erect, draw abdomen in.

2   Darting on to right foot, *demi-plié*, and opening arms in 1st *arabesque*, carry torso forward with back well arched.

3   Executing turn in the air, simultaneously swing both arms and left leg forcefully inward to give impetus to turn, both legs stretched to maximum from thighs to toes.

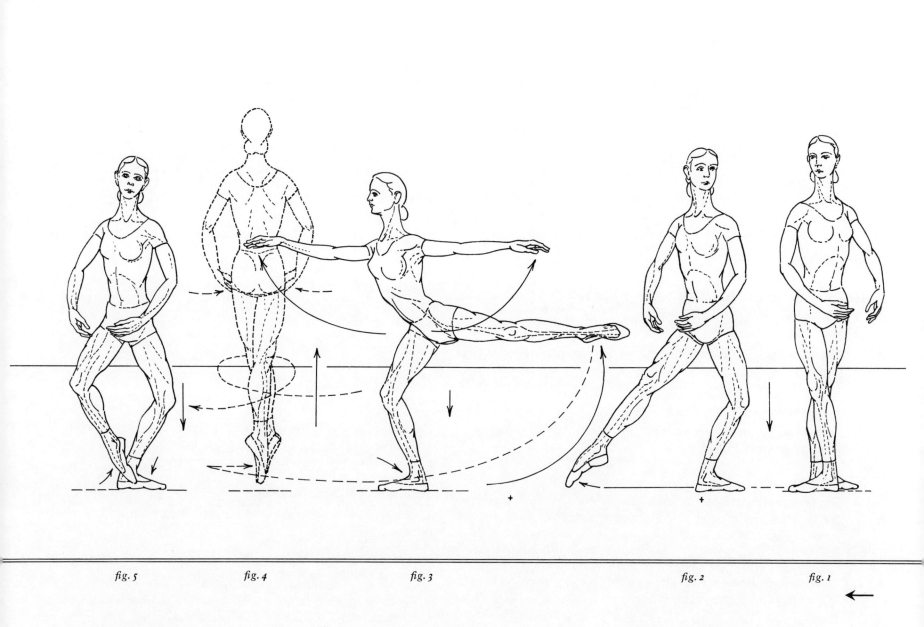

JETÉ EN TOURNANT *(à terre en avant)**

Plate 80. Jeté en tournant (en l'air)*

This movement is executed without pause from preparation to final position.

PREPARATION

5th position, right foot front, right shoulder forward, arms in preparatory position *(fig. 1)*.

EXERCISE

Simultaneously swing torso and right leg forward to 4th position *croisé*, *demi-plié* on right foot, right arm 1st position, left arm 2nd position *(fig. 2)*; quickly draw left foot towards right, replacing it and lifting right pointed foot in front of left leg, bending torso to left, position *effacé*, arms in 1st position *(fig. 3)*; jump from left leg, simultaneously throwing right leg upward *(fig. 4)* and around to right in the air, turning torso back and to the right; jump forward on to right foot *demi-plié*, thrusting left leg upward in back of body in *attitude croisée (fig. 5)*. Both arms move harmoniously during jump and turn, through 1st position into *attitude*.

POSTURE AND MUSCULAR CONTROL

1 Swinging into position *croisé* forward, turn right knee and foot outward.

2 Left foot quickly replaces right; swing both arms forcefully together, gathering momentum for jump.

3 Turning backwards in the air, hold torso erect, back well arched; momentarily hold *attitude* position in the air.

4 A slight muscular tension in the buttocks and thighs effects a light, soft descent on to right foot *demi-plié* (toes reach floor before heel).

---

*According to Cecchetti, *coupé jeté en tournant*.

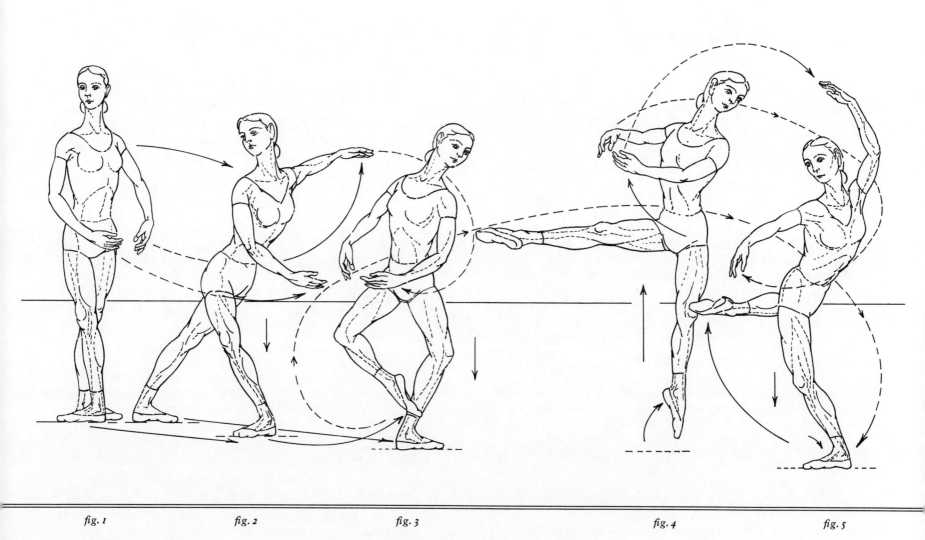

fig. 1   fig. 2   fig. 3   fig. 4   fig. 5

JETÉ EN TOURNANT *(en l'air)**

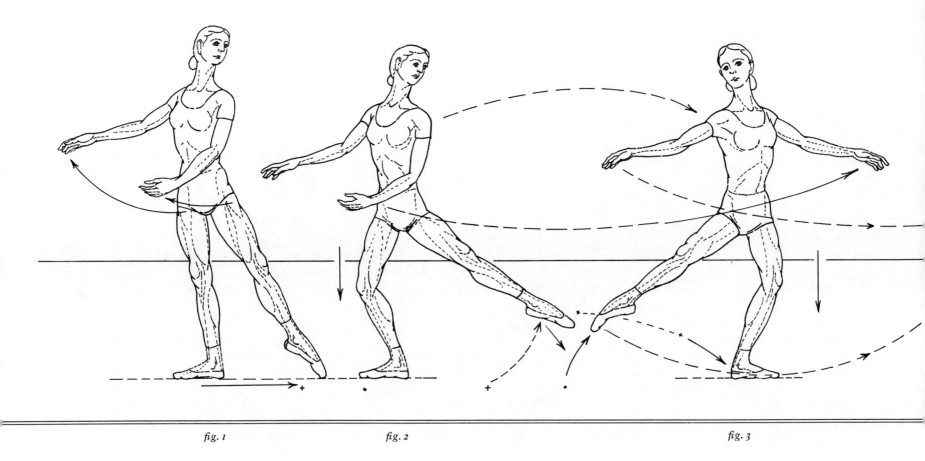

fig. 1   fig. 2   fig. 3

Plate 81. Grand Jeté en tournant Entrelacé (interlaced)*

This movement is executed without pause and is generally preceded by a *chassé* to give impetus to the jump and turn in the air.

---

*Usually abbreviated to *grand jeté en tournant*.

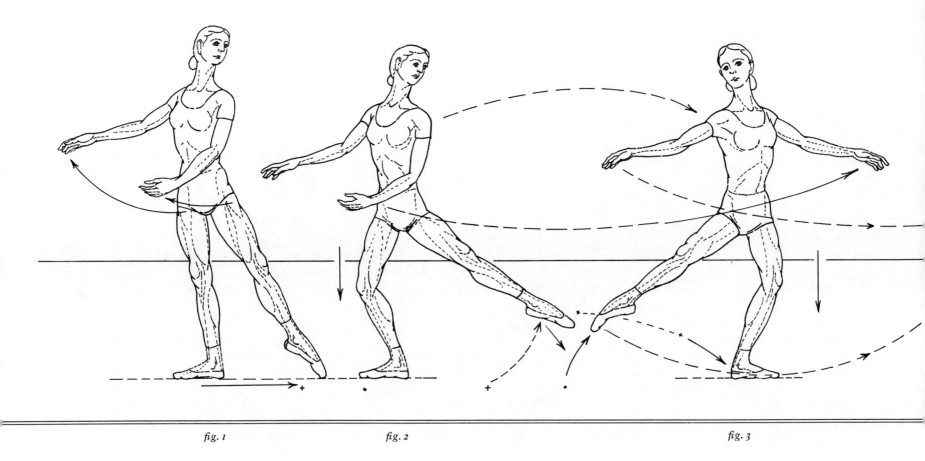[182]

PREPARATION

Stand on right leg, pointing left foot *effacé* back, left shoulder front, both arms to right side, head inclined left *(fig. 1)*.

EXERCISE

Execute *demi-plié* on right leg, raising left leg 45 degrees *(fig. 2)*; step diagonally back on to left foot *demi-plié*, swinging left arm to 2nd position *(fig. 3)*. Jump from left leg, simultaneously swinging

fig. 4

fig. 5

fig. 6

both arms and right leg upward 90 degrees, turning torso to face back *(fig. 4);* simultaneously thrust left leg upward, turning body in the air, back well arched, arms in 3rd position *(fig. 5);* descend on to right foot *demi-plié,* left leg extended back 90 degrees, opening arms into 1st *arabesque (fig. 6).*

POSTURE AND MUSCULAR CONTROL

1   Executing *demi-plié* on right leg, hold torso erect, slightly forward from waistline, left shoulder forward, draw abdomen in.

2   Quickly transfer weight on to left leg *demi-plié,* simultaneously swinging left arm to 2nd position.

3   Simultaneously swing right leg through 1st position and both arms forcefully upward, legs *interlacing* as torso turns in the air.

4   A slight muscular tension in the buttocks and thighs effects a light and soft descent on to right foot *demi-plié* (toes reach floor before heel).

[183]

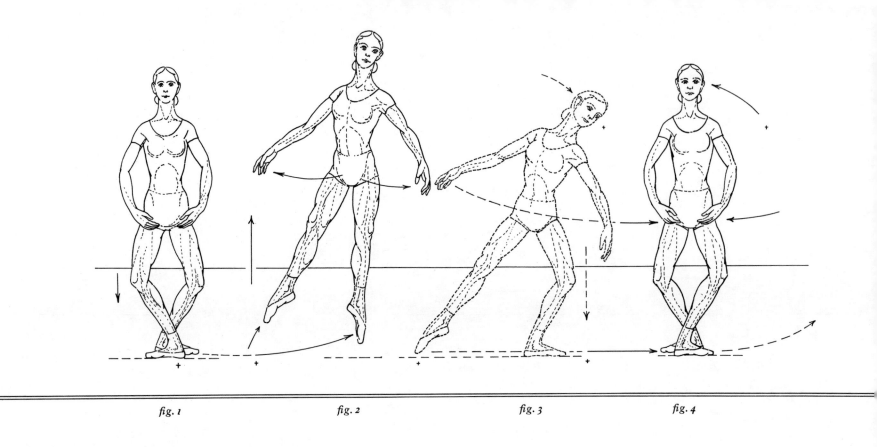

fig. 1   fig. 2   fig. 3   fig. 4

Plate 82. Sissonne Fermée (closed)

Sissonne fermée may be executed in all directions, with and without changing feet in 5th position. *Sissonne fondue* is executed in the same manner, but extended leg finishes *sur le cou-de-pied*, in front or back of ankle, instead of closing in 5th position.

PREPARATION

5th position, right foot front, arms in preparatory position.

EXERCISE

Execute *demi-plié*, distributing weight equally between both feet *(fig. 1)*; jump to left side on to left foot, extending right leg to 2nd position 45 degrees; incline torso to left, opening arms to low 2nd position *(fig. 2)*. As left foot descends to floor *demi-plié* it is followed immediately by right foot, toe sliding on floor back to 5th position, right foot back, *demi-plié*, arms in preparatory position. Straighten knees and bring torso erect *(figs. 3, 4)*.

POSTURE AND MUSCULAR CONTROL

1 Executing *demi-plié*, hold torso erect, draw abdomen in.

2 Jumping to left side, both feet push away from floor, entire body inclines to left. Arms move harmoniously with legs.

[184]

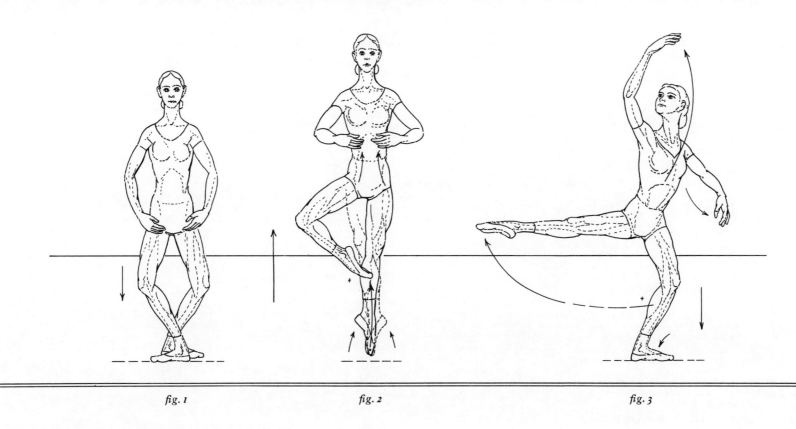

fig. 1   fig. 2   fig. 3

Plate 83. Sissonne Ouverte (open)*

PREPARATION

5th position, right foot front, arms in preparatory position.

EXERCISE

Execute *demi-plié*, distributing weight equally between both feet *(fig. 1)*; jump upward, momentarily straightening both legs in 5th position in the air; raise right leg, toe pointing, in front of left leg, and arms to chest level *(fig. 2)*; jump to left on to left foot *demi-plié*, opening right leg and arms to position *écarté* 90 degrees *(fig. 3)*.

---

*According to Cecchetti, *sissonne retombée:* this movement is taken with leg extending in a *battement* instead of a *développé*.

Sissonne ouverte may be executed forwards, backwards and sideways, also jumping into *attitude* and *arabesque*. It may also be executed with a turn in the air before extending working leg *(sissonne ouverte en tournant)*.

POSTURE AND MUSCULAR CONTROL

1   Executing *demi-plié*, hold torso erect, draw abdomen in.

2   Jumping, both feet push away from floor, right leg lifts and extends 90 degrees without pause.

3   Hold torso erect, inclining to left, in mid-air. Tighten buttocks and thighs to effect a light, soft descent on to left foot *demi-plié* (toes reach floor before heel).

Plate 84. Sissonne Tombée*

PREPARATION

5th position, right foot front, arms in preparatory position.

EXERCISE

Execute *demi-plié*, distributing weight equally between both feet *(fig. 1)*. Jump upward from both feet, lifting right foot *sur le cou-de-pied* in front of left ankle; descend on to left foot *demi-plié (figs. 2, 3)*, immediately extend right leg *effacé* forward and fall *(tombée)* on to right foot *demi-plié*, extending left leg *effacé* back in the air a short distance from floor *(fig. 4)*.

---

*According to Cecchetti, this movement is taken with a *chassé*, and called *temps levé chassé*.

[186]

Arms move harmoniously with legs, passing through 1st position out to low 2nd position.

Sissonne tombée may be executed in all directions, also with a turn in the air before *tombée*.

POSTURE AND MUSCULAR CONTROL

1 Executing *demi-plié*, hold torso erect, draw abdomen in, incline torso to left.

2 Descending on to left foot *demi-plié* and extending right leg forward, torso inclines to right.

3 Weight is transferred from left foot *demi-plié* on to right foot *demi-plié*.

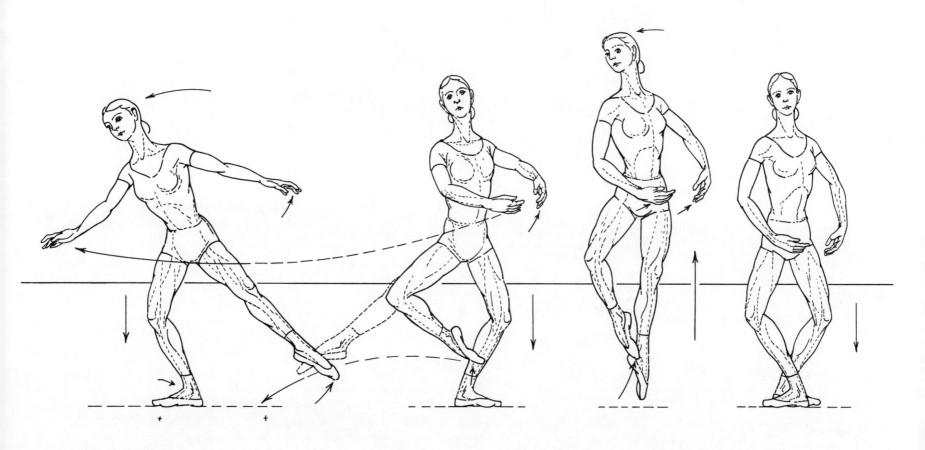

fig. 4   fig. 3   fig. 2   fig. 1

SISSONNE TOMBÉE*

Plate 85. Temps de Cuisse (dessus—over)

Temps de cuisse may be executed *dessous* (under), forwards and backwards.

Preparation

5th position, left foot front, arms in preparatory position.

Exercise

Slide right foot to 2nd position *(battement dégagé)*, opening arms to low 2nd position *(fig. 1)*; quickly close right foot 5th position front *demi-plié (fig. 2)*; immediately spring lightly off both feet towards the left, descend on to left foot *demi-plié*, extending right foot low 2nd position *(fig. 4)*, slide right foot back to 5th position *demi-plié (fig. 5)*.

Posture and Muscular Control

1 Execute *battement dégagé* from 5th position back to 5th position front, *demi-plié*, swiftly and lightly.

2 Springing to the left, both feet push away from the floor, fully pointed, toes barely leaving the ground.

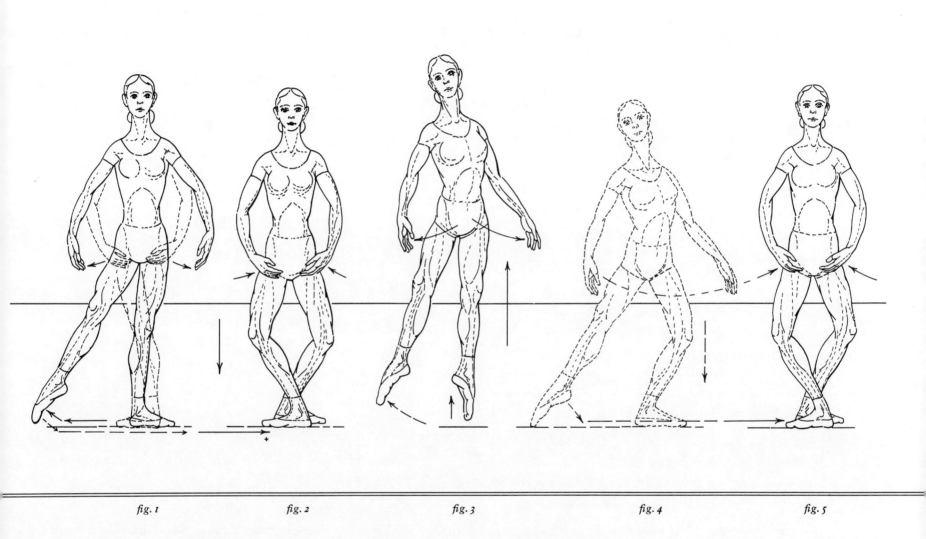

TEMPS DE CUISSE *(dessus, over)*

Plate 86. Soubresaut

A leap from both feet on to both feet.

PREPARATION

5th position right foot front, arms in preparatory position.

EXERCISE

Execute *demi-plié* bending torso forward to left *(fig. 1)*, jump *croisé* forward from both feet, bending torso backward with both legs thrust in back of body, calves and pointed feet pressed together in the air *(fig. 2)*; both feet descend to floor 5th position *demi-plié (fig. 3)*; straighten knees, bring torso erect.

Soubresaut may be executed carrying arms upward at various levels during the jump *(figs. 2, 4)*.

POSTURE AND MUSCULAR CONTROL

1 Executing *demi-plié*, bend torso forward, draw abdomen in.

2 Jumping *croisé* forward, bend torso backward, both feet pressed together pointed to maximum in back of body in the air.

3 As both feet descend to floor torso inclines slightly forward.

[190]

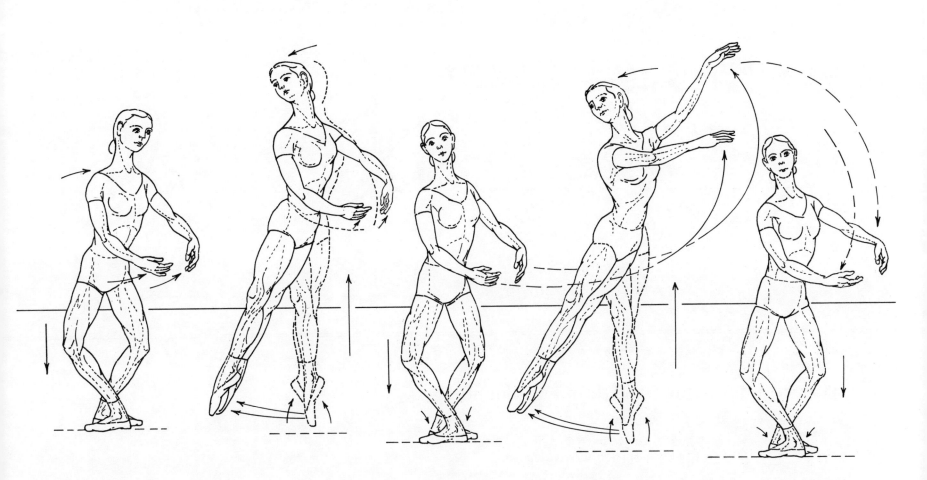

fig. 1   fig. 2   fig. 3   fig. 4   fig. 5

SOUBRESAUT

Plate 87. Sissonne Soubresaut (leaping—bounding)*

PREPARATION

5th position, right foot front, arms in preparatory position.

EXERCISE

Execute *demi-plié*, inclining torso forward *(fig. 1)*; jump forward thrusting both legs upward in back of body, bending torso and head back and moving arms to 1st position *(fig. 2)*. Descend on to right foot *demi-plié*, left leg extended back in the air, carrying left arm upward above head and right arm to low 2nd position, *attitude effacée allongée* (outstretched) *(fig. 3)*.

To execute a series of *sissonnes soubresauts*, *coupé* on to left foot and *assemblé effacé* forward with right leg.

[192]

POSTURE AND MUSCULAR CONTROL

1 Executing *demi-plié*, incline torso forward, draw abdomen in.

2 Jump vigorously forward, left shoulder front, bending torso backward. Muscular tension in buttocks and thighs keeps legs pressed together behind body in the air and effects a light, soft descent on to right foot *demi-plié* (toes reach floor before heel).

*According to Cecchetti, *temps de poisson*.

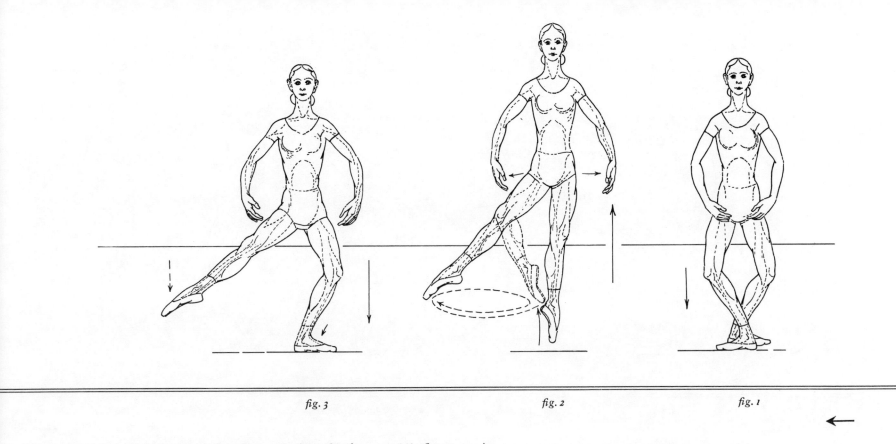

fig. 3   fig. 2   fig. 1

Plate 88. Rond de Jambe Sauté (en l'air, at 45 degrees)

Rond de jambe sauté may be executed *en dedans;* and with working leg extended 90 degrees; and also *en tournant*, the body turning in the air as extended leg executes *rond de jambe*.

PREPARATION

5th position, right foot front, arms in preparatory position.

EXERCISE

Execute *demi-plié (fig. 1)*, jump upward extending straight right leg to 2nd position 45 degrees, quickly execute *rond de jambe en dehors* in the air *(fig. 2)*; left foot descends to floor *demi-plié* as right leg extends to 2nd position 45 degrees *(fig. 3)*.

POSTURE AND MUSCULAR CONTROL

1 Executing *demi-plié*, hold torso erect, slightly forward from waist-line. Distribute weight equally between both feet.

2 Jumping, both feet push away from floor, working leg held straight before and after executing *rond de jambe*, the knee turned out and held stationary from thigh to knee throughout movement.

3 Executing *rond de jambe en l'air*, draw abdomen in.

[193]

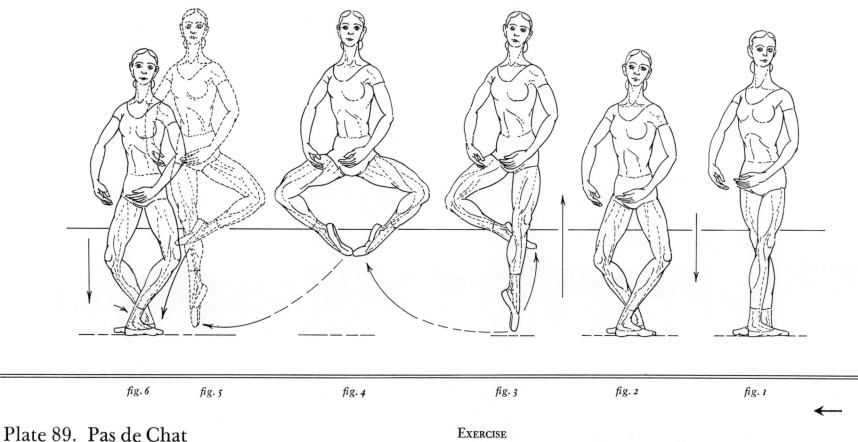

fig. 6   fig. 5   fig. 4   fig. 3   fig. 2   fig. 1

Plate 89. Pas de Chat

The name implies a cat-like movement, a light spring into the air and descent to the floor in 5th or 4th position.

Pas de chat may be executed with various *port de bras* and with change of feet.

PREPARATION

5th position left foot front, left shoulder forward, incline head to left, arms in preparatory position (position *effacé*) (*fig. 1*).

[194]

EXERCISE

Execute *demi-plié* on both feet, lift right foot sharply upward under torso, knee bent, turned out, toe pointing downward (*fig. 3*); immediately jump upward, left leg replacing right in the air under torso, knee bent, turned out, toe pointing downward (momentarily both legs are arrested in the air [*fig. 4*]); right foot descends to floor *demi-plié*, quickly followed by left foot 5th position front *demi-plié* (*figs. 5, 6*).

POSTURE AND MUSCULAR CONTROL

1   In preparation, hold torso erect, shoulders down. Draw abdomen in, lift diaphragm. Move easily into *demi-plié*, executing counter-pull upward.

2   When executing *pas de chat*, hold torso slightly forward from hip-line, with back slightly arched and shoulders held down.

Plate 90. Pas de Chat (with legs thrown back)*

PREPARATION

From 5th position left foot front, arms in preparatory position *(fig. 1)*:

EXERCISE

(a) Execute *demi-plié* on left supporting foot, thrusting right leg back in the air 45 degrees, knee bent, turned out, lean torso slightly forward, incline head to right, lift arms to 1st position *(fig. 2)*;

(b) Jump from left foot, thrusting left leg back in the air, knee bent, turned out, torso bending backward, arms move upward, palms turn downward *(fig. 3)*;

(c) Right foot descends to floor *demi-plié*, quickly followed by left foot, sliding on floor through 1st position to 4th position *croisé* forward *demi-plié*; arms descend, palms downward, torso leans slightly forward, head inclines to right *(figs. 4, 5)*.

POSTURE AND MUSCULAR CONTROL

1 Keep legs together and thighs well turned out when in the air.

2 To prevent strain in arms as they softly rise and fall during movement, hold shoulders down. Relax neck.

*According to Mme Nicolaeva-Legat, *grand pas de chat*.

[195]

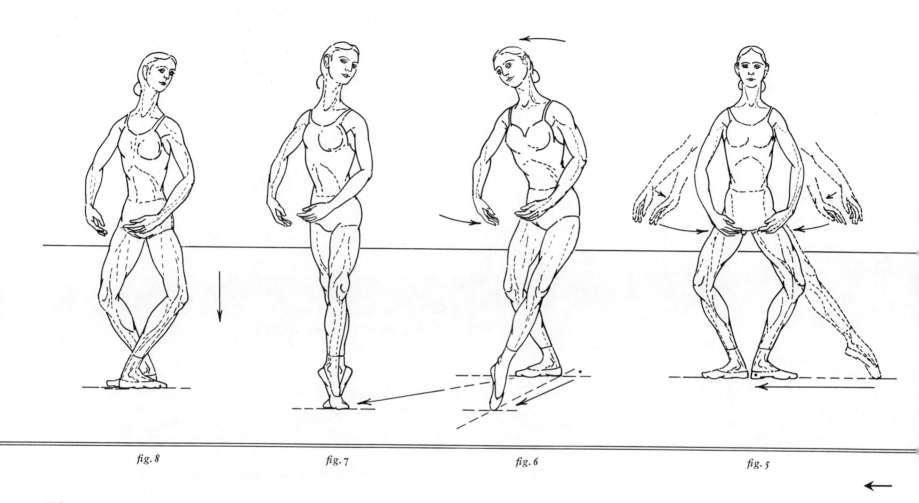

fig. 8   fig. 7   fig. 6   fig. 5

Plate 91. Pas de Basque

(A combination of four movements, performed in three counts.)

Pas de basque may also be executed *en tournant.*

PREPARATION

5th position, right foot front, right shoulder forward, arms in preparatory position *(fig. 1).*

EXERCISE

Preparation for 1st movement (performed in anticipation of 1st count):   Execute *demi-plié,* sliding right foot, toe pointing on floor, *croisé* forward; describe a quarter-circle *en dehors* to right, simultaneously opening arms to 2nd position *(figs. 2, 3);*

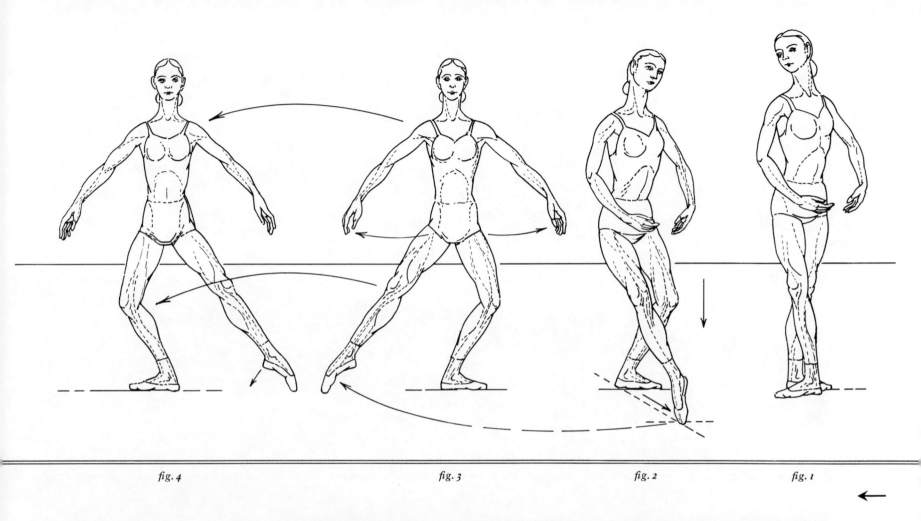

1st movement (performed to 1st count): Transfer weight of body with slight spring on to right foot *demi-plié*, extend left leg, toe pointing on floor, to 2nd position *(fig. 4)*, and slide left foot on floor through 1st position *demi-plié*, arms returning to preparatory position *(fig. 5)*;

2nd movement (performed to 2nd count): Step lightly on to left *demi-pointe croisé* forward, quickly bringing right foot to 5th position *demi-pointes*, arms remaining in preparatory position *(figs. 6, 7)*;

3rd movement (performed to 3rd count): *Demi-plié* 5th position *(fig. 8)*.

Executing *pas de basque* moving backwards from 5th position right foot front, left foot slides *croisé* back, describing a quarter-circle *en dedans, etc.*

POSTURE AND MUSCULAR CONTROL

1 Executing preparation for 1st movement, hold torso erect, slightly forward from waistline, draw abdomen in, center weight on left foot *demi-plié*.

2 Stepping on to right foot *demi-plié*, incline torso and head to right. Stepping on to *demi-pointes croisé* forward, bring left shoulder forward, incline head to left.

[197]

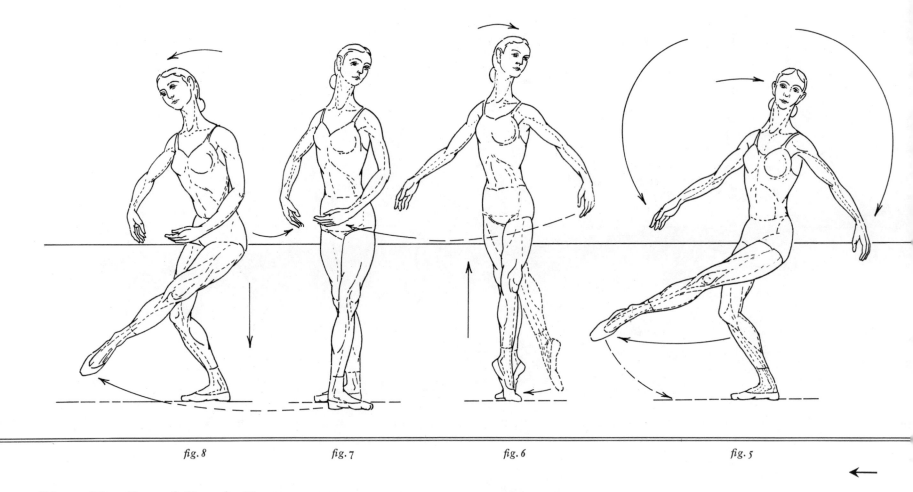

fig. 8   fig. 7   fig. 6   fig. 5

←

Plate 92. Grand Pas de Basque

Preparation

5th position right foot front, arms 2nd position *(fig. 1)*.

Exercise

(a)   Execute *demi-plié* on left leg, simultaneously lowering arms to 1st position and swiftly raising right leg, knee slightly bent, *croisé* forward *(fig. 2)*;

(b)   Right leg swings in a quarter-circle in the air to 2nd position 90 degrees *(figs. 2, 3)*;

(c)   Quickly jump into the air from left foot, raising torso and moving arms up to 3rd position *(fig. 3)*;

fig. 4   fig. 3   fig. 2   fig. 1

(d)   Jump to right on to right foot *demi-plié*, simultaneously developing left leg *croisé* forward in the air, toe passing right knee before extending forward, opening arms to 2nd position *(figs. 4, 5)*;

(e)   Step on to left *demi-pointe croisé* forward, quickly bringing right foot to 5th position *demi-pointes (fig. 6)*, *demi-plié* 5th position.

Preparation for repetition of the movement in reverse *(fig. 8)*.

This movement is executed without pause.

POSTURE AND MUSCULAR CONTROL

1   Executing *demi-plié*, incline torso and arms slightly to the left.

2   Right leg describing quarter-circle swings forcefully upward to 2nd position in the air, compelling torso and arms to rise as supporting foot pushes off the floor.

3   As right foot descends, jumping to right, torso inclines to right, a slight muscular tension in buttocks and thighs effects a light and soft descent to floor *demi-plié* (toes reach floor before heel) *(fig. 6)*.

[199]

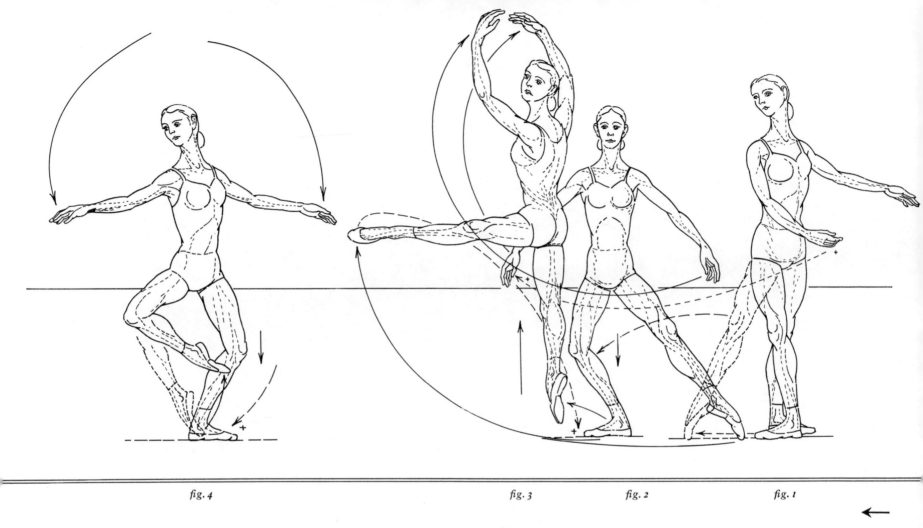

fig. 4

fig. 3   *fig. 2*   *fig. 1*

Plate 93. Grand Saut de Basque

PREPARATION

5th position right foot front, right shoulder forward, right arm 1st position, left arm 2nd position *(fig. 1)*. Extend right leg to right side, opening right arm to 2nd position, quickly transfer weight to right foot *demi-plié*, pointing left foot 2nd position on floor *(fig. 2)*.

EXERCISE

(a) Simultaneously turn torso to right and jump from right foot, forcefully swinging left leg forward and upward 90 degrees, moving arms through 1st position to 3rd position *(fig. 3)*;

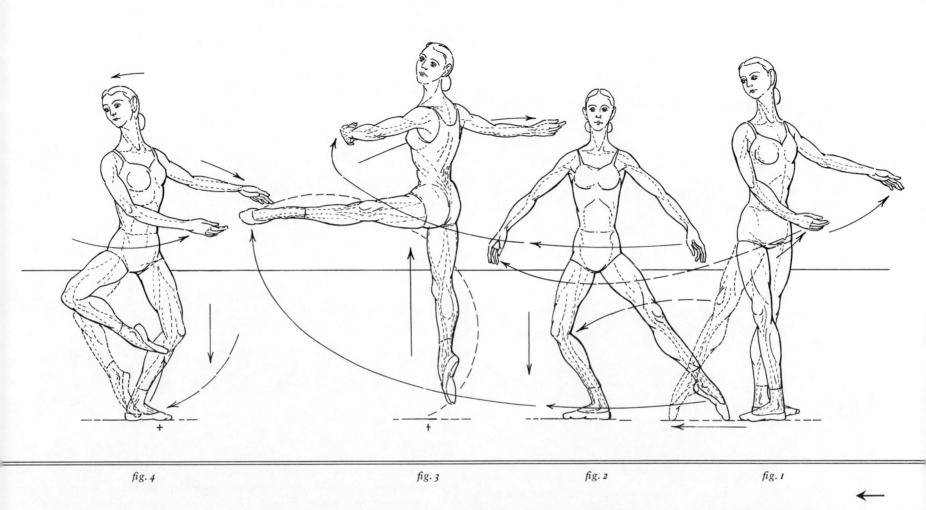

POSTURE AND MUSCULAR CONTROL

(b)   Completing turn, jump on to left foot *demi-plié*, simultaneously lifting right leg directly upward under torso, knee bent, turned out, toe pointing in front of left knee, torso facing forward, arms opening to 2nd position *(fig. 4)*.

Grand saut de basque may also be executed without raising the arms above the head, but with left arm accompanying left leg to 2nd position, terminating with right arm in 1st position *(see plate above)*.

1   Executing *demi-plié* on right foot, left shoulder forward, incline head to left.

2   Swing arms and left leg forcefully upward to 90 degrees, compelling right foot to push off floor.

3   Turning in the air, hold torso erect, slightly forward from hips; as left foot descends to floor, a slight muscular tension in buttocks and thighs effects a light, soft descent to floor in *demi-plié* (toes reach floor before heel).

Plate 94. Pas de Ciseaux

Position *croisé* back, right foot pointing back, arms 2nd position, torso erect, leaning slightly forward *(fig. 1)*.

Exercise

(a) Simultaneously *demi-plié* on left leg, executing *grand battement* forward 90 degrees with right leg, torso bending backwards, arms moving forward (position *effacé*) *(fig. 2)*;

(b) Jump from left foot and thrust left leg forward and upward passing right leg in the air *(fig. 3)*, arms in 1st position;

(c) Right foot descends to floor *demi-plié*, left leg swings back quickly to 1st *arabesque* 90 degrees, right arm forward, left arm in back (left foot passes through 1st position on floor to final position *arabesque*) *(fig. 4)*.

Posture and Muscular Control

1 Execute *grand battement* forward swiftly, bending torso back, both legs stretched to maximum from thighs to toes, passing each other forward in the air.

2 A slight muscular tension in buttocks and thighs effects a light, soft descent to the floor, right foot *demi-plié* (toes reach floor before heel).

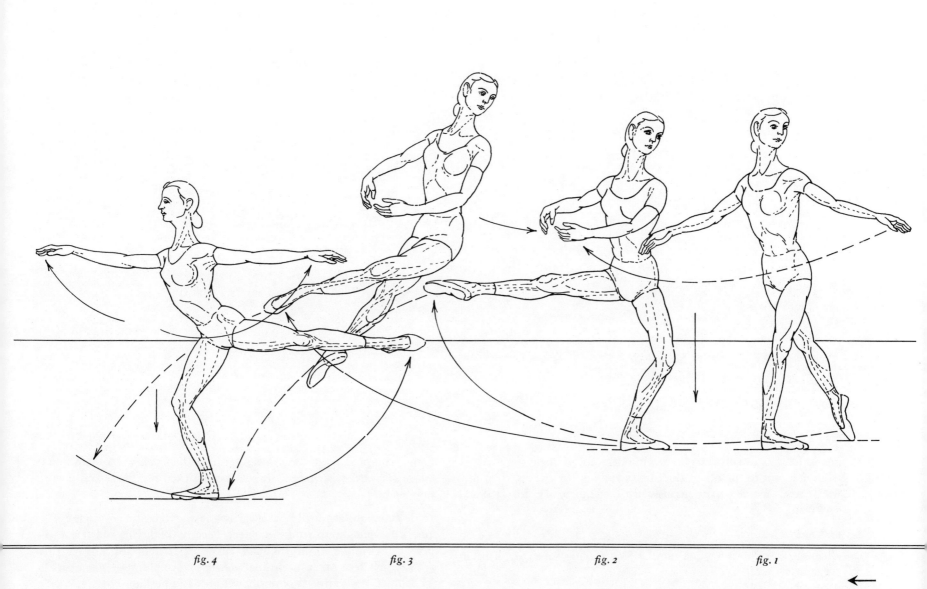

fig. 4   fig. 3   fig. 2   fig. 1

PAS DE CISEAUX

Plate 95. Pas Ballotté*

Pas ballotté is usually executed without pause, transferring weight from one foot to the other, the torso swinging backwards, then forwards, arms moving harmoniously with extending leg, forward and backward.

PREPARATION

5th position right front, position *en face* (facing forward), arms in preparatory position *(fig. 1)*.

EXERCISE

(a) Jumping diagonally forward to right: execute *demi-plié*, jump from both feet, keeping both legs and feet together in the air, left shoulder forward, leaning torso back *(fig. 2); left foot descends to floor *demi-plié*, right foot opens with small *développé* to position *effacé* forward 45 degrees, left arm 1st position, right arm 2nd position *(fig. 3);*

(b) Jumping diagonally backward to left: from 5th position, execute *demi-plié*, jump from both feet, keeping both legs and feet together in the air, right shoulder forward, leaning torso forward *(fig. 2);* left foot opens with small *développé* to position *effacé* back 45 degrees, right arm 1st position, left arm 2nd position *(fig. 3).*

---

*According to Vaganova and Cecchetti. Called *jeté ballotté* by Mme Nicolaeva-Legat.

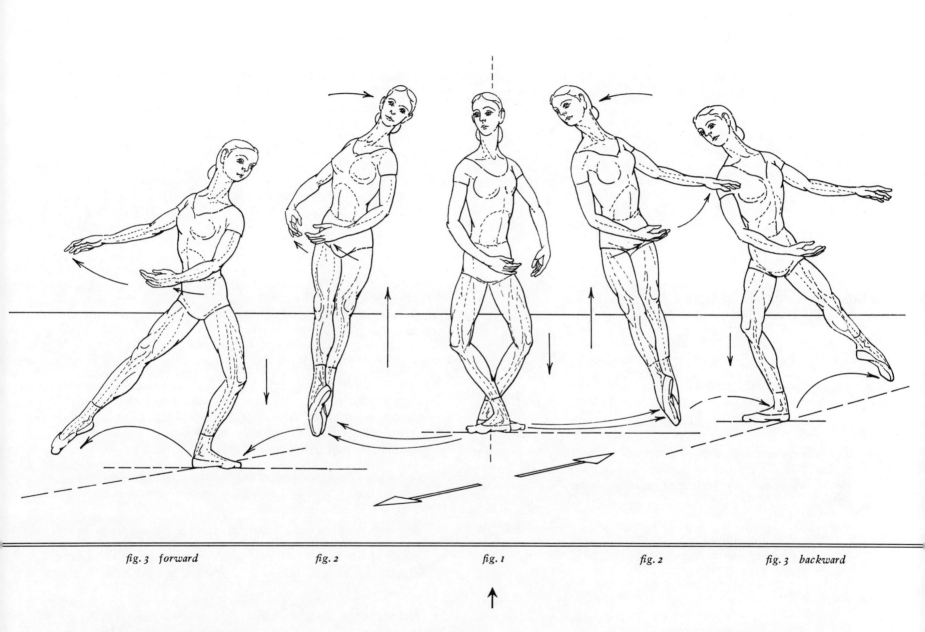

fig. 3 forward   fig. 2   fig. 1   fig. 2   fig. 3 backward

PAS BALLOTTÉ*

Plate 96. Pas Ballonné

(In position *effacé* forward.)

Pas ballonné is executed in all directions, *croisé* and *ecarté*, forward and backward, arms moving harmoniously, according to the direction of the movement, in a variety of positions. It may also be executed *battu*.

Pas ballonné arrondi is a series of *pas ballonnés*, executed alternately *effacé* and *écarté* (according to Mme Nicolaeva-Legat).

Preparation

5th position right foot front, left shoulder forward, arms in preparatory position *(fig. 1)*.

Exercise

Execute *demi-plié*, sliding right foot *effacé* forward; jump moving forward, from left foot, simultaneously extending right leg *effacé*, 45 degrees (momentarily both legs are extended in the air) *(figs. 2,3)*; left foot descends to floor *demi-plié*, simultaneously right knee bends, toe pointing in front of left ankle *(sur le cou-de-pied, fig. 4)*.

From this position the movement may be repeated *(fig. 5)*.

Posture and Muscular Control

1 Both legs are stretched to maximum from thighs to toes in the air.

2 Thigh of working leg remains stationary throughout movement, knee well turned out as foot points in front of left ankle *(sur le cou-de-pied)*.

3 As left foot descends to floor, a slight muscular tension in the buttocks and thighs effects a light, soft descent into *demi-plié* (toes reach floor before heel).

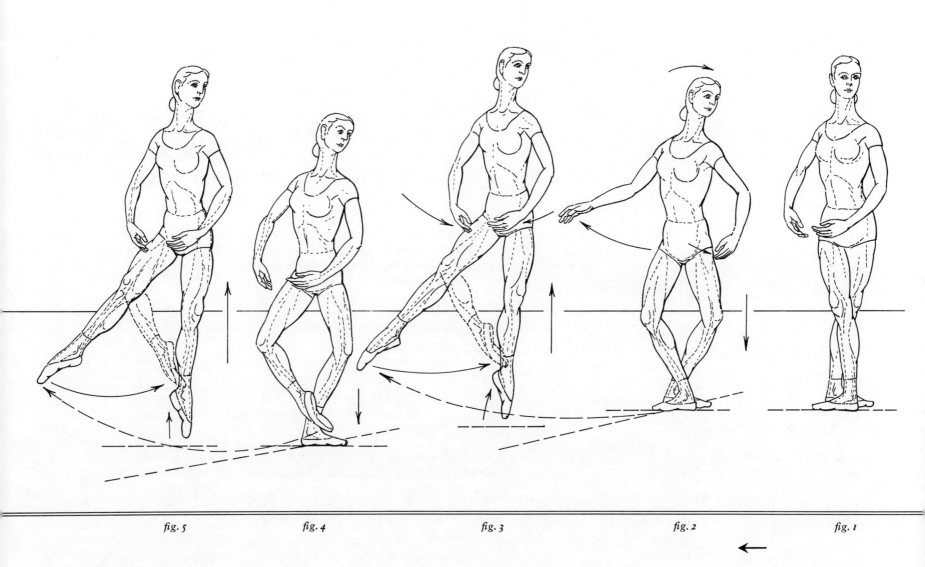

fig. 5   fig. 4   fig. 3   fig. 2   fig. 1

PAS BALLONNÉ

Plate 97. Pas Chassé (effacé en avant—forward)*

Pas chassé is executed in all directions, forward, backward, *croisé* and *en tournant*, arms moving harmoniously, according to the direction of the movement, in a variety of *ports de bras*.

Preparation

5th position right foot front, right shoulder forward, arms in preparatory position.

Exercise

(a)   Execute *demi-plié* on both feet *(fig. 1)*, jump extending both legs and feet 5th position in the air, simultaneously lift right knee, toe pointing in front of left ankle *(fig. 2)*;

(b)   Left foot descends to floor and immediately right foot extends forward, toe pointing and sliding on floor to open 4th position, arms open slightly *(fig. 3)*;

(c)   Weight is transferred on to right foot *demi-plié*, torso bends back *(fig. 4)*.

To continue *pas chassé*, the left leg is drawn towards the right, jumping and extending both legs 5th position in the air, *etc. (fig. 5)*.

---

*According to Cecchetti, *temps levé chassé* into *effacé*.

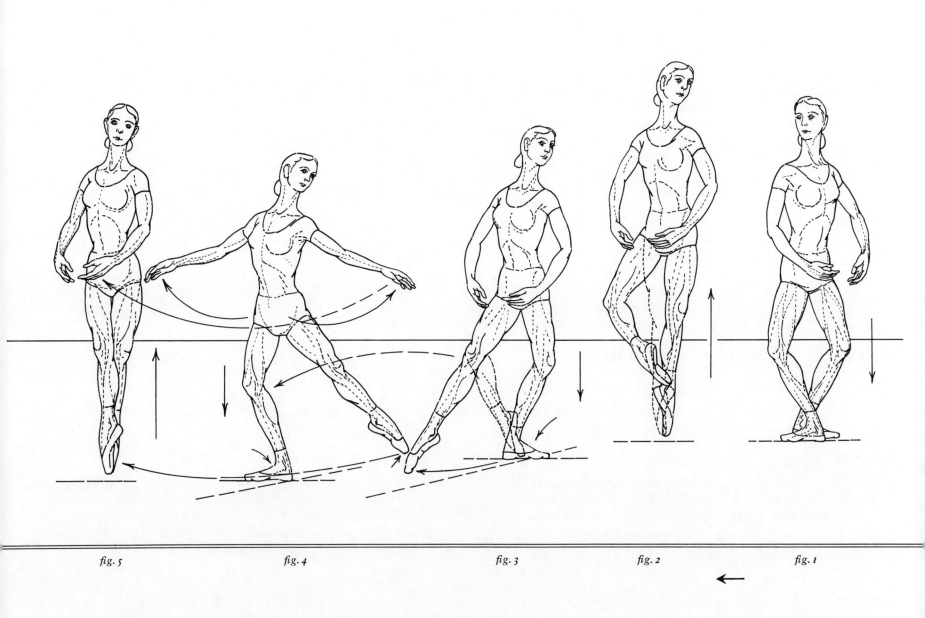

PAS CHASSÉ *(effacé en avant)**

Plate 98. Emboîté en tournant*

A series of half-turns, jumping from one foot to the other, legs changing positions in the air, moving to the right.

This exercise may be executed with the feet *sur le cou-de-pied*, and is so described by Cecchetti. When performed in this manner it is called *petit jeté emboîté* by Mme Nicolaeva-Legat.

---

*According to Vaganova. Called *jeté emboîté* by Mme Nicolaeva-Legat, *emboîté en tournant en dedans* by Cecchetti.

PREPARATION

5th position right foot front, right shoulder forward, right arm in 1st position, left arm in 2nd position *(fig. 1)*.

EXERCISE

Half-turn, jumping to the right to face *back (fig. 2)*: execute *demi-plié* on both feet, jump, straightening right leg in the air, on to right foot *demi-plié*, lifting left leg, knee bent, turned out, toe pointing in front of right leg; simultaneously opening right arm to 2nd position, closing left arm in 1st position *(fig. 3)*.

Half-turn, to face *front (fig. 4)*: jump from right foot, straightening leg in the air, on to left foot *demi-plié*, lifting right leg, knee bent, turned out, toe pointing in front of left leg; simultaneously opening left arm to 2nd position, closing right arm in 1st position *(fig. 5)*.

Continue movement, jumping on to right then left foot, etc.

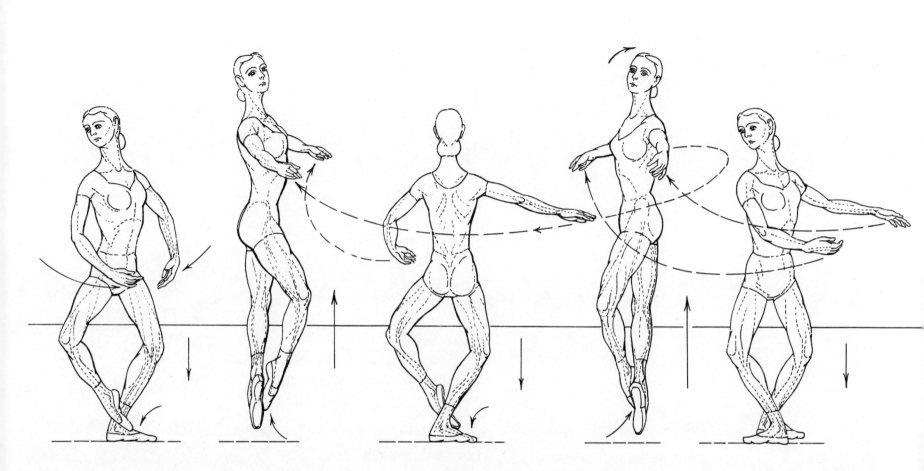

fig. 5　　　　fig. 4　　　　fig. 3　　　　fig. 2　　　　fig. 1

EMBOÎTÉ EN TOURNANT*

Plate 99. Pas Emboîté (en avant—forward)

Jumping forward, legs changing positions in the air.

PREPARATION

5th position right foot front, left shoulder forward, torso erect, leaning slightly back, arms in 1st position; *demi-plié* on both feet *(fig. 1)*.

EXERCISE

(a)   Jump from both feet on to left foot, lifting right leg forward, knee bent 45 degrees *(fig 2)*;

(b)   Jump on to right foot *demi-plié*, quickly lifting left leg forward, knee bent 45 degrees *(fig. 3)*;

(c)   Jump on to left foot, quickly lifting right leg forward, knee bent 45 degrees *(figs. 4, 5)*; continue movement jumping forward, legs exchanging positions in the air.

Pas emboîté en arrière (backward) is executed in the same manner, leaning the torso slightly forward, back arched. *Pas emboîté* may be executed lifting legs to 90 degrees *(grand emboîté)*.

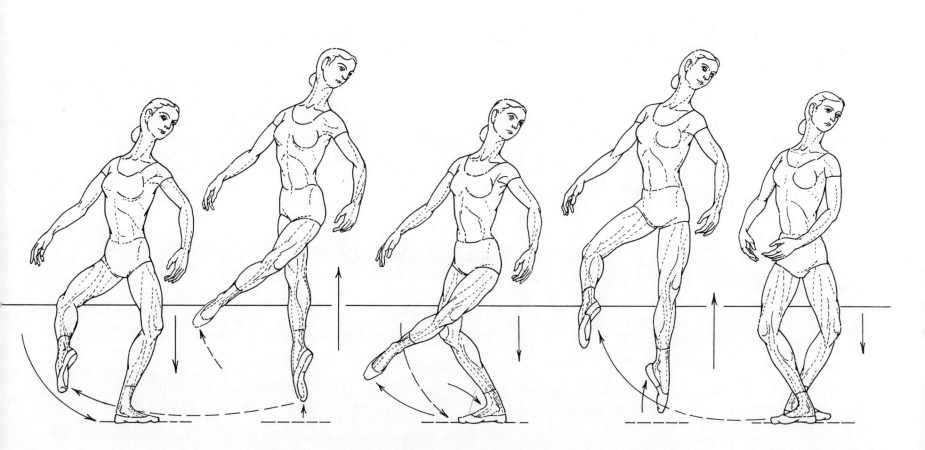

PAS EMBOÎTÉ *(en avant)**

Plate 100. Pas Balancé

5th position, right foot front, arms in preparatory position.

Execute *demi-plié (fig. 1)*, sliding right leg to 2nd position *(fig. 2)*; jump lightly on to right foot *demi-plié (jeté)*, drawing left foot *sur le cou-de-pied* in back of right ankle, bending torso and head to right *(fig. 3)*. Step on to left *demi-pointe*, lifting right foot pointed in front of left ankle, holding torso and head erect *(fig. 4)*. Fall *(tombé)* on to right foot *demi-plié*, raising left foot *sur le cou-de-pied* in back of right ankle, bending torso and head to right *(fig. 5)*.

To repeat *balancé* to left, extend left leg to 2nd position, *etc*.

This movement is executed to a count of three:

1   *Jeté* on to right foot;
2   Stepping on to left *demi-pointe*;
3   Falling on to right foot *demi-plié*.

fig. 5   fig. 4   fig. 3   fig. 2   fig. 1

PAS BALANCÉ*

Plate 101. Royale*

Beaten *changement de pieds—petite batterie* (small beating).

PREPARATION

5th position right foot front, head and torso erect, facing forward, arms in preparatory position; execute *demi-plié* on both feet *(fig. 1)*.

EXERCISE

1 Jump, extending both legs to maximum from thighs to toes in the air, opening them slightly sideways; quickly beat both calves (the right in front of the left) *(fig. 2)*;

2 Legs open slightly sideways in the air *(fig. 3)*, right leg closes in back of left as both feet descend to floor 5th position *demi-plié (fig. 4)*.

Usually this movement is executed with slight *épaulement:* right foot front, right shoulder slightly forward; left foot front, left shoulder slightly forward.

POSTURE AND MUSCULAR CONTROL

1 When executing *demi-plié*, both heels on floor.

2 Jumping, both feet push from floor into the air, barely leaving the ground; the beating is executed swiftly with calves of both legs turned out, stretched to maximum from thighs to toes.

---

*Sometimes called *changement battu*.

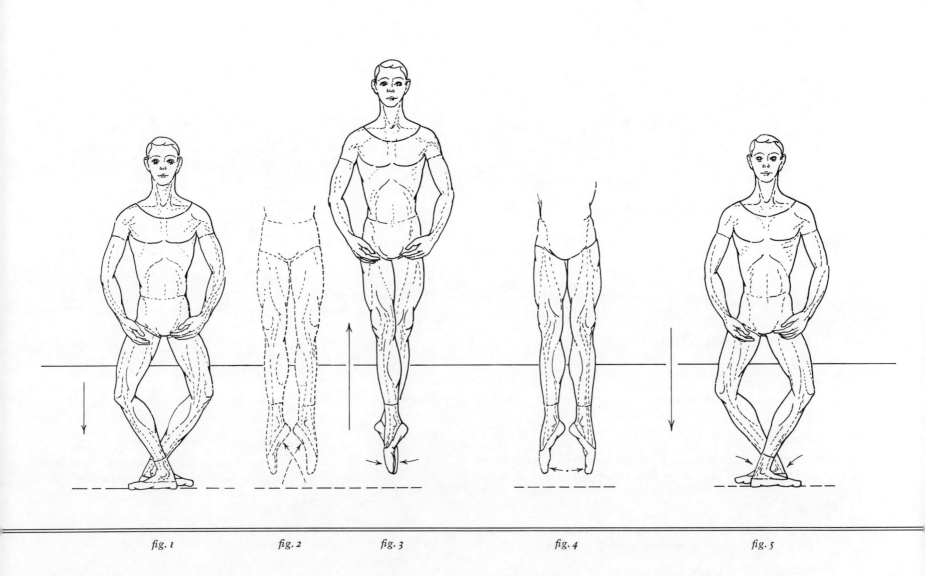

fig. 1   fig. 2   fig. 3   fig. 4   fig. 5

ROYALE*

Plate 102. Entrechat Quatre

(*Petite batterie*—small beating.)

PREPARATION

5th position right foot front, head and torso erect, facing forward, arms in preparatory position; execute *demi-plié* on both feet *(fig. 1)*.

EXERCISE

1 Jump, extending both legs from thighs to toes, a short distance from the floor, open legs slightly sideways in the air *(fig. 2)*;

2 Beat both calves (right leg in back of left) *(fig. 3)*;

3 Open legs slightly sideways in the air *(fig. 4)*;

4 Right leg closes in front of left as both feet descend to the floor 5th position *demi-plié (fig. 5)*.

Usually this movement is executed with slight *épaulement:* right foot front, right shoulder slightly forward; left foot front, left shoulder slightly forward.

POSTURE AND MUSCULAR CONTROL

1 When executing *demi-plié*, both heels on floor.

2 Jumping, both feet push from the floor into the air, toes pointed to the maximum, barely leaving the ground; the beat is executed swiftly with calves of both legs turned out, stretched to maximum from thighs to toes.

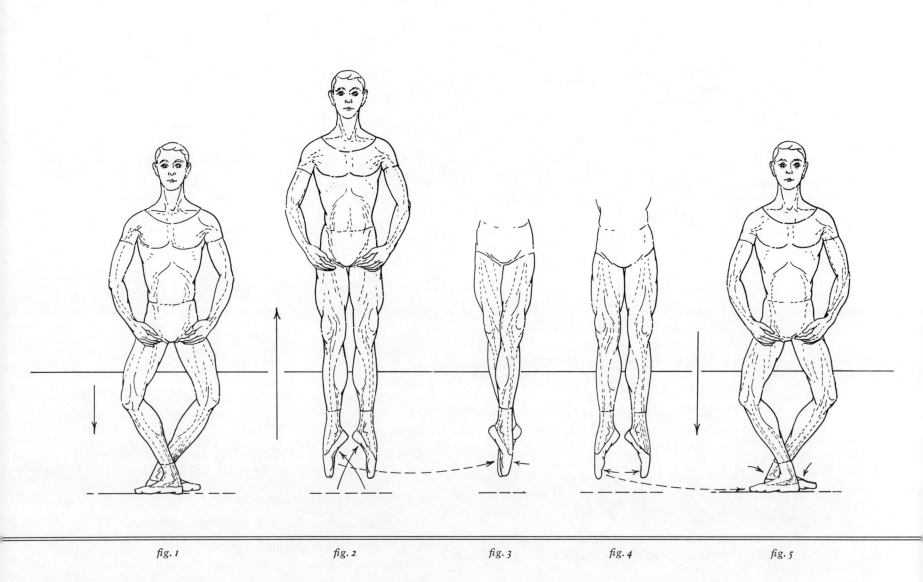

fig. 1   fig. 2   fig. 3   fig. 4   fig. 5

ENTRECHAT QUATRE

[219]

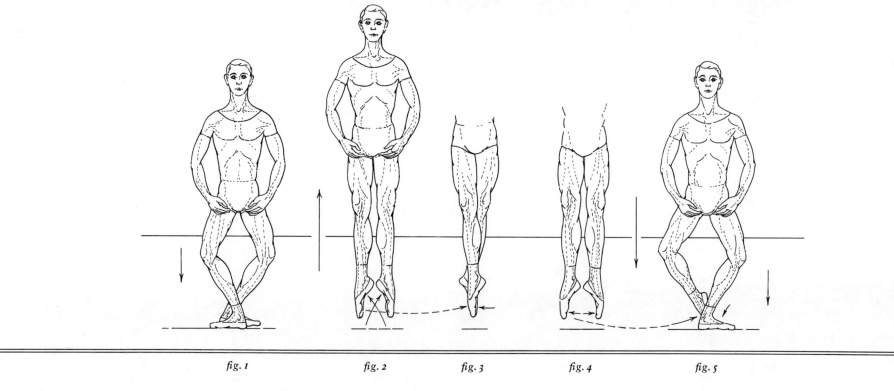

fig. 1   *fig. 2*   *fig. 3*   *fig. 4*   *fig. 5*

Plate 103. Entrechat Trois (derrière—back)

Jumping from both feet, terminating on one foot (*royale*, or beaten *changement*, descending on to one foot).

PREPARATION

5th position right foot front, head and torso erect, facing forward, arms in preparatory position; execute *demi-plié* on both feet *(fig. 1)*.

EXERCISE

1   Jump, extending both legs to maximum from thighs to toes in the air, opening them slightly; quickly beat both calves (the right in front of the left) *(figs. 2, 3)*;

2   Legs open slightly sideways in the air *(fig. 4)*, left leg descends to floor *demi-plié (fig. 5)*;

3   Simultaneously, right foot is lifted, toe pointed, *sur le cou-de-pied* in back of left ankle *(fig. 5)*.

[220]

Usually this movement is executed with slight *épaulement:* right foot front, right shoulder slightly forward; left foot front, left shoulder slightly forward.

This beating movement may be executed *devant*, terminating with right or left foot *sur le cou-de-pied* in front.

POSTURE AND MUSCULAR CONTROL

1   When executing *demi-plié*, both heels on floor.

2   Jumping, both feet push from floor into the air, toes pointing to maximum, barely leaving the ground; the beat is executed swiftly with calves of both legs turned out, stretched to maximum from thighs to toes.

3   As left foot descends, a slight muscular tension in the buttocks and thighs keeps right knee well turned out, and effects a light, soft descent to the floor left foot *demi-plié* (toes reach floor before heel).

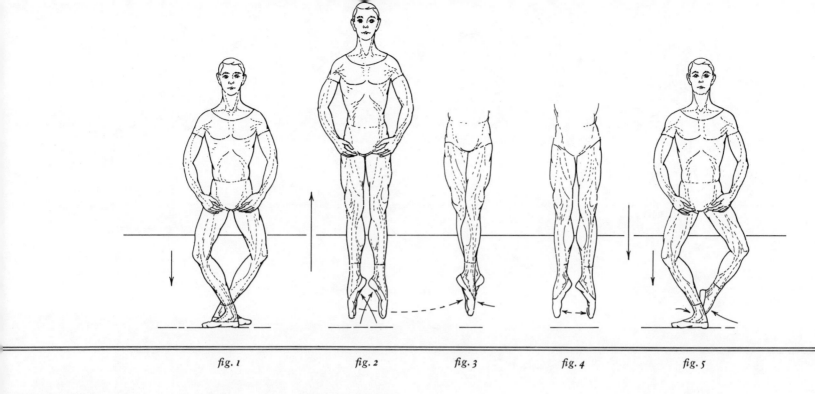

fig. 1   fig. 2   fig. 3   fig. 4   fig. 5

Plate 104. Entrechat Cinq (derrière—back)

Jumping from both feet on to one foot (*entrechat quatre*, descending on to one foot).

PREPARATION
5th position right foot front, head and torso erect, facing forward, arms in preparatory position; execute *demi-plié* on both feet *(fig. 1)*.

EXERCISE
1   Jump, extending both legs to maximum from thighs to toes, opening them slightly sideways in the air *(fig. 2)*;

2   Beat right calf in back of left *(fig. 3)*;

3   Open legs slightly sideways in the air *(fig. 4)*;

4   Right foot descends to floor *demi-plié (fig. 5)*;

5   Simultaneously, left foot is lifted, toe pointed, *sur le cou-de-pied* in back of right ankle *(fig. 5)*.

Usually this movement is executed with slight *épaulement*: right foot front, right shoulder slightly forward; left foot front, left shoulder slightly forward.

This beating movement may executed *devant*, terminating with left or right foot *sur le cou-de-pied* in front.

POSTURE AND MUSCULAR CONTROL
1   When executing *demi-plié*, both heels on floor.

2   Jumping, both feet push from floor into the air, toes pointed to maximum, barely leaving the floor; the beat is executed swiftly with calves of both legs turned out, stretched to maximum from thighs to toes.

3   A slight muscular tension in the buttocks and thighs keeps left knee well turned out, and effects a light, soft descent on right foot *demi-plié* (toes reach floor before heel).

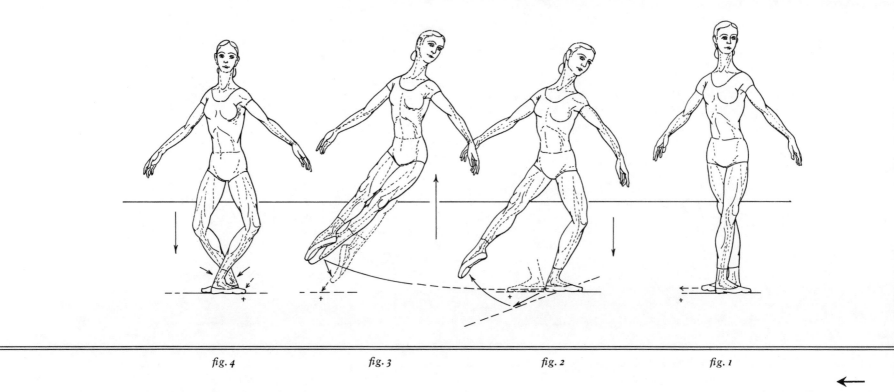

fig. 4   fig. 3   fig. 2   fig. 1

Plate 105. Brisé Fermé (forward)*

Moving forward to the right. (*Petite batterie*—small beating.)

PREPARATION

5th position left foot front, left shoulder forward, arms in low 2nd position (position *effacé*) *(fig. 1)*.

EXERCISE

(a) Execute *demi-plié*, sliding right foot briskly outward, *effacé* 45 degrees *(fig. 2)*;

(b) Immediately jump from left foot, drawing left leg towards right in the air, quickly beat right *calf* in front of left *(fig. 3)*;

(c) Open legs slightly, closing right foot behind left *(fig. 3)*, 5th position *demi-plié*, right arm 1st position, left arm low 2nd position *(fig. 4)*.

[222]

Brisé may be executed in various positions, *e.g.*, with torso turning slightly forward to the right *(écarté)*, and with various *ports de bras*. It may also be executed *en tournant*.

POSTURE AND MUSCULAR CONTROL

1   Torso inclines slightly back, draw abdomen in.

2   Center weight, *demi-plié*, on left foot.

3   Executing beat in the air, both legs are turned out and stretched to maximum from thighs to toes.

4   A slight muscular tension in the buttocks and thighs effects a light, soft descent into 5th position *demi-plié* (toes reach floor before heels).

---

*According to Cecchetti, *brisé dessus*.

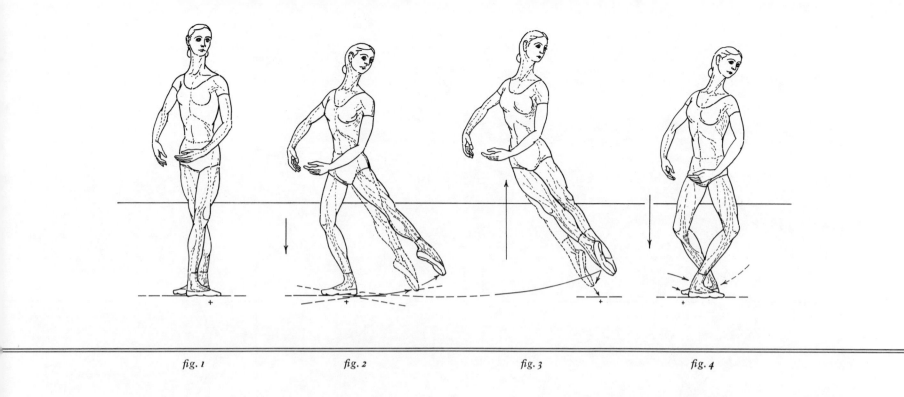

fig. 1   fig. 2   fig. 3   fig. 4

Plate 106. Brisé Fermé (backward)*

Moving backward to the left. *(Petite batterie.)*

PREPARATION

5th position left foot front, left shoulder forward, arms in preparatory position (position *écarté*) *(fig. 1)*.

EXERCISE

(a) Execute *demi-plié*, sliding left leg briskly outward *écarté* back 45 degrees *(fig. 2)*.

(b) Jumping backward, drawing right leg toward left in the air, beat left calf in back of right, closing left foot in front of right, descending to floor 5th position *demi-plié (figs. 3, 4)*.

POSTURE AND MUSCULAR CONTROL

1 Executing *demi-plié*, center weight on right foot, hold torso erect, incline head to left.

2 Back well arched, calves beat swiftly in the air, both legs turned out, stretched to maximum from thighs to toes.

3 A slight muscular tension in the buttocks and thighs effects a light, soft descent into 5th position *demi-plié* (toes reach ground before heels).

---

*According to Cecchetti, *brisé dessous*.

[223]

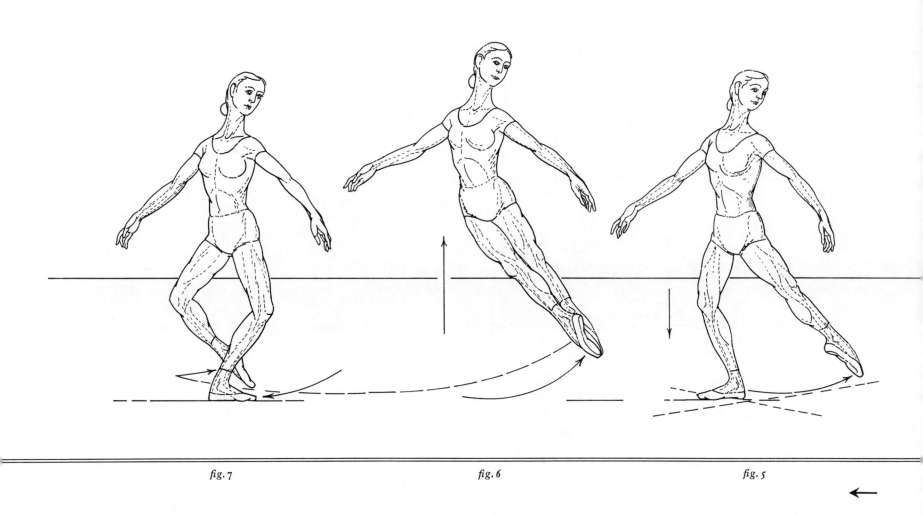

Plate 107. Brisé (dessus—dessous; under—over)*

Executed without pause, moving forward and backward.

PREPARATION

5th position left foot front, left shoulder forward, arms in low 2nd position (*fig. 1*).

EXERCISE

Brisé dessus—jumping forward: execute *demi-plié*, sliding right leg briskly forward position *effacé* 45 degrees (*fig. 2*); jump forward, drawing left leg toward right in the air; beat right calf in front of left (*fig. 3*), right foot descends to floor *demi-plié*, left knee bends, toe pointing *sur le cou-de-pied* in front of right ankle; torso bends forward, leaning towards right hip (*fig. 4*). Arms in 1st position.

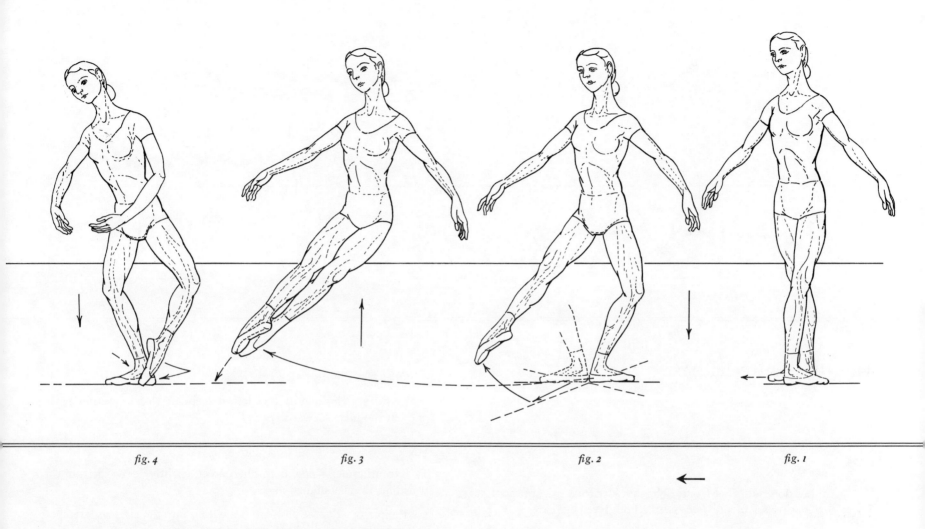

fig. 4   fig. 3   fig. 2   fig. 1

←

Brisé dessous—jumping backward: thrust left leg backward position
écarté back 45 degrees *(fig. 5)*; jump backward, drawing right leg
toward left in the air; beat left calf in back of right, back well arched,
left arm raised, palm held downward, right arm low 2nd position
(fig. 6); left foot descends to floor *demi-plié*, right knee bends, toe
pointing *sur le cou-de-pied* back of left ankle; torso bends backward,
leaning towards left hip *(fig. 7)*.

*According to Cecchetti, *brisé volé en avant* and *en arrière*

[225]

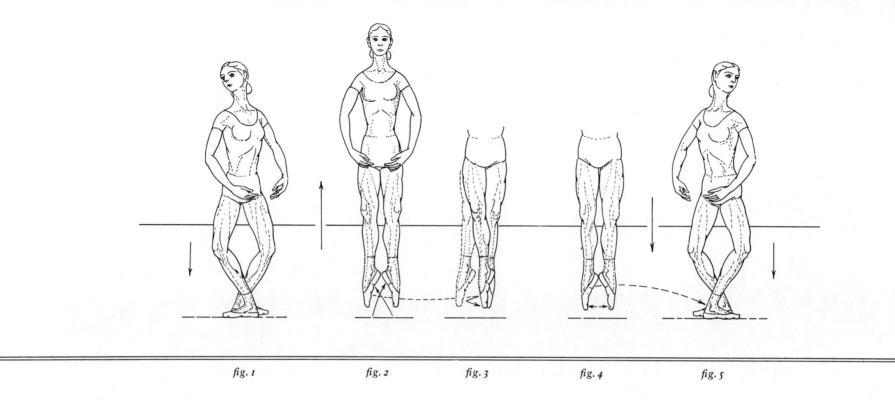

fig. 1   fig. 2   fig. 3   fig. 4   fig. 5

Plate 108. Entrechat Six

(Grande batterie—large beating.)

Preparation

5th position right foot front, right shoulder forward, arms in preparatory position. Execute *demi-plié* on both feet *(fig. 1)*.

Exercise

1 Jump, extending both legs to maximum from thighs to toes, opening them slightly sideways in the air *(fig. 2)*;

2 Beat right calf in back of left *(fig. 3)*;

3 Open legs slightly sideways *(fig. 3)*;

4 Beat right calf in front of left *(fig. 3)*;

[226]

5 Open legs slightly sideways *(fig. 4)*;

6 Right foot closes in back of left, descending to 5th position *demi-plié* left shoulder forward *(fig. 5)*.

Posture and Muscular Control

1 Executing *demi-plié*, hold torso erect, slightly forward from the waistline, draw abdomen in.

2 Jumping, both feet push from the floor into the air, legs stretched to maximum from thighs to pointed toes.

3 With legs well turned out, execute beating swiftly with both calves, during descent to floor.

4 A slight muscular tension in the buttocks and thighs effects a light, soft descent into 5th position *demi-plié* (toes reach floor before heels).

5 The shoulders and torso should remain still during beating movement.

fig. 4   fig. 3   fig. 2   fig. 1   ←

Plate 109. Entrechat Six de Volée*

(*Grande batterie*—large beating.)

This movement necessitates a large and vigorous jump forward, the body and legs remaining momentarily in the air while executing *entrechat six*.

There are various preparatory movements which may lead into *entrechat six de volée*, e.g. *failli, sissonne tombée, pas de bourrée, glissade, etc.*

Preparation

5th position left foot front, left shoulder forward, arms in preparatory position *(fig. 1)*.

Exercise

Execute *demi-plié*, thrusting right leg outward, *effacé* 90 degrees, opening both arms sideways *(fig. 2)*; immediately jump forward swiftly, thrusting left leg towards right in the air; beat right calf in front of left, beat right calf in back of left *(fig. 3)*; right foot closes in front of left, descending to 5th position *demi-plié*, right shoulder forward *(entrechat six) (fig. 4)*.

Posture and Muscular Control

1 Thrusting right leg to 2nd position, weight centered on left foot *demi-plié*.

2 Beating calves in the air, hold torso erect, slightly forward from the waistline, both legs stretched to maximum from thighs to toes.

3 The beating takes place during the descent to the floor.

4 A slight muscular tension in the buttocks and thighs effects a light, soft descent into 5th position *demi-plié* (toes reach floor before heels).

---

*According to Cecchetti, *entrechat six de côté*; according to Mme Nicolaeva-Legat, *grand entrechat cinq volé de côté*.

Plate 110. Entrechat Sept (finishing en attitude)

(Grande batterie—large beating.)

PREPARATION

5th position right foot front, right shoulder forward, arms in preparatory position. Execute *demi-plié* on both feet *(fig. 1)*.

EXERCISE

1 Jump, extending both legs to maximum from thighs to toes, opening them slightly sideways in the air *(fig. 2)*;

2 Beat right calf in back of left *(fig. 3)*;

3 Open legs slightly sideways *(fig. 3)*;

4 Beat right calf in front of left *(fig. 3)*;

5 Open legs slightly sideways *(fig. 4)*;

6 Left foot descends to floor *croisé* forward *demi-plié (fig. 5)*;

7 Simultaneously right leg is thrust in back of body, knee bent *(attitude croisée* back).

Executing *entrechat sept* finishing *en attitude*, arms move upward passing through 1st position to *attitude croisée*.

Entrechat sept may be finished in various positions: *effacé* or *croisé*, in *arabesque*, *à la seconde*, etc.

POSTURE AND MUSCULAR CONTROL

1 Executing *demi-plié*, hold torso erect, draw abdomen in, incline head to the right, center weight on both feet.

2 Beat swiftly with calves of both legs turned out, stretched to maximum from thighs to toes. Beat is executed during descent to floor.

3 Descending to left foot *(attitude croisée)*, hold torso erect, slightly forward from waistline, back well arched.

4 A slight muscular tension in the buttocks and thighs effects a light, soft descent to left foot *demi-plié* (toes reach floor before heel).

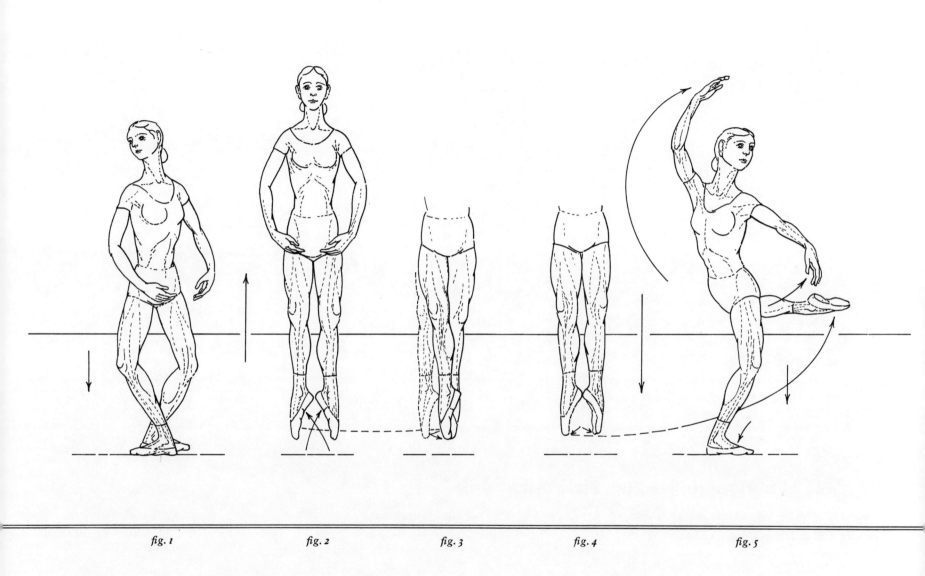

fig. 1   fig. 2   fig. 3   fig. 4   fig. 5

ENTRECHAT SEPT *(finishing en attitude)*

fig. 6

fig. 5

←

Plate 111. Cabriole (in position effacé—forward)

(*Grande batterie*—large beating.)

Cabriole may be executed forward and backward, in the following positions: *croisé, effacé, écarté;* in *arabesque,* and from various preparations: *failli, coupé, sissonne tombée, etc. Cabriole fermée* is executed with a smaller jump and beat, with the foot closing immediately.

PREPARATION

Position *croisé*, left foot pointing forward, left shoulder forward, arms in 1st position *(fig. 1)*.

EXERCISE

(a) Execute *demi-plié* on left foot, torso leaning forward to right *(fig. 2)*; simultaneously swing right leg quickly forward and upward to 90 degrees, and arms through 1st to position *effacé* (bending torso back) *(fig. 3)*;

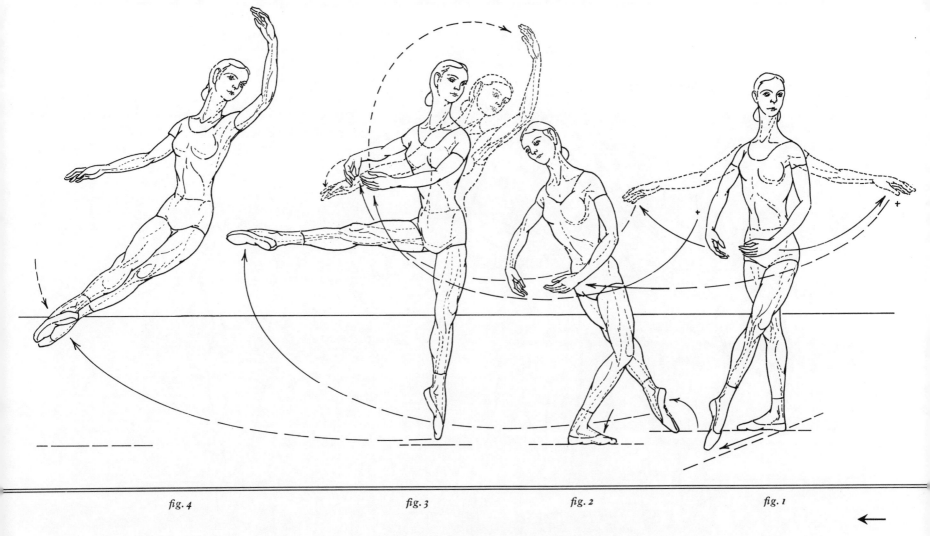

fig. 4   *fig. 3*   *fig. 2*   *fig. 1*

(b) Immediately jump from left foot, swinging left leg forward and upward, both calves beat in the air, right in front of left, left arm raised above head, right arm in 2nd position (*fig. 4*);

(c) Left foot descends to floor *demi-plié*, right leg is raised and momentarily held extended in the air 90 degrees (position *effacé* forward), before returning to 5th position *demi-plié* (*figs. 5, 6*).

POSTURE AND MUSCULAR CONTROL

1 Transfer weight on to left foot *demi-plié*, right foot passes on floor through 1st position, swinging forcefully upward (*grand battement* to 90 degress), back well arched.

2 As calves beat in the air, both legs are turned out and stretched to maximum from thighs to toes.

3 A slight muscular tension in the buttocks and thighs effects a light, soft descent to floor on left foot *demi-plié* (toes reach floor before heel).

[231]

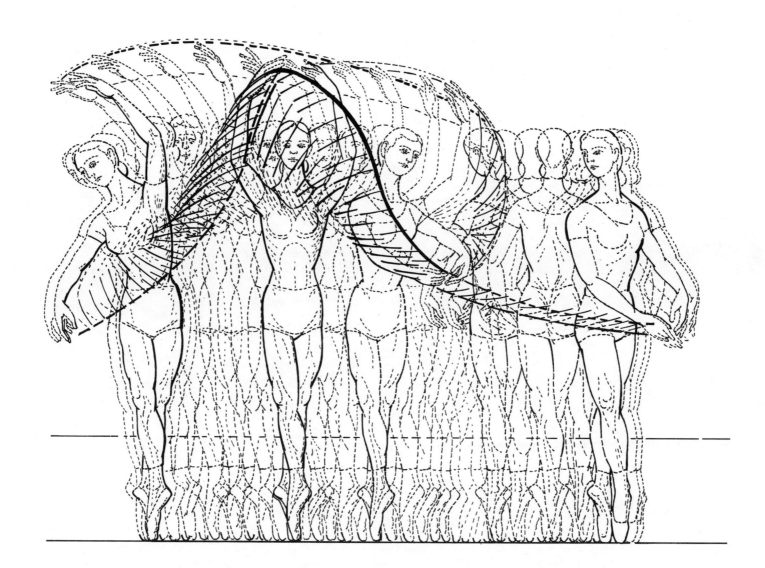

Space Development of a Pas de Bourrée on Pointes

Part IV: Dance on Pointes

Introduction to Dance on Pointes

The student should have completed two or three years' continuous training, consisting of at least one lesson a day, before attempting to dance on point. Her muscles are then able to execute movements on point correctly and without strain. The elementary student begins by facing the bar in 1st position, resting both hands lightly on the bar, and at first executes all the fundamental movements in this manner (see p. 234), before attempting to perform them in the center.

For example, executing *demi-plié* and *relevé* on to points in 1st position: the foot is supported on as many toes as possible, and not exclusively on the big toe. The movement may be executed in two ways, of equal value: pressing into the floor with both heels in *demi-plié* and rising on to point with a slight spring, lifting both heels off the floor; or slowly rising through *demi-pointe* on to full point, and slowly descending through *demi-pointe* to 1st position. The latter is more difficult and requires greater strength and a very pliable shank in the ballet shoe.

As the student gains strength, she begins to perform a wider range of movements on point: for instance, turns, starting with those on both feet—*soutenu en tournant*, first with half turns, then with complete turns—and when these have been mastered, single *pirouettes* from 4th position. Eventually, she will learn to perform on point almost all the movements described in this book, but the fundamental exercises described in the following section must always be performed at the beginning of each class to prepare the muscles for the more complicated movements.

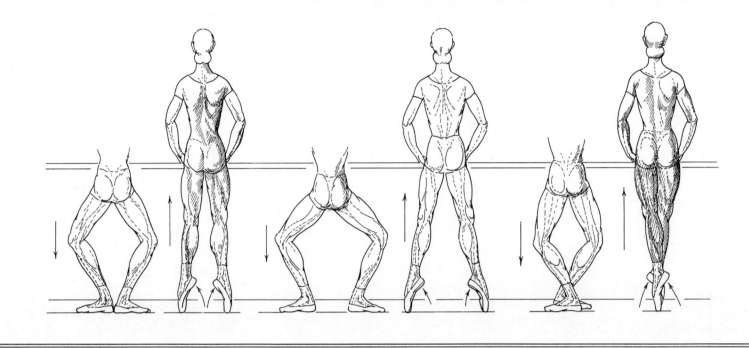

figs. 1-2   *first position*   figs. 3-4   *second position*   figs. 5-6   *fifth position*

Plate 112. Relevés (facing the bar)

RELEVÉ—1st position

PREPARATION

1st position. Execute *demi-plié*, distributing weight equally between both feet, keeping heels on floor.

EXERCISE

Spring on to toes of both feet *(relevé)*, lower heels to floor 1st position *demi-plié (figs. 1, 2, 1)*.

RELEVÉ—2nd position

PREPARATION

2nd position. Execute *demi-plié*, distributing weight equally between both feet.

EXERCISE

Spring on to toes of both feet *(relevé)*, lower heels to floor 2nd position *demi-plié (figs. 3, 4, 3)*.

RELEVÉ—5th position

(Soussus—springing on to pointes or demi-pointes in any direction.)

Relevé in 5th position or *soussus* may be executed in the center travelling forwards, backwards and sideways.   (See page right.)*

PREPARATION

5th position. Execute *demi-plié*, distributing weight equally between both feet, heels on floor.

EXERCISE

Spring on to toes in 5th position, drawing legs and feet closely together, right foot in front of left; return heels to floor 5th position *demi-plié (figs. 5, 6, 5)*.

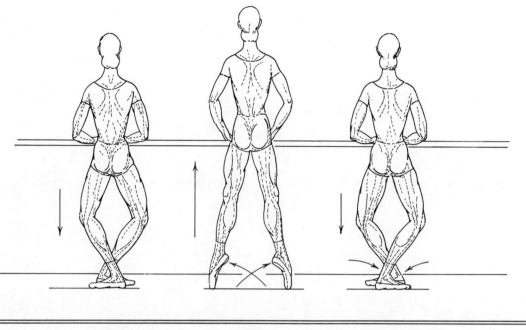

fig. 1   *fig. 2*   *fig. 3*

Plate 113. Échappés (facing the bar)

(With change of feet each time in 5th position.)

RELEVÉS—(facing bar)

POSTURE AND MUSCULAR CONTROL

1   Executing *demi-plié*, hold torso erect, draw abdomen in, knees turned out in direct line over center of feet.

2   Before springing on to toes, feet press into floor, a slight muscular tension in thighs keeps legs and feet turned out, held firmly together, eliminating strain from neck and arms *(figs. 5, 6)*.

3   On *pointes*, both legs stretched to maximum, calves and heels brought forward, weight distributed equally on the toes, avoiding pressure on big toes and rolling inward.

Échappé may be executed without change of feet, or moving backward, forward, sideways and turning. Also in positions *croisé* and *effacé*.

PREPARATION

5th position right foot front. Execute *demi-plié*, distributing weight equally between both feet *(fig. 1)*.

EXERCISE

Slide and spring into 2nd position on *pointes (fig. 2)*; return to 5th position right foot back, lowering heels to floor *demi-plié (fig. 3)*.

POSTURE AND MUSCULAR CONTROL

1   Executing *demi-plié*, heels on floor 5th position, hold torso erect, draw abdomen in.

2   Before sliding and springing into 2nd position on *pointes*, feet press into floor.

3   Both legs turned out and stretched to maximum in 2nd position on *pointes*.

[235]

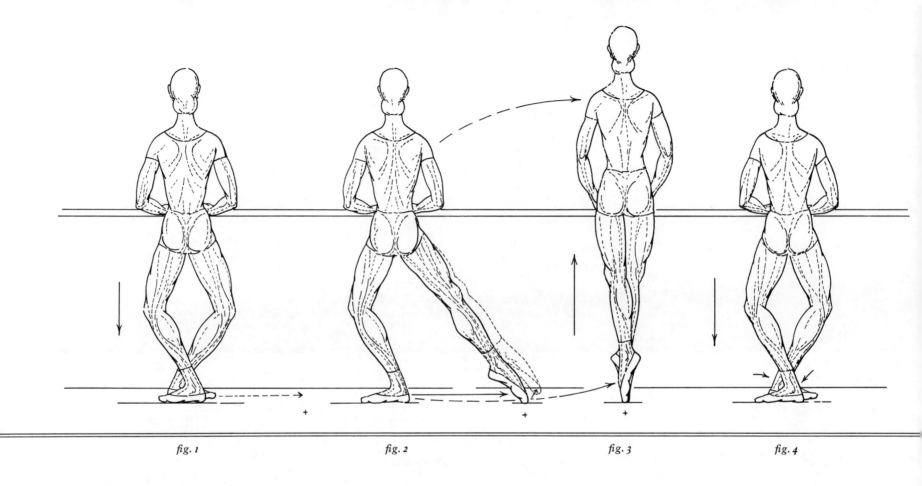

fig. 1   fig. 2   fig. 3   fig. 4

Plate 114. Glissade (on pointes, facing the bar)*

(Without change of feet, moving to right.)

Glissade may be executed with change of feet in 5th position, and in all directions.

Preparation

5th position, right foot front.

---

*This bears no relation to the Cecchetti *glissade sur les pointes*.

[236]

Exercise

Execute *demi-plié (fig. 1)*, sliding right leg to right side, toe pointing on floor, to 2nd position, barely leaving the ground *(fig. 2)*; step on to right toe, quickly drawing left foot on *pointe* to 5th position back *(fig. 3)*, lower heels to floor 5th position *demi-plié (fig. 4)*. To continue movement, slide right leg to 2nd position, *etc*.

Posture and Muscular Control

1   Executing *demi-plié*, center weight on left foot, hold torso erect, draw abdomen in.

2   Springing on to right toe, quickly drawing left foot to right, 5th position, tighten thighs, holding legs and feet firmly together.

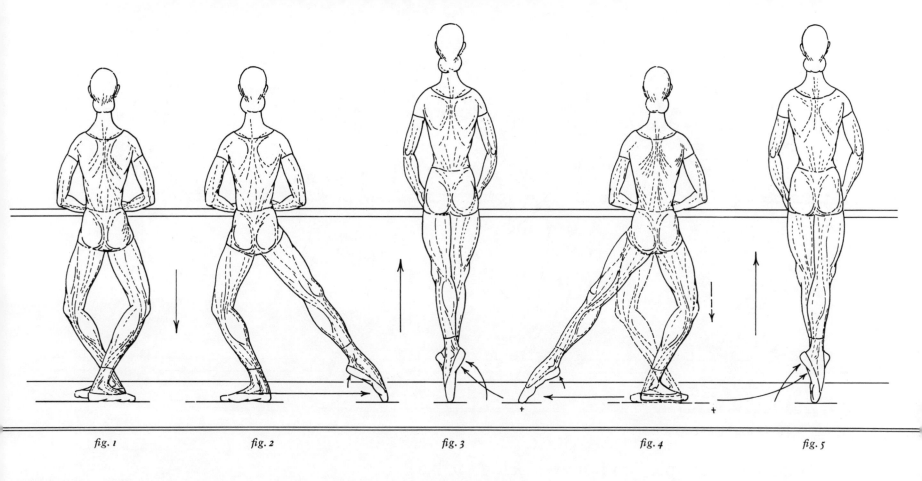

fig. 1   fig. 2   fig. 3   fig. 4   fig. 5

Plate 115. Assemblé Soutenu (on pointes, facing the bar)

PREPARATION

5th position left foot front.

EXERCISE

Execute *demi-plié* sliding right leg, toe pointing on floor, to 2nd position *(figs. 1, 2)*. Draw right leg back to left, simultaneously springing on to *pointes* 5th position right foot front *(fig. 3)*; lower heels to floor 5th position *demi-plié*; slide left leg, toe pointing on floor, to 2nd position *(fig. 4)*. Draw left leg back to right, simultaneously springing on to *pointes* 5th position left foot front *(fig. 5)*.

POSTURE AND MUSCULAR CONTROL

1 Executing *demi-plié*, weight centered on left foot, hold torso erect, draw abdomen in.

2 Springing into 5th position on *pointes*, legs and feet held firmly together, tighten thighs, eliminate strain from neck and arms.

[237]

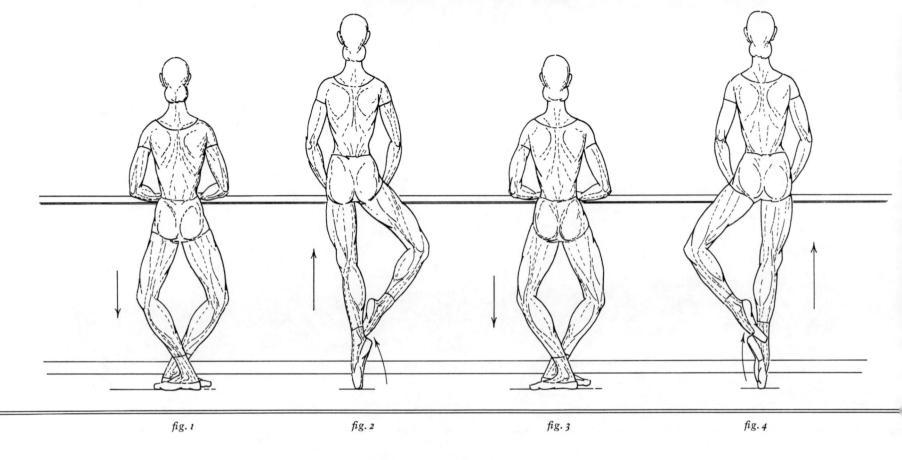

fig. 1   fig. 2   fig. 3   fig. 4

Plate 116. Sissonne Simple (on pointes, facing the bar)*

(Without changing positions of feet.)

PREPARATION

5th position right foot front, execute *demi-plié* on both feet *(fig. 1)*.

EXERCISE

Spring on to toes of left foot, simultaneously lift and point right foot *sur le cou-de-pied* front of left ankle *(fig. 2)*; simultaneously lower both feet 5th position *demi-plié*; spring on to toes of right foot, simultaneously lift and point left foot *sur le cou-de-pied* back of right ankle *(fig. 4)*; simultaneously lower both feet 5th position *demi-plié* *(fig. 1)*.

[238]

POSTURE AND MUSCULAR CONTROL

1   Executing *demi-plié*, hold torso erect, draw abdomen in, center weight equally between both feet, pressing them into the floor in preparation for springing on to toes.

2   Supporting leg stretched to maximum on point, lifted leg, knee turned out, toe pointing in front of supporting ankle.

---

*Called by Cechetti *relevé devant et derrière*.

fig. 1   fig. 2   fig. 3   fig. 4

Plate 117. Sissonne Passer la Jambe (on pointes, facing the bar)*

PREPARATION

5th position right foot front, execute *demi-plié* on both feet *(fig. 1)*.

EXERCISE

Spring on to toes of left foot, simultaneously lifting right leg, knee bent, toe pointing, in front of left leg to knee *(fig. 2)*; right foot passes in back of left leg, simultaneously lower both feet, right foot back, into 5th position *demi-plié (fig. 3)*.

Spring on to toes of right foot, simultaneously lifting left leg, knee bent, toe pointing, in front of right leg to knee; left foot passes in back of right leg, simultaneously lower both feet, left foot back, into 5th position *demi-plié (fig. 1)*.

This movement may be executed moving forward, closing working leg 5th position front.

POSTURE AND MUSCULAR CONTROL

1 Executing *demi-plié*, hold torso erect, draw abdomen in, weight centered on both feet.

2 Supporting leg stretched to maximum on *pointes*. The toe of the working leg keeps contact with the supporting leg, knee well turned out.

---

*Called by Cecchetti, *temps relevé passé en arrière*.

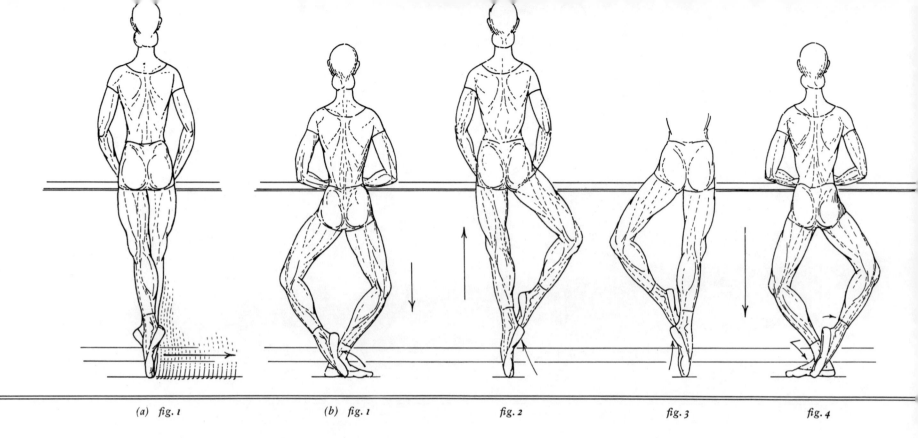

Plate 118. Pas de Bourrée (facing the bar)

A series of small even steps on *pointes*, moving to the right.

PREPARATION

5th position right foot front, execute *demi-plié* on both feet.

EXERCISE

Spring on to toes 5th position *(fig. 1a)*, drawing legs and feet firmly together; step to right on to right toe, left foot quickly moves in back of right, and continue a series of very small even steps moving to the right.

POSTURE AND MUSCULAR CONTROL

Keep knees flexible but not bent, effecting a smooth and continuous movement.

PAS DE BOURRÉE (with change of feet)

PREPARATION

5th position right foot front.

EXERCISE

Execute *demi-plié* on right leg, simultaneously lifting left foot, pointing *sur le cou-de-pied* in back of right ankle *(fig. 1b)*. Step on to left point, straightening the knee, and lift right pointed toe in front of left ankle *(fig. 2b)*. Step on to right point, straightening the knee, and lift left pointed toe in front of right ankle *(fig. 3b)*. Step on to left foot *demi-plié*, lifting right pointed toe *sur le cou-de-pied* in back of left ankle *(fig. 4b)*.

Index*

*An alphabetical listing of plates including a page reference for details of technique and terminology and for the alternate terms given for the technique illustrated in this work.

Index

A Note on the Type

This book was set in Janson, a typeface long thought to have been made by the Dutchman Anton Janson, who was a practicing typefounder in Leipzig during the years 1668–1687. However, it has been conclusively demonstrated that these types are actually the work of Nicholas Kis (1650–1702), a Hungarian, who most probably learned his trade from the master Dutch typefounder Dirk Voskens. The type is an excellent example of the influential and sturdy Dutch types that prevailed in England up to the time William Caslon (1692–1766) developed his own incomparable designs from them.